Storage Concepts

Storing and Managing Digital Data

Edited by

Peter Manijak

Martin Stewart

Pavel Vild

HDS ACADEMY

Storage Concepts
Published by
HDS Academy, Hitachi Data Systems
Copyright © 2012 by Hitachi Data Systems Corporation.

Corporate Headquarters
750 Central Expressway
Santa Clara, California 95050-2627 USA
www.HDS.com
Regional Contact Information
Americas: +1 408 970 1000 or info@hds.com
Europe, Middle East and Africa: +44 (0) 1753 618000 or info.emea@hds.com
Asia Pacific: +852 3189 7900 or hds.marketing.apac@hds.com

Acknowledgements

Executive editor:	Peter Manijak
Development editor:	Martin Stewart
Editor:	Pavel Vild
Copyeditor:	Rebecca George
Graphical work:	Vojtech Marek
	Jiri Zavadil
	Tina Pankievich
Consultants and specialists:	Dr. Miroslav Kotrle
	Radim Petrzela
	Jiri Zeman
	Tomas Bucek
Project managers:	Cecil Chamberlain
	Jaroslav Fojtik

Produced and developed by HDS Academy in cooperation with MHM computer a.s.
© Hitachi Data Systems Corporation 2012. All Rights Reserved.

ISBN-13: 978-0615656496 (HDS Academy, Hitachi Data Systems)
ISBN-10: 0615656498

Contents

Foreword

Data. It's a word we all know and use regularly, but how does it impact our personal and professional lives? We live in an era of technology that places information at our fingertips. Technology empowers us to create anything from digital photographs, films and symphonies to advanced medical images and space systems. Data grows exponentially and stretches further each day. It makes the highest achievements possible and connects us like never before.

But how do we store this ever growing data — the countless files created daily around the world? The answer depends on the data owner. Individuals need to store files in an easily accessible location and maximize free space for new files. Small businesses face more complex issues with the data they use and store, but it is critical to store their data. Midsized businesses and large corporations face far greater concerns. Their information, or data, is a corporate asset that needs to be stored, managed and protected — plus there are government compliance regulations that impact the process.

For years, many IT professionals have seen data storage as a mystery. Larger businesses employ dedicated storage administrators or contract with professional services consultants to perform the more complex procedures and manage the all important data. Most IT professionals know a lot about servers but very little about storage systems. However, these specialized systems are a modern day necessity for the storage of data. In this regard, an IT administrator (or other responsible party) must have at least elementary knowledge of common problems related to data storage and storage systems.

This book covers the basic areas of data storage. Each chapter is written as an independent section, so you do not have to read the chapters in serial order to glean knowledge on a particular topic; feel free to jump from one chapter to another and select only the chapters that interest you.

The book is for anyone who would like to understand the cornerstones of data storage technology and the significance of basic terminology used in connection with storage systems. We recommended this book for students or starter administrators, as well as experienced IT workers who want to deepen their knowledge in data storage. Some individuals do not work directly with storage systems but need to communicate with personnel in IT; the book is suitable for this audience as well.

Our intent is not to provide a detailed manual for coping with the technologies of individual manufacturers, concrete commands, scripts and procedures, or to compare equipment from different vendors in the market. We respectfully leave these next steps to you.

After reading this book, you should understand the basic rules of data storage and get a systematic overview of modern tools and technologies. You will also be acquainted with the economic viewpoint of technology operation, and for this reason, you will better understand the essence of IT investments.

If the subject of data storage systems piques your interest and you want to deepen your knowledge after reading this book, you can search for additional information through data storage companies such as Hitachi Data Systems (www.hds.com).

We wish you a successful first step in the amazing world of data storage and storage systems.

Peter Manijak
HDS Academy Director

Conventions used in the book

In this book, we have adopted various conventions to provide you with clarity and an enjoyable reading experience as you explore the concepts and architecture of storing and managing digital data. The content is logically structured into nine chapters and written in simple language suitable for readers whose native language is not English. Each chapter starts with an overview to introduce you to a new topic and ends with a summary to help you consolidate the knowledge you have gained. The text is supplemented with pictures and diagrams to illustrate the content through examples. Throughout the book, you will encounter practical hints marked with the **Instructor's Tip** icon and highlights marked with the **Remember** icon:

The Instructor's Tip icon marks additional information that provides you with a new perspective on a given topic. Exploring the topic from different points of view should make it easier for you to understand the complex principles and concepts of data management and storage systems.

The **Remember** icon accompanies summaries of what was discussed in the preceding section. You should pay special attention to these summaries since they contain the most important information you should remember after reading this book

Brief introduction to data management and storage systems

1

What are you going to learn in this chapter?

- What kind of data we have
- The importance of data for business
- Data and information — what's the difference?
- How data looks from the perspective of a storage system
- How to distinguish between physical and logical level of data processing
- The concepts of data consistency and data integrity

Introduction to data management

The changing forms of data

Before we get to storage systems and their components, let's take a closer look at data itself. There are not many people who realize that whenever they take a picture with their camera or send a document by email they bring large amounts of data into existence. This data needs to be stored and backed up somewhere, which of course creates an increasing demand for data storage. Few people nowadays are satisfied with mere conservation of data on their personal computer hard drives. More people want unlimited access to their data through the Internet and the ability to share that data with their friends and families. This common goal creates a lot of space for business, and that's why companies offer a wide range of services focused on data backup and sharing. To get an idea of the amount of data handled nowadays, simply look at social networks, media sharing websites and other similar sites.

However, common users aren't the only ones generating data; institutions like banks, hospitals and telecommunication companies also generate data. This is the point where it all gets interesting. Unlike common users, these companies are highly dependent on data, since data is the crucial element that enables them to do their business. Imagine a bank that loses Internet banking transaction data. Even if the bank lost data collected in the past fifteen minutes, it would lose huge amounts of money and face potentially devastating consequences.

In this chapter, we'll talk about data and its importance. You'll see simple examples that should help you understand the depth and complexity of technology connected with data storage. To give this topic a bit of structure, we'll divide data into subgroups and list characteristics these subgroups possess. The division is not an exact science since the boundaries between types of data are often blurred. However, this approach will help you become familiar with key terms that we'll look at in detail later.

Common user data:

- Photos uploaded to web galleries or social networks

- Movies uploaded to services like YouTube.com

- Documents created by online applications like Google Docs

- Email communication stored on the Internet

- Data backed up to online storage such as Microsoft Sky Drive

- Personal web pages and blogs

- Increasingly popular cloud systems and online applications

All this data can be considered important, at least from the user's point of view, and deserves careful and secure handling. However, limited access to these types of data — for example, during hardware maintenance — usually doesn't create any financial loss to the end user. If you can't access your photo gallery for an hour once a year, it most likely won't cost you a lot of money. For large institutions that store ongoing financial transaction data, this disruption can have sometimes devastating consequences. To prevent data loss, you need to employ several basic concepts — various techniques for data backup and data replication. The key term in the storage technology is *redundancy*. Data needs to be stored as several copies in several locations to ensure no disaster can affect its availability.

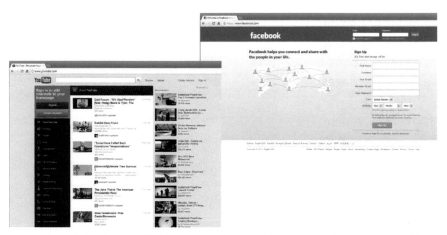

Figure 1.1 — Services like YouTube and Facebook have to store huge amounts of data.

Basically, redudancy is achieved through techniques commonly called **data replication**. Data can be replicated on the basis of in-system replication or remote replication to a storage system located in another town or even country. The process of data replication is rather complex, and there are many tools for creating duplicates or clones of data. That's why we dedicated a whole chapter to this topic. Aside from data replication, there's also hard drive mirroring, which we'll discuss further when we talk about RAID technology.

Business sector data:

- Accounting, invoices and financial records
- Databases that contain data about clients
- Email communication
- Digitalization of printed documents
- Archiving

Data that contains information about clients' personal information or financial transactions plays a crucial role for business. Imagine a telecommunications company that cannot store data about phone calls, sent text messages or data traffic. When this company loses such data, it's unable to invoice the customer and request payment for the provided services. A malfunction in the storage system could therefore mean serious financial loss for the company. In this case, it is not enough to have the data backed up several times. The concept of redundancy doesn't solve this problem. On this level, it's a matter of course that the company doesn't lose any data that was stored before the storage system failure; the key is to ensure business continuity to bring all the applications back online as fast as possible. Each company that needs the highest data availability possible also needs a disaster recovery plan. This brings us to two other key storage systems terms: **business continuity** and **disaster recovery**.

An institution that's highly dependent on the availability of its data must be prepared to deal with all possible risk situations, such as natural disasters, cyber attacks, failure of public infrastructure. For example, imagine a fire destroys all infrastructure's servers and storage systems — how long would it take to bring the essential components back online? How extensive would the loss of data be? All these criteria need to be considered in a business continuity plan.

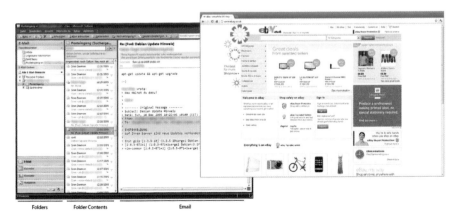

Figure 1.2 — Businesses are dependent on a properly working data storage system.

State institutions data:

- Databases and other structured data
- Audio and video records (CCTV, court records)
- Hospital records
- Confidential and classified data
- Archiving and digitalization

With this type of data, we can demonstrate other aspects that need to be taken into consideration when designing a storage solution for the customer. We have already mentioned redundancy, business continuity and disaster recovery. When it comes to legal requirements, however, there are some other verticals that need to be considered. Private businesses and state institutions typically have a policy that governs how long data must be retained. For medical records, it can be several decades. The data from court trials also needs to be archived over a long period of time. On the other hand, data from CCTV cameras and the like do not have to be stored for longer than several weeks or months. When we talk about data, we also talk about its **lifecycle**. When we have a storage system, it must be able to retain data over a long time with the possibility of easy data migration to other devices. Legally mandatory **data retention** does not apply only to data generated by state institutions — even companies are legally bound to keep records on their accounting for several years.

 The term data lifecycle applies to all data that comes into existence, while a data retention period applies only to certain types of data and is governed by law.

Another thing to mention here is that long-term data retention is often inversely proportional to high data availability. This means we have to store certain data for, let's say, forty years, but its fast availability is not so important. Therefore, we do not have to store this data on the fastest and most efficient hard drives — we can use archiving storage systems that are based on cheaper and less sophisticated hardware such as magnetic tape technology.

Figure 1.3 shows how data lifecycles work and what types of technology are used according to data availability demands. For most frequently accessed data, we will use the most powerful hardware, for example the most up-to-date storage systems equipped with SSD disks or fast SAS hard drives. For data that does not have to be available as quickly, we can use less powerful and less expensive storage systems with SATA hard drives. There are also special storage systems designed especially for archiving; these systems use data compression and are equipped with less powerful but more reliable hard drives. For legacy data and backed up data, we can use offline tape systems. Data stored on these devices cannot be accessed immediately, and it can take hours to get data ready for use.

Data Lifecycle

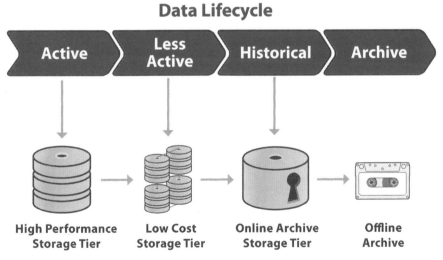

Figure 1.3 — Data lifecycle diagram.

We can illustrate how the data lifecycle works by using accounting as an example. Every company is legally bound to keep records. Accounting data of the ongoing quarter is stored on their high peformance tier because the accountants are working with this data frequently. After the quarterly financial statement, the data is moved to a low cost storage tier because it is not accessed or modified that often. Once there is a new financial year, the old data is transferred to an online archive storage tier and stays there for another five years, which is required by law. At this stage, the data is still accessible online. After five years, the company migrates the legacy accounting data to the offline archive, most likely based on tape technology. The data lifecycle is closely related to the changing value of information over time.

Structured and unstructured data

What is the difference?

In addition to dividing the data according to purpose, it's possible to divide the data according to structure. **Structured data** can be stored in rows and columns while unstructured data cannot. Structured data, therefore, consists of mostly databases, such as client databases, balance sheets and phonebooks. **Unstructured data** refers to computerized information that either does not have a data model or does not have one that's easily usable by a computer program. The term *unstructured data* distinguishes such information from data stored in a structured form in databases or annotated (tagged) in documents.

The ongoing information explosion has consumed huge amounts of expensive and valuable resources, both human and technical. The management of unstructured data is a major problem. To manage and process structured data with clearly defined columns and rows (mostly databases and tables) you can use software for analysis. Then people can use this data for interpretation. As for managing and processing unstructured data, you need more sophisticated software able to work with just one file type (for example, with MP3 files or Microsoft® Word documents). The computer analysis of unstructured data does not always provide satisfying results and there is often a need for human factor intervention. In other words, there must be a person to organize, manage, process and analyze this data. Some examples of unstructured data are:

- Medical images such as MRI scans and x-rays

- Photographs and diagrams

- Digital documents such as check images and contracts

- Electronic assets such as presentations, emails and design documents

To have a general idea of the structured and unstructured data ratio, refer to Figure 1.4, which illustrates the exponentially growing demand for data storage.

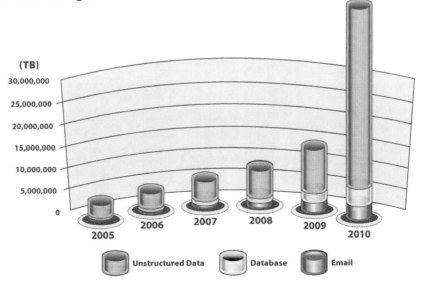

Figure 1.4 — Structured and unstructured data ratio, growing demands on data storage capacity, HDS statistics.

In this section, we discussed several types of data. You learned that different levels of importance can be attributed to data, at least from the perspective of business and storage systems. The trick is ensuring that data is safely stored and available for creation of several copies. Whenever you send an email or upload a picture to a web gallery, you create at least two, maybe even three or four copies, because the service provider cannot afford losing your data just because of technical failure. This, of course, demonstrates that the need for storage space is increasing, because all data must be duplicated multiple times. This is called **redundancy** and it is a key word that will be mentioned many times throughout this book. Other terms worth remembering are **business continuity** and **disaster recovery**. We will talk about these in detail later.

Data plays a crucial role in business nowadays. It is said that if a bank computer system failed for two or three days and the bank could not store transactions, it would cause a panic and the bank would most likely collapse. This is just one example of how important data is!

New trends in data management: cloud computing

To better illustrate the development of storage systems and the demand for more and more storage capacity, we can take a look at cloud computing, increasingly popular among companies and users. You probably know that on the Internet there are various services that offer disk space, often for free, with the possibility to upgrade to a larger storage area for little money. You can then use this storage space as you wish — to back up your photos, documents and applications, and access them from any computer connected to the Internet. This type of service can be seen as a predecessor to newly emerging cloud computing. Cloud computing goes even further — it not only offers disk space at your disposal, but also the possibility to use the computing power of the data center to run your online applications. The idea is that you do not have to install the software on your computer but you can use online software on the cloud. The advantages of cloud computing are clear:

- The user does not have to worry about licensing and software costs.

- The user has the same working environment on any computer in any location that is connected to the Internet.

- The user does not need powerful hardware to run certain applications; all the data processing and computing is done by a remote computer that is part of the cloud solution.

- All online applications are automatically updated.

- Systems are scalable and *pay as you go* — you can buy the exact amount of services you need.

- There is a low risk of data loss.

Figure 1.5 — An example of cloud technology, iCloud solutions provided by Apple. Among its competitors is Google, which offers Google Apps such as Google Docs.

On the other hand, there are disadvantages — the biggest problems can be the dependency on the solution provider, possible security risks and Internet connection issues. Furthermore, the applications available on cloud solutions usually do not offer the full functionality of the software you install on your computer, especially because of limitations in Internet connection speed and latency. This whole area is not very old and only the future will show if this type of data and application access prevails.

Data and information

Why should we distinguish the two?

In the last section, we discussed what forms data can take and its importance to businesses. Before we continue, let's define the term *data* itself and make a clear distinction between data and information. This should help you understand more clearly the way data is handled in computers and storage systems. We can say that data is a physical and written representation of information, knowledge and results of any real world observation.

From an information technology point of view, data:
- Is a succession of written characters, which can be represented by numbers, letters or symbols. These characters may seem strange or meaningless at first glance, but they serve to organize the data.
- Does not have to bear any useful information.
- Must be processed, organized and structured in order to extract information.
- Is easily processed by modern electronic devices. It's the language of computers and storage systems.

On the other hand, *information* is a more complex term. Information:

- Is a meaningful interpretation of certain parts of data

- Does not have to be written in characters

- Cannot be easily processed by electronics devices

- Has value that is not linear, but constantly changing

- Is a commodity and can be bought or sold

When we compare these two definitions, we see that information is superior to data. We do not store information to get data, but we store data to preserve and pass the information on. We can also see that the value of information is different from person to person. The same set of data can be interpreted differently by different individuals. What is meaningful for one person does not have to be meaningful for somebody else. When we have a company that stores various types of statistical data, the data can serve financial analysis, accounting or marketing strategy development. The data will be the same; the output may be different. When we talk about storage systems, we are talking strictly about data, processed in binary code, which consists only of ones and zeros. A storage system cannot help us extract any kind of information. Storage systems work only with raw blocks of data. Storage systems themselves cannot see whether the data we store includes databases, films, music files or other data types. It's important to remember that a storage system sees only those ones and zeros.

Levels of data processing

Logical and physical layer

Distinction between data and information can also help us understand the more complex distinction between logical and physical levels of data. This distinction can be more difficult to grasp because it is quite abstract. Generally speaking, we can say that the physical level is the hardware level, with a primary focus on where exactly raw blocks of data are stored on a hard drive, how they are optimized for input and output (I/O) performance, and mutual communication among hardware components on the lowest level. The logical level of data, however, can be understood as a virtual interface working as a bridge between the lowest level hardware operations and the user. The user of the logical construct can be the server, the application or the person using the equipment. This may sound confusing, but there are many practical implementations of this abstract concept. The key terms that will help you understand how physical and logical levels of data work include **physical unit, logical unit, partition, volume, file system and microcode** (to an extent).

 In most of modern systems, the physical level of data processing is hidden from the user. The user either does not have the possibility to control this level or can partially make changes using tools that are able to influence the physical level through the logical level.

Hard drive partitioning

Hard drive partitioning, well known from ordinary personal computers, can be a good way to explain the distinction between how logical and physical levels actually work. In a model situation, we can have a laptop running Microsoft® Windows® software. If you click on the *My Computer* icon, you can access your file system where files are organized in a tree structure. On the top of this tree, you have icons of installed hard drives, CD/DVD drives and memory card drives. Each of these drives is attributed a letter that serves as an address valid within the operating system. A hard drive usually has *C:* and *D:* addresses. A DVD drive usually has an *E:* address. Though rare in modern computers, a floppy disk drive usually has an *A:* address. You may notice that on many computers with this type of configuration, you can have two icons of hard drives (*C:* and *D:*) while you know that there is only one physical drive installed inside. Why is this happening? Why is there not only one icon representing the whole drive? It is because somebody, perhaps you or a vendor, partitioned the disk into two logical disks. In the computer, there is just one piece of hardware, but the user of this hardware, which in this case is the operating system and you indirectly, will see figure 1.6.

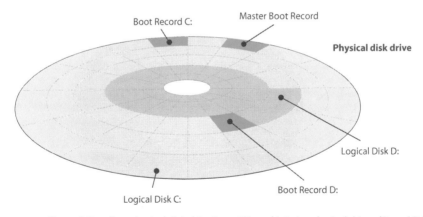

Figure 1.6 — One physical disk drive is partitioned into two logical drives (C: and D:).

Now you may ask what the joining element between physical hard drive and logical hard drives is. In this case, it is the metadata stored on the first physical sector of a hard drive that contains the Master Boot Record (MBR) table with information on the partitioning of the disks, their proportions and their status (i.e., whether they are formatted and contain some kind of file system). The MBR table is able to address only disk drives with a capacity of up to 2TB. For bigger disks, there is a new standard called a GUID partitioning table (GPT). This is, however, not very important for us at the moment.

Why would people partition their hard drives? There can be several reasons:

- OS and application system files may be separated from user files for purely organizational reasons.

- It is easier to create a backup image of a partition that contains the operating system. (It is not very practical to create an image of the whole disk.)

- You may want to install different file systems and operating systems on a single drive.

- You may want to encrypt one partition that contains important data.

Volume

Compared to the term *partition*, the term *volume* is more general as it describes any single accessible storage area with a single installed file system. The term *volume* is mostly used in the context of operating systems, but we can encounter this term even when we use software for managing storage arrays. Volume will always be interpreted as a logical layer because it is not connected directly with physical operations. When we have a physical hard drive with two or three partitions, the first partition can contain a New Technology File System (NTFS) used by the Windows NT series, the second partition can be formatted with the ext3 file system used by Linux operating systems and the third partition can remain unformatted, without a file system — perhaps because we have not yet decided what to do with this disk space. When we boot Windows, we see only one volume, because Windows systems cannot access and use the Linux ext3 file system (at least not without third party utilities that may enable access to partitions that use different file systems). Windows also cannot use unformatted disk space. When we boot Linux, we see two volumes — one with the ext3 file system and one with the NTFS, because Linux is able to access disk space that is using the NTFS (even though Linux does not use the NTFS for its installation by default settings). The third partition cannot be called *volume* because it does not have a file system installed, and thus does not comply with the definition of the term *volume*.

The term *volume* does not even have to be connected with partitions. If you insert a CD with music or a DVD with film, it will be again called a *volume*. The same applies to USB pen drives, memory cards or legacy floppy disks. They are not partitioned, and yet they are recognized as volumes by an operating system.

The term *volume* is then again part of the logical level of data and it comprises the terms *partition* or *disk drive* and *file system*. The term *volume* can be understood as a logical interface used by an operating system to access data stored on the particular media while using a single instance of a file system. A volume, therefore, cannot contain two or more file systems.

We have learned that you can split one physical hard drive into two or more logical drives through a technique known as partitioning. If the logical volume contains a file system, an operating system sees it as a volume. It is very important to note that a partition (or volume) can also be created from two or more physical hard drives. If you have two physical hard drives and you want to create one unified volume, then you can join them together, creating a single logical disc that will have the capacity of both physical hard drives. This technique is called **concatenation of hard drives**.

File system

We have mentioned that volume is defined by two things — it must be a single storage area and it must have some sort of *file system* installed. We have encountered the term file system quite a lot throughout the last few paragraphs without describing what it actually is. In simple words, a file system is a way in which files are named, organized and stored on the hard drive. Again, it can be described as some sort of logical interface between the user layer (individual files, for example, .mp3 music files and .avi video files) and the physical layer that contains only ones and zeros. File system translates raw binary data into what we see when we open a file explorer in our preferred operating system. A file system is, therefore, also a way of storing file attributes and metadata that contain additional information about the file and are used by the operating system. This information can bear details such as access permissions to users, a read only attribute, and the date of file creation and modification. Please note that the file system is closely connected with the user's operating system choice. If you prefer to run Windows, you must use NTFS. If you wish to run Linux, you must employ a different type of a file system, probably ext3.

To sum it up, a file system serves these purposes:

- It sets up the way files are named. Applications such as text processors and video players use these names to access files. These applications do not *see* where the particular file is physically stored on the hard drive.

- Applications access the file system using an application programming interface (API) and make requests, such as copy, paste, rename, create directory, update metadata and file removal.

- A file system is always installed on a homogenous storage area that is, in the context of operating systems, called a volume.

- A file system stores information about where data is physically located.

- A file system stores metadata that contains additional information.

- A file system maintains data integrity and allows you to set access restrictions and permissions.

- A file system can offer advanced functionalities, such as file compression, encryption and keeping track of various versions of a single file (older and newer, using volume shadow copy technology).

There are more features of a file system, but the ones we discussed are among the most important. Please note that storage systems do not work with file systems, but with blocks. Blocks consist of raw data that can be seen as a sequence of bytes or bits. Blocks can have various lengths, meaning the number of bytes or bits that can be stored in one block depends on the block's size. In a storage system, you have special hardware processors that determine where to store the particular data depending on a storage system's configuration and settings.

Figure 1.7 shows how a file system works in general terms. To have a better idea how a particular file system works, we can take a closer look at the NTFS used by Windows.

To understand how this particular system works, please refer **to Figure 1.8**, where you can see the Windows boot procedure. The MBR is stored on the first sector of a hard drive. This record contains disk partitioning information, and also tells BIOS which partition is active and bootable. The boot sector can be found on each partition and contains information about the file structure (in Windows it is a tree structure). The NT loader is a set of instructions describing how to use the file system and in which order to load all the drivers and libraries. At the end of this process, we have a running operating system. Note the difference between kernel mode and user mode. In kernel mode, the operating system has direct access to installed hardware. In user mode, applications access these devices via the operating system and its drivers.

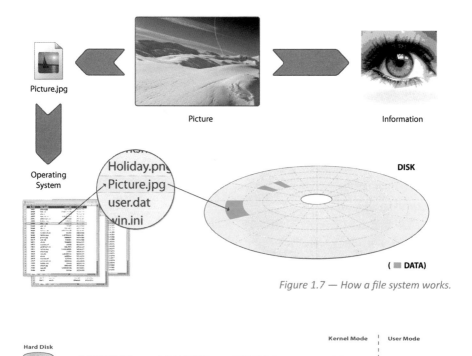

Picture.jpg

Picture

Information

Operating System

Holiday.png
Picture.jpg
user.dat
win.ini

DISK

(■ DATA)

Figure 1.7 — How a file system works.

Hard Disk

Kernel Mode | User Mode

Master Boot Record → Boot Sector → NT Loader → Operating System → Applications

Figure 1.8 — How the NTFS works.

Logical units on a storage system

We are already familiar with conceptual distinction between physical and logical levels of data. Now it is time to reveal why this is so important when it comes to storage systems. In very broad terms, we can see a storage system as a rather complicated and sophisticated bunch of hard drives based on different technologies (according to requirements on performance). This bunch of hard drives creates a large storage area that is further partitioned into smaller storage areas that are to be linked to individual servers. Usually, you have several servers with running applications connected to one storage system. The partitions you create on a storage system are basically logical units that are striped across a large number of physical hard drives. When we talked about partitioning, you learned that you can split one physical drive into several partitions. On a storage system, this works the other way around — you usually connect several physical hard drives, or their parts, to create one partition. This partition or logical unit is then assigned a unique identification number, which is called a ***logical unit number (LUN)***. Remember this definition because we will be talking about LUNs many times throughout this book. The LUN created on the storage system physical hard drive is then linked to a server. This is called ***mapping***. We create a logical unit and then we map it to a server. When we map a LUN to a server, the server then sees this LUN as a physical disc and is able to perform read and write operations as if it really were a single physical hard drive.

From this description, we can see that physical and logical layers work on several levels. You have physical hard drives on a storage system and then you create a logical unit and map it to a server, which sees it as if it were a physical hard drive. The server installs a file system on this *physical* drive, making it *logical* to the user, which can be an application or an actual person sitting in front of the server.

Though this is already a very complex topic, it is actually just the beginning. Storage systems today create so many virtualized logical layers that it is easy to get lost. At this point, it is also good to mention why storage systems work on so many virtualized logical layers — it is because of performance. In the next chapter, we'll explain how we achieve performance through virtual logical layers.

To summarize, LUNs represent a logical abstraction or a virtualization layer between the physical disk device/volume and the applications. Storage administrators can assign access and privileges on the basis of LUNs.

A logical unit that is created on a storage system over several physical hard drives is mapped to a server using LUN identification.

In the context of storage systems, logical units are often referred to as LUNs. The term LUN can, therefore, be used to describe just the unique identification number or the logical unit itself.

Key words to remember are **LUN and mapping**.

Microcode

In terms of mere definition, *microcode* is built-in software that works on the lowest layer of instructions, directly controlling hardware equipment. It is important to note that *microcode* is a term used not only with computers and storage systems but with all electronic devices that are based on microprocessor technology. As a cell phone or digital camera user, you may have encountered the procedure of a firmware update — you connect your cell phone or digital camera to a computer and it downloads new internal software (firmware) from the Internet. The term *firmware* can be, in most cases, interchangeable with the term *microcode*. However, firmware installed in your digital camera or even in your washing machine usually contains microcode and some kind of user interface (menu, icons, etc.), while the term microcode can be interpreted as the most basic software, with no graphical user interface (GUI). Microcode is usually stored on a high performance memory chip, which can be either *read only* or *read and write*.

In relation to storage systems, we can differentiate between two types of microcode:

- Microcode stored on individual hard drives: In storage systems, it is common to update microcode stored on each individual hard drive to fix bugs and increase performance of the whole system.

- Microcode on a storage system that also contains an integrated user interface, either a command line interface (CLI) or a GUI. In this case, it is possible to rewrite or update the microcode. Some storage system vendors use the term *firmware* instead of microcode.

Microcode, in a way, represents the interface between the physical hardware and the user, and can be represented by another piece of hardware, application or even end user. It can also be seen as a set of instructions that governs the relationship between the physical layer and the logical layer.

Remember that when we talk about storage systems, the term *microcode* refers to the built-in software that contains basic tools for managing disk arrays. To perform more complicated operations (LUN mapping, RAID group setup, replication, etc.) you need additional software provided by a storage system manufacturer. Storage systems do not require an operating system to run; they use microcode instead.

Data consistency

Data consistency plays a crucial role in any data storing device. To have consistent data basically means you have valid, usable and readable data. In other words, you need to have all ones and zeros in the right order to be able to read data. If something goes wrong in the storage device and just one bit of information is changed, then the whole sequence of ones and zeros becomes unreadable and useless for the end user, which can be an application running on the server. Therefore, it is vitally important to employ various technological means to maintain data consistency and prevent data corruption.

When we use a computer at home, we usually have just one hard drive installed. If this hard drive malfunctions and one sector becomes unreadable, we have little protection and are likely to lose the whole file stored on this bad sector. However, all modern hard drives have bad sector detection tools included in their microcode, and when one particular sector on the disks shows signs of possible failure, the hard drive automatically moves the data from this sector to a more secure place on the platter. Another way to make sure your data remains consistent is to back it up regularly to a data storing device.

The problem of data consistency is even more painful on large storage systems. Due to redundancy concepts, there is virtually no risk of data inconsistency caused by a single hard drive malfunction; the problem is connected with ongoing data transactions. Imagine a situation where a bank operates a server that runs an Internet banking application. This application stores data on an enterprise storage system. The internet banking service is used by many users and there is a large number of transactions made every second. If the server or the storage system loses power, there would be at least one incomplete transaction that hasn't been stored in time. When the bank gets the power back, this incomplete transaction is likely to cause database inconsistency. It can be very difficult to restore data consistency, and that is why storage systems offer sophisticated software tools that in most cases are able to achieve this result.

When we are talking about data consistency, we can differ among:

- Point-in-time consistency

- Transaction consistency

- Application consistency

Point-in-time consistency means that data is consistently "as it was" at any single instant in time. Point-in-time consistency is maintained, for example, in synchronous (continuous) data replication, where data is stored at the same time on two independent storage systems. At any single point-in-time, the data must be the same on both storage systems.

To understand transaction consistency, you must first understand the term *transaction*, which is a logical unit of work that may include a number of files or database updates that occur "in one shot." *Transaction consistency* is described in the example above — the data will not be transaction consistent if there was an in-flight transaction at the time of device failure. In other words, if there was a transaction "hanging somewhere in the air" that was not processed before the shutdown of the storage system, it would be lost. If this happens, the storage system is able to identify that there was a lost transaction and offers the storage administrator various possibilities for fixing the problem.

Application consistency is similar to transaction consistency — there are just more streams of transactions belonging to a single application. If we have an application that uses different kinds of databases and files, we need to keep all streams of transactions consistent.

Data integrity

While data consistency deals with data readability and usability based on the correct sequence of ones and zeros (if there is one mistake in the sequence, the whole file is corrupted and unreadable), data integrity describes accuracy, reliability and correctness in terms of security and authorized access to the file. To put it in a different way — to maintain data integrity, we have to ensure data in a database is not altered. If we lose data integrity, data is still readable and technically usable, but it is not correct. If we disrupt data integrity, we replace one sequence of ones and zeros with another sequence of ones and zeros that also makes sense to the storage system (i.e., data is consistent) but alters the information carried by the data in an undesirable way.

Data can be altered either by unauthorized user access or incorrect application and it can endanger previously stored data by overwriting it instead of, for example, keeping both copies of the file (the original and the altered version).

It is important to maintain integrity and trustworthiness for the entire lifecycle of the data. The reason is that the differences among the various versions of a single file or a single database entry can also carry useful and, in some cases, essential information. To ensure data integrity, we have a large set of tools ranging from permissions and restrictions of access to a single file or a single database entry (we can set the data to *read only* and forbid writing operations), and we can also employ data integrity policies that consist of a set of rules and govern access and possible data alterations.

Storage administrators must take data integrity into consideration when designing data architecture, and they must be trained on how to set rules governing data integrity. Data integrity becomes a complicated matter especially when it comes to structured data, or databases.

Thanks to cheaper and more powerful hardware, we have more and more data coming into existence every day. This, together with increasing dependency of people and businesses on quick access to data and information, brings an exponentially growing demand for storage.

Having read this chapter, you should be able to understand what kinds of data exist and what their importance is to companies and individuals.

You should be able to name and describe the basic principles of data management and terms connected with data storage systems. In later chapters, we will discuss each of these terms in detail and you will see what the technology behind these concepts is and how it works.

Storage components and technologies

2

What are you going to learn in this chapter?

- How a hard drive works
- What means of hardware redundancy we have
- How to describe midrange storage system architecture and components
- How to determine factors directly influencing the performance of a storage system
- How midrange and enterprise storage systems differ

Overview of disk array components

In the first chapter, we discussed data and its importance. You learned the basic principles, and now it's time to get to something slightly more technical — we'll look at the storage system itself to see how these principles work when we implement them. By now you should know that the very basic component of each storage system is a hard drive, a piece of hardware well known from any personal computer. We know that a hard drive is a device that stores data. Simply put, a storage system is a highly sophisticated, state-of-the-art piece of technology that connects dozens or even hundreds of physical hard drives to create a **disk array**. Other components of a storage system include disk array controllers, cache memories, disk enclosures, power supplies, fans and racks. A disk array provides increased availability, resiliency and maintainability by using additional, redundant components (controllers, power supplies, hot-swappable spare hard drives, etc.). If one component of a storage system fails it does not affect the functionality of other components and it doesn't cause loss of data. We call this **dual-controller architecture** or **full redundancy**; these concepts are implemented to have **no single point of failure**. To help you understand how exactly this works, we will start by taking a look at a hard drive and its construction. Then we will describe how these individual hard drives are interconnected and how this influences availability and reliability of data. Once you're familiar with this concept, we'll move to other storage system components and their descriptions.

How does a hard drive work?

A *hard disk drive (HDD)* is a nonvolatile storage device that stores data on a magnetic disk. This is the basic definition. A nonvolatile storage device, unlike a volatile storage device, is able to retain data even when the computer is not switched on — when it is disconnected from a power supply. Data is written on the disk by magnetizing particles within a magnetic material in a pattern that represents the data. The hard disk is able to read back this data by detecting the magnetic patterns created during the write process.

Key components of a disk drive are (see Figure 2.1):

- Platter
- Spindle
- Actuator arm assembly
- Read/write (R/W) head
- Controller

The data is stored in binary form (ones and zeros) on the platters in the shape of circular discs, which are coated on both sides with magnetic particles. The platter itself is made of nonmagnetic material, usually glass, aluminum or ceramic. The data can be read and written by an actuator arm with an R/W head. A spindle holds one or more platters and is connected to a motor that spins the platters at a constant number of revolutions per minute (rpm). The set of platters spins in a sealed case, called a head disk assembly. The velocity of the spinning platters is one of the most important aspects that influences I/O data speed. Common disks spin at 4,800rpm, 5,400rpm and 7,200rpm. The slower drives are typically used in laptops because they consume less power than the faster ones. For use in servers, we see hard drives that have platters spinning at 7,200rpm, 10,000rpm or even 15,000rpm. These hard drives are more expensive and their components must be more durable to maintain a high level of reliability.

The space between the head and platter is so minute that even a dust particle can disrupt the spin. HDDs are manufactured in clean rooms in which air quality, temperature and humidity are tightly controlled. The sealed cover also prevents intrusion of any dust.

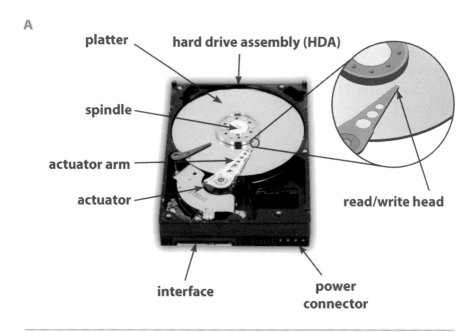

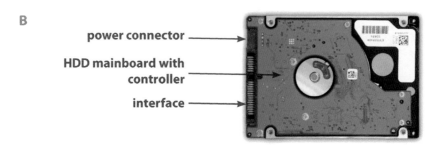

Figure 2.1 — A hard drive and its components.

The read/write head of an HDD reads data from and writes data to the platters. It detects (when reading) and modifies (when writing) the magnetization of the material immediately underneath it. Information is written to the platter as it rotates at high speed past the selected head. The data is, therefore, written in circles called tracks. The tracks are then divided into sectors, which represent the smallest usable space on the hard drive.

An actuator arm with an R/W head is another component that high-ly influences the performance of a hard drive. The actuator arm must quickly find the data on the platters; this is called **seek time**. Average seek times range from 8 – 10ms for common hard drives. However, in the most modern hard drives designed for use in servers, it can be only 3 – 5ms.

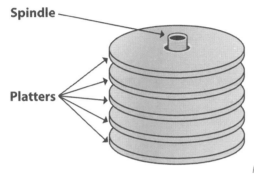

Figure 2.2 — Spindle and platters.

As we already know, performance of an HDD can be measured by velocity of platters in revolutions per minute and by seek time in mil-liseconds. There are two more basic parameters:

- **Capacity**: The number of bytes an HDD can store. The current maximum capacity of an HDD is 4TB.

- **Data transfer rate**: The amount of digital data that can be moved to or from the disk within a given time. It is dependent on the performance of the HDD assembly and the bandwidth of the data path. We can further differentiate between the internal transfer rate from platters to cache (buffer), which is measured within the HDD assembly, and the external transfer rate from the cache to the bus. The average external transfer rates range from 50MB – 300MB per second. See Figure 2.3.

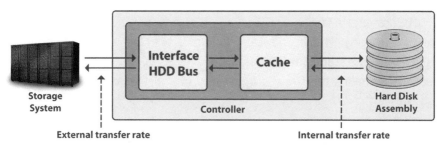

Figure 2.3 — Internal and external transfer rate.

A hard drive is connected to other components of a computer or storage system via an interface. The most common types of interface are:

- Parallel advanced technology attachment (PATA)

- Serial advanced technology attachment (SATA)

- Small computer systems interface (SCSI)

- Serial attached SCSI (SAS)

At this point, it is important to emphasize **that common hard drives used in personal computers cannot usually be used in storage systems**. Storage systems usually support only a few types of hard drives (with strictly determined parameters such as capacity, rpm and interface). These hard drives are equipped with more electronic systems to increase performance. The microcode of these drives contains highly sophisticated monitoring tools that are able to determine the condition of the hard drive and predict possible failures or malfunctions. Hard drives to be used in disk arrays are usually supplied by the manufacturer of the particular storage system. They are sealed in a special plastic drawer that is hot swappable. This hard drive component can be easily plugged in and out of a storage system with no additional equipment, such as a screwdriver.

Parallel advanced technology attachment)

PATA was a standard used to connect HDDs to computers, based on parallel signaling technology. PATA cables are bulky and up to 18in long, so they can be used only in internal drives, which is a serious limitation. The PATA interface became obsolete for a few reasons. Firstly, the data transfer rate is limited to 133MB/sec. Secondly, the hard drive connected via this interface is not **hot-swappable**, which means that if you want to connect or disconnect a drive to the computer, you have to power it down. Especially in the storage systems business, it is necessary that all hard drives (and other components) are hot-swappable. When one hard drive fails, you can replace it without rebooting the whole system.

Figure 2.4 — A PATA cable.

Serial advanced technology attachment

SATA evolved from PATA. It uses serial signaling technology. SATA became a standard mainstream technology used to control and transfer data from a server or storage appliance to a client application. Today, SATA is also a standard in all personal computers. Compared to PATA, SATA has the following advantages:

- Greater bandwidth

- Faster data transfer rates — up to 600GB/sec

- Easy to set up and route in smaller computers

- Low power consumption

- Easier manipulation

- Hot-swap support

Figure 2.5 — SATA cable.

Small computer systems interface

SCSI is a parallel interface standard used to transfer data between devices on both internal and external computer buses. Compared to PATA and SATA, SCSI can offer faster data speeds, multiple devices can connect to a single port and there is a certain level of device independence. A SCSI interface works not only with hard drives, but also with other hardware such as DVD-RW drives. There are some disadvantages, though. SCSI interfaces do not always conform to industry standards, and SCSI is more expensive than PATA and SATA. SCSI is rarely found in personal computers, but it can be found in servers and storage systems. SCSI has recently evolved into SAS.

Serial Attached SCSI

Serial Attached SCSI evolved from the previous SCSI standards; it uses serial signaling technology. SAS is a standard used to control and transfer data with SCSI commands from a server or storage appliance to a client application. SAS can offer even faster data transfer rates than SCSI. This standard also has the lowest power consumption. SAS cables are similar to SATA cables. A SAS bus is compatible with older SATA hard drives. It is thus possible to connect a SATA hard drive to a SAS bus. It is not, however, possible to connect a SAS hard drive to a SATA bus.

SAS technology is very current and suitable for enterprise applications. It offers increased performance and inexpensive implementation (compared to Fibre Channel), and it natively supports redundancy features such as dual bus for connection to two independent/interconnected controllers. Remember that SAS serves not only for connecting a hard drive to a controller within an expansion unit, but also for connecting expansion units to a storage system back end interface.

To sum it up, PATA and SCSI interface technologies are becoming obsolete. SATA can be found in most modern personal computers. Both SATA and SAS hard drives are suitable for use in servers and storage systems.

Solid-state drive (SSD) — a hard drive with no platters

A solid-state drive is a data storage device that uses solid-state memory to store persistent data with the intention of providing access in the same manner of a traditional block I/O hard disk drive. SSDs are different from traditional HDDs, which, as discussed earlier, are electro-mechanical devices containing spinning disks and movable read/write heads. SSDs, in contrast, use microchips that retain data in non-volatile memory chips and contain **no moving parts**. Compared to HDDs, SSDs offer a wide range of advantages. Due to the absence of moving parts, they consume less power, thus producing less heat, which lowers demands on storage system cooling operations. These drives also provide lower access time and latency. The major disadvantages are their price and the limited number of writes over the life of the device. SSDs use the same interface as HDDs, and thus easily replace them in most applications.

Connecting hard drives together

RAID levels and their function

You have learned how a hard drive looks and what its components are. You have also learned that when you interconnect multiple hard drives you get **a disk array**. Now it's time to find out how this is done. The key word is ***redundancy***.

The technology behind connecting hard drives together is called redundant array of inexpensive (or independent) drives **(RAID)**. The trick is to combine several **physical hard drives** to create a single **logical disk** that can be further split or partitioned into LUNs, as mentioned in the previous chapter. The physical hard drives connected in one RAID group must be of the same make and the same capacity — they must be identical. The outcome of all this is that an operating system does not see individual hard drives, but just one logical disk that combines the capacity of all individual hard drives. See Figure 2.6

RAID provides the following advantages:

- Data consistency and integrity (security, protection from corruption)

- Fault tolerance

- Capacity

- Reliability

- Higher speed and better performance

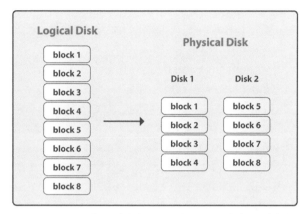

Figure 2.6 — A logical disk is a combination of physical disks.

Different types of RAID can be implemented, according to application requirements. The different types of RAID implementation are known as RAID levels. Common RAID levels are: RAID-0, RAID-1, RAID-1+0, RAID-3, RAID-5 and RAID-6. Each RAID level is a combination and application of four features, or parameters, which are **data striping, data mirroring, data spanning and parity distribution**. Selection and implementation of RAID levels is closely connected with performance requirements and amount of redundancy.

Data striping

Data striping is one of the basic techniques that help us achieve increased performance of a storage system. With one hard drive configuration, you store your files sequentially on the platter. When you wish to access particular data, the R/W head on the actuator must find the correct place on the spinning platters, and then it reads the sequence of bits. This can be further complicated by data fragmentation, when one file is stored on several locations within a single hard drive. This is how data is accessed on personal computers. On a storage system, performance of this sequential access to data is far from sufficient. Data striping provides a solution to this problem.

Imagine that you have, for example, five hard drives and a single file. You can divide this single file into five parts, and then you can store each part on one of those five hard drives. When you want to access this file, it will be read from five hard drives at once, combining their performance. In a storage system, you concatenate these five drives into a single logical disk that can be further partitioned and mapped to a host (server). Whenever you store something on this logical drive, a RAID controller installed in a storage system will stripe the data and distribute it to the physical drives in the fashion that will ensure the highest possible performance. Remember, by data striping, you can achieve increased read and write speed, but you cannot improve seek time performance (with the exception of solid state drives with no moving parts). The significant disadvantage of data striping is the higher risk of failure — when any of the above mentioned five physical drives fails, you will not be able to access your data anymore. In other words, there is no redundant data that could be used for reconstruction of files stored on the damaged hard drive. So data striping must be combined with other techniques to ensure there is no data loss. See Figure 2.7

Data mirroring

Data mirroring is efficient and the easiest way to prevent data loss due to malfunction or failure of one or more physical drives. The principle of data mirroring is quite simple — read and write operations of data are conducted simultaneously on two physical hard drives. One file is automatically saved on two physical drives. This not only ensures a high level of data redundancy, but it also provides increased read performance, because data is accessed on both drives. This performance boost, however, is not as significant as in data striping. This is why these two techniques — data striping and data mirroring — are implemented together. Storage system data mirroring works on the hardware level in the RAID controller. Note that because the data is written in duplicates, the created logical disk is just half the size of the actual installed capacity of physical hard drives. The major disadvantage is costly application.

Data spanning

Data spanning, or linear data writing, is the simplest way of storing data. It does not offer any increase in performance and no level of redundancy and it is therefore not suitable for enterprise application. It can, however, be practical for home use or in small servers. The whole trick is to concatenate several physical drives to create one logical disk. The data is then written on this disk sequentially. In other words, when one physical hard drive gets full, the data is stored on the next available physical drive. This can be useful when you want to have a unified logical disk on several hard drives with no demands on increased performance. The main advantage of data spanning implementation is that you do not need a hardware RAID controller. The other advantage is that the system that consists of several physical hard drives is easily scalable; when you run out of space, you can easily add more physical hard drives. The last advantage is that if one physical hard drive fails, the data on other hard drives is not lost [except for the file(s) that are overlapping both physical hard drives]. Data spanning is also used on CDs and DVDs. When you are making a backup image of your data, it often happens that capacity of one backup medium is not enough. You will therefore back up your system on several DVDs.

Parity

The last procedure for RAID implementations uses parity data to balance the disadvantages of data striping and data mirroring. Data striping offers no redundancy and data mirroring is costly because you can only use half of the physically installed capacity. If you want to overcome these issues and get the best of all the above mentioned techniques, you should use parity. In simple terms, parity data contains information that can be used to reconstruct and recalculate data on a failed hard drive. Using parity requires at least three physical hard drives. You would concatenate these drives to create a single logical disk. The logical disk offers two–thirds of the physically installed capacity. Whenever you perform write operation on this logical disk, the RAID controller stripes data on two physical hard drives and then, using sophisticated algorithms, calculates parity data to be stored on the third physical drive. Note that you can also stripe parity data. In this case, the RAID controller calculates the parity data and then stores data and parity stripes on all three physical hard drives. Parity data works by complementing actual data. The advantages are obvious — you save money, and you have a good level of redundancy and performance. The disadvantage is that, if one disk fails, it takes time to reconstruct the data from the parity. However, the RAID controllers used in modern storage systems are powerful enough to overcome even this issue, and when a disk fails, it provides fast reconstruction times and prioritized immediate access to required data.

Just a Bunch of Discs (JBOD)

This method of interconnecting hard drives cannot really be included in RAID levels since it offers neither redundancy nor better performance. In fact, *JBOD* is a term used for implemented data spanning. Data is written and read sequentially. When one disk gets full, data is stored on another disk in succession. Aside from the benefits we mentioned in the data spanning section, there is another advantage — you are not limited to using hard drives of the same make, capacity and interface — you can use whatever hard drive you have. JBOD is implemented in small servers or in computers that are designed to work with large amounts of data, for example, computers for video editing.

RAID-0

In RAID-0, data is spread evenly across two or more disks, data is stored just once without any backup copy. RAID-0 is easy to implement and offers increased performance in terms of data access (more disks equals more heads, which enables parallel access to more data records). This RAID level has no redundancy and no fault tolerance. If any disk fails, data on the remaining disks cannot be retrieved, which is the major disadvantage.

With a three disk implementation, one third of the data is sequentially written to each disk. In other words, if you store a file to a logical disk that consists of three physical disks connected in a RAID-0 level, this file is then divided into three pieces, and each piece is stored on a separate disk. We can see that RAID-0 uses only **data striping**.

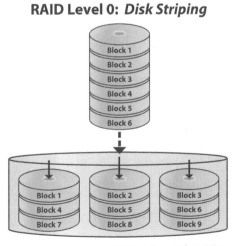

RAID Level 0: *Disk Striping*

Figure 2.7 — Disk Striping.

RAID-1

RAID-1 implements **mirroring** to create exact copies of data on two or more disks. In this way, it can offer increased availability of the data, resistance to a disk failure and, thus, a good level of redundancy. RAID-1 is easy to implement, and it reduces the overhead of managing multiple disks and tracking the data. It provides fast read/write speed because the system can read from either disk. If a disk fails, RAID-1 ensures there is an exact copy of the data on the second disk. This RAID level also has some disadvantages. The most important is limited capacity — in RAID-1, the true storage capacity is only half of the actual capacity, as data is written twice. This also makes RAID-1 implementation more expensive — it doubles the costs.

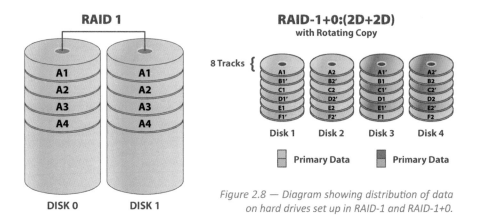

Figure 2.8 — Diagram showing distribution of data on hard drives set up in RAID-1 and RAID-1+0.

RAID-1+0

RAID-1+0 is an example of multiple, or **nested**, RAID levels. A **nested** RAID level combines the features of multiple RAID levels. The sequence in which they are implemented determines the naming of the nested RAID level. For example, if RAID-0 is implemented before RAID-1, the RAID level is called RAID-0+1. RAID-0+1 combine the features of RAID-0 and RAID-1 by mirroring a striped array. The advantages of this connection are obvious — you get fast read/write speed and data protection based on redundancy of data. The only disadvantage is high implementation cost.

RAID-5 and RAID-6

RAID-5 consists of a minimum of three disks (two data and one parity). RAID-5 distributes **parity** information across all disks to minimize potential bottlenecks if one disk fails. If failure occurs, parity data from the other disks is used to recreate the missing information. RAID-5 is the most common and secure RAID level that balances performance, security and cost. It ensures fast read speed and data recovery if a disk failure occurs. The disadvantage is that extra overhead is required to calculate and track parity data. It offers slower writes because it has to calculate parity before writing data.

To implement RAID-6, at least four disks are required. This configuration is very similar to RAID-5, with an additional parity block, allowing block level striping with two parity blocks. The advantages and disadvantages are the same as RAID-5, except the additional parity disk protects the system against double-disk failure. This feature was implemented to ensure the reliability of the SATA drives. **The key value** is that two parity drives allow a customer to lose up to two HDDs in a RAID group without losing data. RAID groups configured for RAID-6 are less likely to lose data in the event of a failure. RAID-6 performs nearly as well as RAID-5 for similar usable capacity. RAID-6 also gives the customer options as to when to rebuild the RAID group. In RAID-5, when an HDD is damaged, the RAID group must be rebuilt immediately (since a second failure may result in lost data). During a rebuild, applications using the volumes on the damaged RAID group can expect severely diminished performance. A customer using RAID-6 may elect to wait to rebuild until a more opportune time (night or weekend), when applications will not require stringent performance. See Figure 2.9 for reference.

RAID-5:(3D + P)
Data is striped with parity over RAID members.

Disk 1   Disk 2   Disk 3   Disk 4

Figure 2.9 — Data distribution across hard drives connected in RAID-5 and RAID-6 groups.

RAID-6:(6D + 2P)
Data is striped with parity over RAID members.

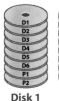    

Disk 1   Disk 2   Disk 3   Disk 4   Disk 5   Disk 6   Disk 7   Disk 8

The last few pages provided you with fundamental redundancy concepts based on RAID implementation. You should also understand the direct connection of RAID implementation to the performance of a storage system.

You now know what a hard drive is and how it works. You also know basic principles of interconnecting hard drives together. In the next pages, we will essentially build up a midrange storage system, taking a look at all the components and their architecture.

Remember the key principles: data striping, data mirroring, redundancy and parity. You will hear about these often.

RAID level range

In the previous paragraphs, we described the most common RAID levels in their minimal configuration. For example, we know that for

RAID-5 you need at least three hard drives — two for data and one for parity. However, this configuration can be extended. When we use a distributed parity, we can, for example, have seven hard drives used for data and one for parity and the result will still be RAID-5. Usually it is more advantageous to use a higher number of hard drives than allowed by a minimal configuration, especially for performance reasons. The more hard drives you have in a parity group, the more data stripes created, which offers higher read speed. Storage systems from various vendors support different RAID level configurations. These RAID level configurations are also often called a RAID level range. The RAID parity group is a building block of a RAID group. In other words, if you create a RAID-5 group in an eight disk configuration (7D+1P) — this will be your parity group. Several parity groups will then make a RAID group. Remember that hard drives used in one RAID group must be of the same make, capacity and interface.

Relative RAID performance

The table below shows the performance levels for different RAID configurations relative to RAID-1+0 (2D+2P), which is assumed to be 100% for reads and writes. The illustration is not meant to be a recommendation or imply that one RAID group is better than another RAID group, but to illustrate how performance of a RAID group should be matched to the type of performance an application needs.

RAID Level	Random Read, Sequential Read	Sequential Write	Random Write
RAID-1+0 (2D+2P)	100 %	100 %	100 %
RAID-5 (3D+1P)	100 %	150 %	50 %
RAID-5 (7D+1P)	200 %	350 %	100 %
RAID-6 (6D+2P)	200 %	300 %	66.7 %
Note	Proportional to the number of disks	Proportional to the number of data disks	–

The second column shows that the random read and sequential read performance is proportional to the number of disks, because the disks can be accessed simultaneously. With sequential writes, there are no reads involved as with random writes. Therefore, the performance is proportional to the number of data disks.

As for the random writes column, the reason for the performance difference between RAID-6 (6D+2P) and RAID-5 (7D+1P) is that RAID-6 (6D+2P) must process 1.5 times (see below) more disk I/Os than RAID-5 (7D+1P). Therefore, the random write performance in RAID-6 (6D+2P) is 33% lower than with RAID-5 (7D+1P). The number of disk I/Os in RAID-5 random writes is four (old data/old parity reads, new data/new parity writes). The number of disk I/Os in RAID-6 random writes are six [old data/old parity (P)/old parity (Q) reads, new data/new parity (P)/new parity (Q) writes].

The values listed in the table were collected using the Hitachi Adaptable Modular Storage 2000 family system. The table is meant to illustrate that different applications may require different performance characteristics from its RAID group.

Software and hardware RAID

To implement RAID, you need specific means, which can be either software or hardware based. For purely software RAID implementation, you need just an operating system and perhaps some third party application, which will simplify the procedure. The advantage is the cost — this solution is very cheap. The software based RAID implementation will, however, show lower performance than other solutions. Other disadvantages include dependency on the operating system, slow and problematic reconstruction of data if one hard drive fails and limitation to only a few basic RAID levels in their minimal configuration. Since this solution is purely software based, there is no dedicated hardware responsible for all the operations. All operations are controlled by the central processing unit (CPU), which also calculates parity information. Performance of the CPU is therefore diminished. As a result, this type of solution is applicable only in home environments and is not suitable for application in business environments.

Some manufacturers of mainboards for personal computers offer dedicated RAID chip controllers. This is, in most cases, just marketing because all the computing is done by the CPU. This type of solution also does not usually support interfaces other than SATA or the now obsolete IDE.

Hardware RAID controllers, on the other hand, offer much more than their software counterparts. They include dedicated processing units for parity data calculation, and they have cache memory for improved I/O operations. If one disk fails, the reconstruction is automatic and faster. You do not need any additional software, and you can configure the RAID array and perform all the operations by accessing the built-in microcode interface. Hardware RAID controllers can ensure data consistency by adding an independent backup battery that is connected to cache and keeps it alive in case of power disruption. When the power is back online, data in the cache is stored on the hard drive, and the user does not lose any data. A hardware RAID controller is usually employed in servers or in high performance professional computers. In storage systems, you always have a powerful integrated RAID controller modified to support a large number of individual hard drives.

On personal computers, it is possible to combine software RAID with hardware RAID. On the hardware level, you can create two 1+0 RAID groups that can be further joined in RAID-0 on the software level.

In this way, you can stripe data across a striped and mirrored disk array, gaining additional performance. This type of solution is possible, but not implemented very often because of software RAID downsides. It is enough to know it is theoretically possible.

Spare disks

In any storage system you must have spare hard drives so that if one disk in a RAID group fails, there is another one ready to take over. The damaged hard drive is later manually replaced with a new disk.

There are two methods that support sparing out of RAID group data:

- **Correction copy**

- **Dynamic sparing**

Correction copy occurs when a drive in a RAID group fails and a compatible spare drive exists. Data is then reconstructed on the spare drive. Figure 2.10 shows how the reconstruction is conducted depending on the RAID level implemented.

Dynamic sparing occurs if the online verification process (built-in diagnostic) determines that the number of errors has exceeded the specified threshold of a disk in a RAID group. Data is then moved to the spare disk, which is a much faster process than data reconstruction. See Figure 2.11 for details.

Notice that the speed of reconstruction of a failed disk depends on the implemented RAID level. If we have a RAID-1 level, which uses only mirroring and no parity information, the whole process of reconstruction is simple, because the system just copies the data from the mirrored drive to the spare disk. With RAID-5, the reconstruction will take longer, because lost data must be calculated from the remaining disks and parity information. In RAID-6, we have double-disk failure protection — if two disks fail, the procedure takes even longer than in RAID-5. In Figures 2.10 – 2.13 all the diagrams are marked with an "**I/O is possible**" title. This means the data is accessible even during the process of reconstruction. Performance of storage will be affected, but you have immediate access to your data because requested data reconstruction is prioritized during the process. Remember that in the event of double-disk failure on a RAID level other than RAID-6, you lose all the data and you are not able to reconstruct it using conventional means. That is why RAID technology is usually combined with other techniques to ensure redundancy and high availability. The most common of these techniques is data replication, which will be discussed in its own chapter.

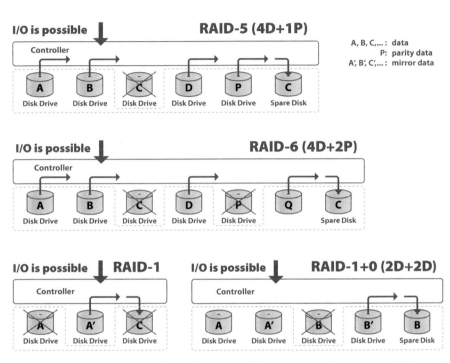

Figure 2.10 — This diagram shows the process of data reconstruction in event of failure of one or more hard drives. In RAID-6 we have two parity disks: P and Q.

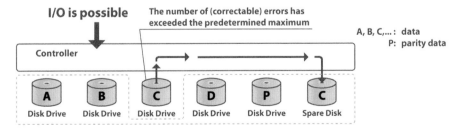

Figure 2.11 — Dynamic sparing operations.

Sparing can be set in such a fashion that storage system controllers check the health of the installed hard drives and anticipate possible future failure. Each hard drive has built-in diagnostics that monitor and store various parameters, for example, Spin-Up Time, Start/Stop Count and Seek Error Rate. When the possible future failure is detected, the storage system automatically moves data to the spare disk. This saves time, especially because copying data is always faster than recalculating data from the parity.

Built-in diagnostic capability is part of all modern hard drives, even those used in personal computers. This technology is called Self-Monitoring, Analysis and Reporting Technology (**SMART**). To access data collected by a hard drive controller, you need special monitoring software able to read and evaluate this data.

Note that diagnostics used in storage systems are more sophisticated than SMART.

On most modern storage systems, correction copy can have two parameters set by a storage system administrator. These two parameters are *copy back* and *no copy back*, and they influence the behavior of the storage system once the failed drive is manually removed from the storage system and replaced by a new hard drive. Depending on the settings, the storage system can move data from the spare disk that was used for data reconstruction to this new drive, or it can set this newly added hard drive as a new spare disk while the former spare disk becomes the regular member of the RAID group.

In Figure 2.12, you can see the diagram of "copy back settings." A copy back procedure takes less time than data reconstruction, but it can still have a minor impact on the storage system performance. That is why it should be conducted when the system is not on high load, for example at night. Copy back parameter can also be used with dynamic sparing technology.

Choice of either *copy back* or *no copy back* usually depends on the storage system administrator alone. Since performance is not gained from either of these parameters, the selected option mainly has organizational impact.

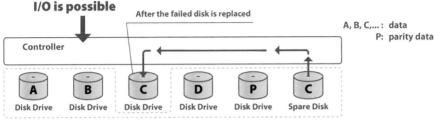

Figure 2.12 — Correction copy with "copy back" parameter.

As you can see in Figure 2.13, if parameter *no copy back* is selected, after a dynamic sparing process or correction copy, the spare disk becomes a permanent member of the RAID group and a copy back does not occur. The replacement disk becomes the new spare disk.

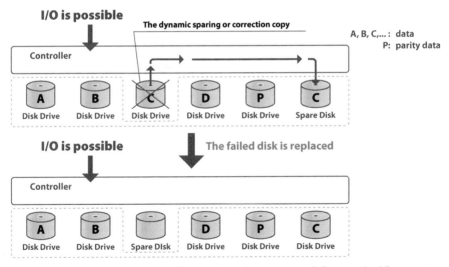

Figure 2.13 — Sparing out with "no copy back" parameter.

Storage system hard drive enclosures

A *disk enclosure* is another component of a storage system. In terms of definition, we can find two possible interpretations:

• The most widely accepted description is a chassis with a single hard drive and additional electronics (e.g., interface conversion board). A good example of this is an external hard drive, which is basically a small box with a SATA drive and a chip that converts a SATA interface to USB.

• In relation to storage systems, a disk enclosure can be understood as a hot-swappable hard drive unit. See Figure 2.14.

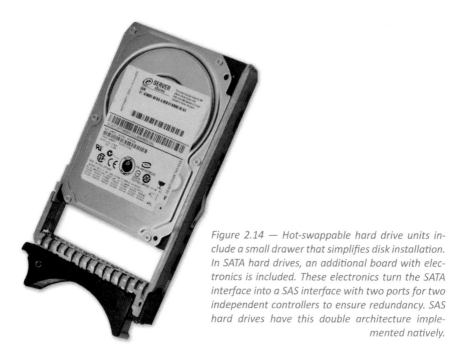

Figure 2.14 — Hot-swappable hard drive units in-clude a small drawer that simplifies disk installation. In SATA hard drives, an additional board with elec-tronics is included. These electronics turn the SATA interface into a SAS interface with two ports for two independent controllers to ensure redundancy. SAS hard drives have this double architecture imple-mented natively.

For storage systems, the term *hard drive enclosure* often covers not only the hot-swappable disk chassis, but the whole expansion unit that is basically a rack for installing many individual physical hard drives. In other words, in the context of storage systems, the terms *hard drive enclosure* and *expansion unit* are interchangeable.

An expansion unit or disk enclosure (based on SAS architecture), consists of following components:

- Individual hard drives (SAS, SATA, SSD)

- Expander (buses and wires for connecting the drives together)

- Power supplies

- Cooling system (fans)

- Chassis

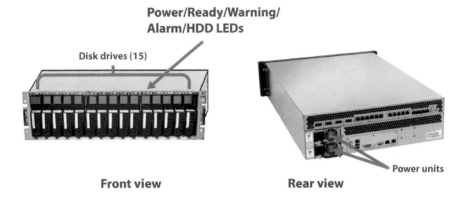

Figure 2.15 — Front and rear view of an expansion unit/disk enclosure, Hitachi Adaptable Modular Storage 2000 family.

In Figure 2.15, you can see how a typical expansion unit looks. Note that we usually have two types of expansion units — a **standard expansion unit**, which can usually accommodate 15 hard disks, and a **high density expansion unit**, which can accommodate up to 50 hard drives. In high density expansion units, the disks are installed vertically and are not directly accessible from the front panel. The advantage is that you save space. The disadvantage is more complicated access to individual disks and demand for more powerful cooling system (more disks generate more heat). Also notice the status LED lights that are a standard part of regular expansion units and serve for monitoring purposes. Another reason each disk is accompanied with LED lights is localization of a particular hard drive. Imagine that one disk in the enclosure fails. The reconstruction process starts immediately and a spare disk is used. An illuminated LED marks the failed disk that needs to be manually replaced. In high density expansion units, this is more complicated since you need to pull out the whole expansion unit from the rack, remove its cover and then localize the failed hard disk.

On the rear side of an expansion unit, you can see ports for connecting the enclosure to the back end controller of a storage system. These ports can be based either on Fibre Channel or SAS technology, whichever is more efficient. We will describe the operations and differences of these two technologies in detail later in this chapter. You can also see power cord outlets.

In midrange storage systems, the first enclosure is usually part of the base unit, together with other components. In some storage systems, the base unit enclosure uses the first few hard drives for storing system administration software. The remaining capacity of these hard drives cannot be used for user data.

We know that each SAS disk is equipped with two SAS connectors. An expansion unit has two expanders — each one is connected to one SAS connector on each hard drive. If we use a SATA hard drive, we need an additional device that will convert one SATA port into two SAS ports. All this is done to meet cause of redundancy requirements. Storage systems are also equipped with double architecture — every component in a storage system is duplicated to maintain the no single point of failure requirement. This means that we also have two back end controllers that are connecting expansion units. Any hard drive is, therefore, connected to both back end controllers via expanders and SAS cables. *See Figure 2.16.*

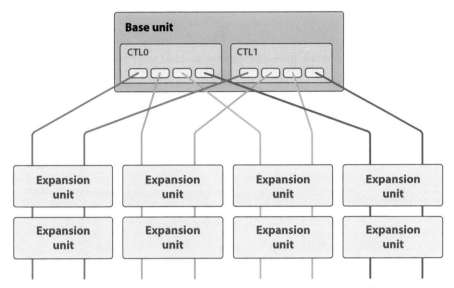

Figure 2.16 — Each expansion unit is connected to both controllers.

Back end architecture

A midrange storage system contains main controller boards that are equipped with components that can be put into three categories:

- **Front end** (connection to hosts or other storage systems)

- **Cache** (works as a buffer, has major influence on performance)

- **Back end** (connection to hard drive enclosures, RAID operations)

Since we are building a midrange storage system step by step from hard drives to complex solutions, the back end is another component. Please refer to Figure 2.17 to see how the individual components are connected.

When we are talking about back end architecture, we should know that there are two basic ways of interconnecting individual disks in enclosures. One is based on **Fibre Channel** technology and uses **Arbitrated Loop** topology. This architecture is, however, becoming obsolete, and that is why we will pay more attention to **SAS technology**, which is becoming a standard in back end architecture. More information about Fibre Channel Arbitrated Loop can be found later in this chapter.

Individual components of SAS back end architecture are depicted in Figure 2.17:

- **DCTL/RAID** — Disk controller with RAID processor. Determines where to store the particular data coming from host via front end and cache. Takes care of striping and calculates parity data. In event of disk failure, it will control data reconstruction.

- **SAS controller** — Together with SAS buses, it provides the interface for connecting enclosures with individual hard drives.

- **WL/cable** — SAS wide link; a type of SAS cable.

- **Expander** — Serves for connecting individual hard drives.

- **AAMux** — Multiplexer that changes SATA interface to SAS interface (SAS encapsulation).

- **CTL0 and CTL1** — Names of the controllers; notice double architecture.

- **Cache** — High-speed memory; a key component that stands between back end and front end.

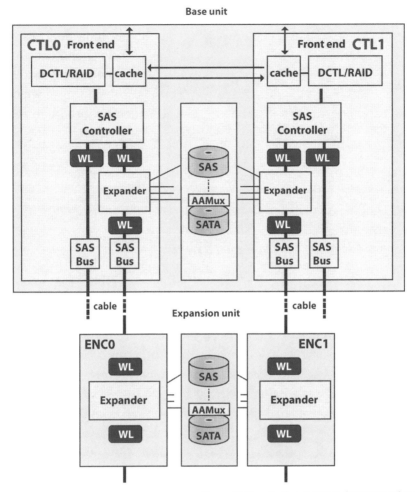

Figure 2.17 — Back end SAS architecture scheme.

Fibre Channel Arbitrated Loop (FC-AL) architecture

To understand operations and advantages of SAS back end architecture, we need to become familiar with back end architecture based on the Fibre Channel Arbitrated Loop. Even though this solution is becoming obsolete and is not used in new models of storage systems anymore, it is still present in installations that run applications on older equipment. Note that SAS back end architecture is quite new — introduced in 2008.

The name Fibre Channel Arbitrated Loop is derived from the three basic parameters that define this type of architecture:

- **Fibre Channel** — Data is transferred through fiber optic cables in the form of light impulses. These cables are made from glass or plastic.

- **Loop** — All the hard drives are sequentially connected to a cable structure that resembles a loop. A loop connection is an alternative to a point-to-point connection.

- **Arbitrated** — Only one hard drive can communicate with the controller at a time. On the loop, the *token* is circulating. A token, which is essentially a bit of data, determines which hard drive can communicate with the controller. If you need to write data on a particular disk, you need to wait until the token reaches this disk, because only then is the communication possible. In other words, only the hard drive that has the token can communicate with the controller. When the I/O operation is finished, the token moves to another hard drive. Since data is usually not read or written in a sequential manner, you have a longer response time because you have to wait for the token to reach its destination hard drive. This is the element of arbitration. See Figure 2.18.

In FC-AL technology, you have a single link for one path that supports a 4Gb/sec transfer speed. To meet redundancy requirements, each hard drive is connected to two loops, each one belonging to one controller (CTL0 and CTL1).

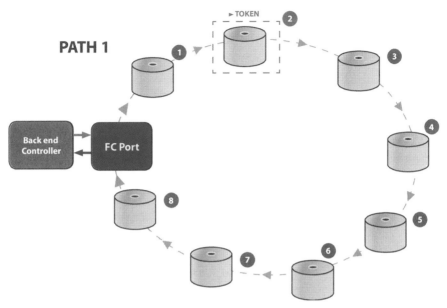

Figure 2.18 — Fibre Channel Arbitrated Loop back end architecture. Only one hard drive can communicate with the controller at a time. A token determines which device can communicate with the controller; other hard drives have to wait for their turn.

Do not confuse Fibre Channel Arbitrated Loop, which is becoming obsolete, with Fibre Channel itself. Fibre Channel can deliver speeds up to 12.75Gb/sec and is suitable for application over distance, since Fibre Channel cables can be up to 100km long. A Fibre Channel connection is often used between servers and storage system (front end). It is also the building block of Storage Area Networks (SANs) that represent the storage system networking infrastructure.

SAS back end architecture in detail

In comparison with FC-AL, SAS can provide a point-to-point connection, where hard drives communicate directly with controllers. The controller does not have to wait until the token reaches the destination hard drive because, in SAS back end, there is no such thing. In the configuration with four SAS links, there can be four hard drives communicating with the controller at the same time, each with a data transfer rate of 3Gb/sec. We know that FC-AL can deliver 4Gb/sec. In SAS architecture we can, therefore, reach three times higher performance. FC-AL provides good performance with larger chunks of data written sequentially, while SAS performs much better with random I/O operations. We can illustrate this with an example: imagine that you have a train and a car. Train cargo transportation is efficient when you have lots of load directed to one destination. On the other hand, the car will be more efficient with small loads to multiple locations. Since storage systems must handle more "small" random I/O operations, SAS back end architecture offers better performance.

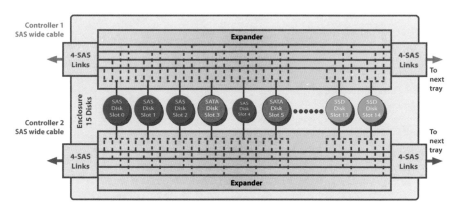

Figure 2.19 — SAS back end architecture. Hard drives are connected to expanders, which are placed in enclosures. In this picture, we can see an example of a four SAS link expander.

SAS based back end solutions provide other advantages in addition to those we have already mentioned. SAS hardware is cheaper than FC-AL hardware, thus it is more powerful technology for less money. SAS is also able to handle failures more efficiently than FC-AL because it uses component level reporting. When a hard drive fails, this particular drive is mapped out and the failure is reported by a system monitoring tool. FC-AL, on the other hand, does not report at the component level, but it reports any failures at the loop level. The outcome is that it takes longer to correct the malfunction. The SAS solution, therefore, boasts higher availability and allows for greater redundancy.

SAS also natively supports full duplex. Full duplex communication means that both devices (controller and hard drive) can talk to each other at the same time. In other words, both devices are able to transmit and receive I/O simultaneously. A half duplex solution is similar to communication over walkie talkies — only one side can talk at a time. Fibre Channel technology delivers half duplex or full duplex depending on the system architecture.

Cache

We have described individual hard drives in detail and how they are connected together. You learned that the hard drive is the component that stores data, and its performance is measured in transfer data rate. In paragraphs dedicated to RAID, you learned that data striping can increase performance of a storage system — the storage system performs more I/O operations per second. I/O operations are basically read and write requests coming from the host, which is the server. Nevertheless, hard drives are still the major bottleneck in storage systems. Their performance is not sufficient, simply because of the limitations of their construction. When you want to perform I/O operations with a hard drive, you have to wait for the platter to turn into the right position and for the actuator to move the head on the spot where you want to write or read data. You may object that solid-state drives already overcame these limitations, but they are still very expensive and their limitation is somewhere else — solid-state drives offer a reduced number of writes per one memory unit, compared to common hard drives with platters. The technology of solid-state drives is advanceing, but it still needs perfection. **The component that drastically improves storage system performance is cache.**

In storage systems, cache is volatile high-speed memory that can temporarily store data. Volatile means that this type of memory is erased when the power is turned off. Let's compare it with the perfor-

mance of a hard drive — hard drives connected in RAID with data striping and cache:

- **A standalone hard drive** can deliver external transfer data rates
  ranging from 100MB/sec – 300MB/sec. If we take 150MB/sec as
  the average value, the average seek time is 5ms.

- **RAID-5 in 3D+1P** configuration increases data transfer rates to
  approximately 450MB/sec for read operations (data is read from
  three drives). The write speed also increases, but not as drastically, since there is time required to calculate parity data and this
  data also must be written (on four drives). You still have 5ms seek
  time because of the construction limitations of a hard drive.

- **Cache** can offer speeds up to 8GB/sec (8,000MB/sec) with access
  time under 1ms. You can, therefore, see that cache speed is significantly higher.

When a host server makes write requests to the connected storage
system, it has to wait at least 5ms for the platters and actuator to turn
to the right position, plus time for the data transport itself. Another
read or write operation cannot be performed until the ongoing one is
marked as completed. Instead, it must be queued, which slows down
the whole system. Furthermore, you do not usually have a single server connected to a single storage system — you can have hundreds of
them. Response time of a storage system without cache would not be
sufficient. **Response time** is defined as the duration of the cycle when
a server makes a request for a write operation and the storage system
sends confirmation that this write operation has been successfully completed.

The reason cache improves performance of a storage system is based
on the assumption that some of the data stored in a storage system
is accessed more often than other data. This frequently accessed data
can, therefore, be temporarily stored in high performance memory that
is expensive and can have limited capacity compared to non-volatile
storage devices. This function of a storage system is especially useful

for read operations. For write operations, cache operates more as a buffer. With cache implementation, whenever the server makes a write request, data is written to cache and then to the installed hard drives. The storage system, however, will send the confirmation of the successful write as soon as the data is stored in cache. The storage system waits to collect more write requests to one destination, thus making the write operations more efficient since several write commands are sent in one batch instead of sending several write requests to the disks. The transfer of data from cache to the physical drives is solely dependent on a storage system. The host gets the information of a successful write when data is stored in cache, considers the whole operation completed and immediately sends another request. That's why cache dramatically reduces a storage system's response time.

Two kinds of cache can be implemented: global cache for both read and write operations or dedicated cache that supports either read or write operations, but not both. Modern systems are equipped with global cache.

In midrange storage systems, the cache provides capacity of at least 8GB – 16GB. Cache is the component that lies between the storage system's front end and back end.

Note, that individual hard drives also have small built-in cache to improve their performance. Capacity of this built-in cache ranges from 8MB – 64MB. This cache basically works on the same principles as cache in a storage system. Built-in cache improves performance of the external data transfer rate compared to the internal data transfer rate.

Cache operations

Cache operations are controlled by the CPU and interface board that are usually part of the front end. Because the capacity of cache is limited, efficient data management is of crucial importance. To maintain uninterrupted and fast data flow from the host to the back end hard drives and vice-versa, the storage system's microcode contains algorithms that should anticipate what data is advantageous to keep (for faster read access) and what data should be erased. There are two basic algorithms that affect the way cache is freed up:

- Least Recently Used (LRU) — Data that is stored in cache and has not been accessed for a given period of time (i.e., data that is not accessed frequently enough) is erased.

- Most Recently Used (MRU) — Data accessed most recently is erased. This is based on the assumption that recently used data may not be requested for a while.

The capacity of cache is shared by two basic kinds of data — read data, coming from the hard drives to the servers, and write data, coming from the servers to the hard drives. The ratio of cache available for read and write operations is dynamically adjusted according to the workload.

Other algorithms govern the behavior of cache when it is getting full or is underused. When the cache approaches the value set by the microcode, dirty data is immediately sent to the hard drives for write. *Dirty data* is a term for write data that has been confirmed to the server as written but has not been written to actual hard drives yet.

Other operations are based on configuration. Storage systems are usually supplied with software for cache management and cache partitioning. Cache partitioning can be useful because various applications running on servers have various requirements on cache. Optimal configuration of cache highly influences performance of the whole storage system and the whole infrastructure.

Cache data protection

Cache is volatile memory dependent on a constant power supply, and it contains write data that appears to the server as if it has already been written, but is in fact still in cache and not yet on the hard drives. This all means that cache is an extremely sensitive and potentially vulnerable component that requires careful handling. Since the storage systems are based on double architecture that provides no single point of failure, cache must also be equipped with the means that ensure redundancy. The first technique of data protection in cache is **cache mirroring**. Both independent controllers (CTL0 and CTL1) have their own cache module. Both these modules are of the same size and technical specifications. Thanks to cache mirroring, the cache modules on both controllers contain the same data. This brings protection in the event of a controller or cache module failure. However, it does not solve the dependency on electricity.

To overcome dependency on constant power supply, we have batteries installed in a storage system. In case of power failure, all components of a storage system shut down immediately. Installed batteries only keep data in cache alive. Depending on the capacity of installed batteries, data can be kept in cache up to 36hrs.

Some storage system vendors equip their devices with a **cache vaulting** functionality. The storage system that supports cache vaulting must be equipped with more powerful batteries. In the event of power failure, batteries support not only data in cache, but also other components of the base unit. The only subsystems that shut down immediately are connected expansion units. Data from cache is then dumped on dedicated hard drives called *vault drives*. When the data is safely placed on the hard drives, the whole system shuts down. When the power is back online, cache is restored using the cache image stored on the vault drive.

Front end architecture

When we talk about the storage system front end, we usually mean the interface board with individual ports that connect the storage system to the SAN with servers. The main component, therefore, is the **interface board**. The interface board bears controllers for the particular port. Common front end ports are:

- **Fibre Channel (FC)** — The medium is optical fiber wire that supports high speeds. Fibre channel is usually the best option you can go with when building a SAN.

- **Fibre Channel over Ethernet (FCoE)** — The medium is metallic (copper) wire, but the network protocol is still based on Fibre Channel. This solution is cheaper but cannot offer as high a transfer speed as Fibre Channel. There are also limitations in copper wire length. This port is becoming obsolete and in modern storage system it is replaced by the iSCSI port.

- **iSCSI** — Interface that connects the storage system to the LAN. The advantage is that customers do not have to invest money in building a SAN, and can instead use their network infrastructure. This solution is suitable for smaller companies that use only one or a few midrange storage systems. The medium is always metallic (copper) wire.

Aside from the interface board, the front end includes the main **CPU** and random access memory (RAM) used for calculating and conducting instructions connected with storage system operation. The main CPU and RAM complete the instructions coming from the microcode and administration software, which serve for RAID group creation, LUN mapping, LUN resizing, replication, etc.

The front end interface board and CPU are also responsible for managing **paths**. In relation to storage systems, the term *path* describes which way the stream of data goes from an application to individual LUNs. For redundancy purposes, we usually need two paths from a server to one LUN. One of these paths goes via CTL0, and the other goes via CTL1. Similarly, back end enclosures (with individual hard drives) are connected to back end controllers.

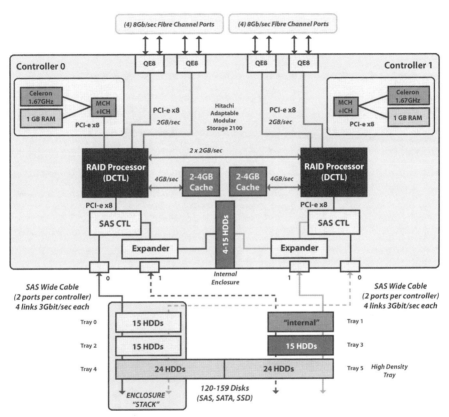

Figure 2.20 — Overview of the whole mainstream midrange storage system architecture and components using Hitachi Adaptable Modular Storage 2100 as an example. In the front end, we have QE8 Fibre Channel port controllers that are part of the interface board. These controllers are mainly responsible for conversion of FC transfer protocol into PCIe bus used for internal interconnection of all components. The storage system in this configuration is not equipped with FCoE or iSCSI ports because they are optional. Notice the CPU and local RAM memory (not cache). This processor is the microcode engine or the I/O management "brain."

LUN ownership

Earlier we discussed that, in a storage system, we have to configure data paths. The data path starts in a server that has two FC ports for connection to two FC ports on a storage system — one port is located on CTL0 the other one is on CTL1. From the interface board, data is sent to cache. The DCTL/RAID processor then takes care of data striping and sending the stripes to their destination physical hard drives.

On the user level, we have to configure where the path leads — we have to map the LUN to a server. From one server to one LUN, we have two paths for redundancy. When one path fails, data can be transferred through the second path. As you learned, in a storage system we have double architecture with two controllers for redundancy, but so far, we have not mentioned that double architecture also equals double performance if no malfunction occurs. Since the storage system is accessed from several servers, there are also several paths leading to different LUN destinations. Imagine you have five servers accessing five LUN destinations. This makes 10 data paths. To use all hardware means efficiently, each controller is assigned a certain number of LUNs. When we create LUNs, we must also set **LUN ownership, or decide which controller will be responsible for which LUN**. This way we can split the workload efficiently between two controllers.

Data will then be transferred primarily through the path that leads to the controller that **owns** the particular LUN. The second path is used as a backup. In event of failure of the path that leads to owning controller (let's say CTL0), the backup path is used. However, the backup path leads to CTL1, which is not set as a LUN owner. Therefore, data is transferred internally to CTL0, bypassing the malfunctioning FC port.

The path failure is depicted in Figure 2.21 on the next page. This configuration, when one controller is dominant and the second one is for backup purposes, is called *active-passive architecture*.

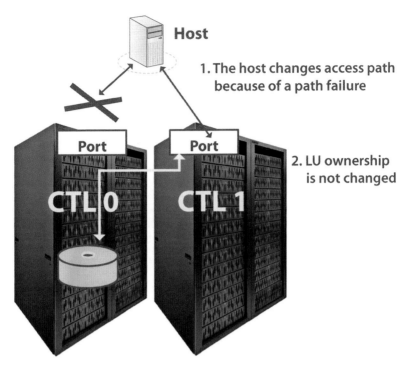

Figure 2.21 — Active-passive architecture. In the event of a path failure, LUN ownership does not change. Data is transferred via the backup path to CTL1 and then internally to CTL0, bypassing CTL0 front end ports. This diminishes performance because of internal communication.

Active-passive architecture means that only one connection (path) to a device can be active at a time. Other paths are passive with respect to that device and waiting to take over if needed.

In an active-passive storage system, if there are multiple paths to one LUN, one of them is designated as the primary route to the device. The other one is designated for backup purposes only.

Modern storage systems, however, add the functionality of **active-active architecture**, which brings several major advantages. In active-active architecture, you can use more than one path to a single LUN simultaneously.

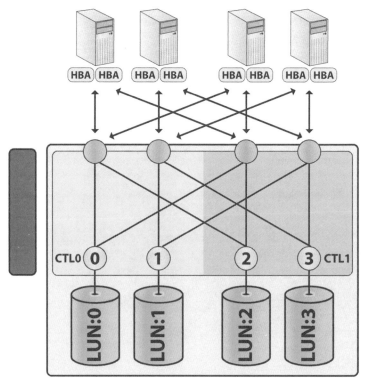

Figure 2.22 — Multiple paths to a single LUN are possible. LUN ownership automatically changes in the event of path failure. Unlike active-passive architecture, active-active architecture offers equal access to the particular LUN via both paths. This means the performance is not influenced by what path is currently used.

If both paths are working correctly, both of them can be used for communication. In Figure 2.22, you can see that one path from the first server to LUN:0 is connected directly, and the second path to the same LUN leads via CTL1 and also include internal communication. This requires communication overhead; however, this overhead has been reduced drastically through the implementation of modern PCIe buses in modern storage systems. The PCIe interface allows fast internal communication between CTL0 and CTL1.

In the event of path failure in active-active architecture, LUN ownership can be **dynamically changed**. When the storage administrator creates the LUN, ownership to the controller is assigned automatically.

In the event of path failure, LUN ownership is automatically switched to another controller, and the particular LUN is mapped directly via this controller. This mapping is more performance efficient since internal communication performance overhead is eliminated completely and the path goes straight through the controller. Active-active architecture enables other techniques that allow performance increase, such as **controller load balancing**.

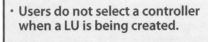

· Users do not select a controller when a LU is being created.

· If necessary, LU ownership can be changed manually afterwards.

Administrator

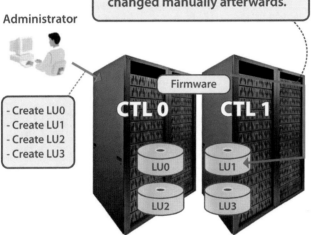

Firmware

CTL 0   CTL 1

- Create LU0
- Create LU1
- Create LU2
- Create LU3

LU0   LU1

LU2   LU3

Figure 2.23 — Active-active architecture. No need to configure LUN ownership manually. Communication goes either via CTL0 or CTL1. In the event of path failure, no bypassing as depicted in Figure 2.21 is necessary; therefore there is no communication overhead.

The active-active front end design of modern storage system controllers allows for simultaneous host access of any LUN on any host port on either controller with very little added overhead. A host accessing a LUN via a port on CTL0 can have most of the I/O request processed completely by CTL1 with little intervention by the main CPU and DCTL processors in CTL0.

Controller load balancing

Simultaneous use of multiple paths to a single LUN together with LUN ownership dynamic allocation are two major features of active-active front end architecture. When employed together, they can eliminate bottlenecks and balance workload on both controllers. Imagine a situation where CTL0 is 75% busy while CTL1 is only 15% busy. To reach optimal usage of hardware means the load balancing monitoring tool, which is part of the microcode, can change the LUN ownership to the less busy CTL1, which will be used for data processing. You could object that both paths could be used simultaneously, so LUN ownership is not necessary, and simple usage of both paths would solve the problem. This is not true, though. You need to realize that the DCTL processor is the exact location where the bottleneck is created. The DCTL processor must calculate all the parity data, and it rules where the data is to be distributed in terms of physical hard drives. Remember that the LUN is still only virtualized space within one RAID group. To avoid overloading a single DCTL processor, the LUN ownership is changed and the less busy controller takes over. Figure 2.24 depicts how is this all done. Read the description of all the components carefully to avoid getting lost in the complexity of the diagram.

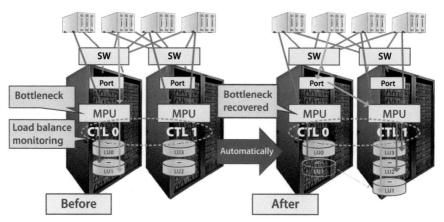

Figure 2.24 — Controller load balancing diagram. Black boxes at the top of the pictures are host servers. SW stands for switches, which are part of the storage area network (discussed in the next chapter). MPU stands for microprocessing units (DCTL together with MPU). If one MPU is too busy while the other one is underused, LUN:1 ownership is automatically changed to CTL1 and the corresponding path is redirected.

At this point, it is good to mention that one more element plays a role in using several paths simultaneously. If you have one host server connected to a single LUN via two paths, then the server's OS will see two mapped LUNs because it has no chance to realize that there is only one LUN connected via two paths. That's why there must be an additional software layer installed on the host server. This software layer is based on dynamic link provisioning and enables the server to work with the mapped LUN via two paths. Note that dynamic link provisioning cannot get the information that one particular controller is too busy. That is why the storage system must redirect the path to a less busy controller, exactly as in Figure 2.24. Notice that the green arrow in the *After* diagram is redirected within the storage system, even though it would be better to change LUN ownership and communicate directly via the second path. This example demonstrates that even active-active architecture is still imperfect.

Fibre Channel ports and their configuration

A midrange storage system usually offers at least four Fibre Channel ports on both controllers that are used for connection to other devices in network. These devices can be:

- **Host servers**, usually connected via Fibre Channel switches. LUNs are mapped to servers so that applications running on these servers can use the allocated capacity.

- **Another midrange storage system used for data replication**. On the connected storage system there are pair LUNs. In data replication, the source LUN is marked as P-VOL (primary volume) and destination LUN is marked as S-VOL (secondary volume that contains exact replica of data on P-VOL).

- **A storage system with virtualization capabilities**. This is usually an enterprise storage system able to virtualize space on the midrange system and use it as extended capacity. This is especially useful if you have several storage systems from various vendors and you need to consolidate your infrastructure to lower costs. Virtualized capacity is then managed through the enterprise system software tools.

Depending on the type of midrange storage system and vendor, Fibre Channel ports can be configured as either **an initiator** or **target**. Some modern midrange storage systems do not require any settings at all and automatically configure the Fibre Channel ports according to the connected device. In enterprise storage systems, you usually have to configure ports manually. Setting the Fibre Channel port as the target serves for connecting host servers or systems with virtualization capabilities. In the case of a storage system replication pair, the P-VOL initiates the communication when replicating data to an S-VOL. On the source storage system, therefore, we set the Fibre Channel port as initiator, and on the destination storage system, we set the Fibre Channel port as the target.

iSCSI interface

iSCSI interface is an alternative to Fibre Channel interface. Fibre Channel ports are powerful, efficient and can be used for transmitting data over long distances. However, their disadvantage is that they require the entire network infrastructure to be built on Fibre Channel technology, using Fibre Channel optical wires. This means that you have to build a new SAN, and all the components, such as switches, servers and other storage systems, must support Fibre Channel. This can be costly. To balance output performance and costs, it is possible to use iSCSI front end ports that are often optional parts of a midrange storage system. The first letter in iSCSI means Internet. This technology is therefore built on a combination of TCP/IP and SCSI protocol. Through the technique of encapsulation of SCSI instructions to TCP/IP protocols, data can be transmitted without special requirements on a network environment (i.e., a specialized SAN network). This allows you to connect your storage system to a LAN or WAN (especially Internet) using common Ethernet cabling. The advantage is that you can use your infrastructure and you do not have to invest in costly Fibre Channel components. The downside is that the performance of this solution is much lower. Therefore, iSCSI connections are usually implemented in small companies that use only a few midrange storage systems. Any storage system equipped with iSCSI ports also offers Fibre Channel ports, so it is not complicated to upgrade to a Fibre Channel infrastructure if needed.

Remember that a midrange storage system consists of two controller boards, CTL0 and CTL1, which contain all the components. Components, according to their tasks and roles, can be attributed to the front end or back end. Between front end components and back end components there is cache, which has a major impact on the performance of the whole system because it offers high processing speeds compared to hard drives.

Enterprise storage systems

So far we have been discussing midrange storage systems. Some vendors call their midrange products **modular** storage. Midrange or modular systems are well suitable for application in small or medium sized businesses and organizations. They are powerful in processing I/O requests from a limited number of servers. One application accessing a storage system makes one thread that needs to be processed. For companies that have a large number of servers running many applications, enterprise storage systems are more suitable since they deliver significantly higher performance when it comes to **multi-thread processing**. In other words, enterprise high-end storage systems are able to process a large number of I/O requests simultaneously. Note that enterprise storage systems can also be called monoliths. That is because enterprise systems are installed in proprietary racks of non-standard dimensions, which are supplied from the particular storage system vendor.

Enterprise storage systems offer a higher level of **reliability, scalability and availability**. We know that midrange storage systems have two independent controller boards, which contain components that can be attributed to front end, cache or back end. In enterprise storage systems, these components are installed on dedicated boards that can be replaced individually. They are also often hot swappable, so there is no need to turn off or reboot a storage system when replacing. In enterprise storage systems, you would have one board for the DCTL controller, one board for cache, boards for individual front end ports, etc. This also means that you can install more than one instance of the component, which makes enterprise storage systems more flexible and more scalable. In case you decide to upgrade your enterprise storage system, for example, with additional ports or cache, you just need to order the specific board that is then installed into the **grid switch** that provides the platform and interface for mutual communication of the installed components. For redundancy reasons, whichever component you order is always duplicated to maintain no single point of failure. The set of two identical components that are to be installed in the grid switch is called an *option* or *feature*. You can, therefore, order one cache option that will consist of two identical modules, one for CTL0 and one for CTL1.

Enterprise storage systems can offer additional performance by providing:

- **A large storage capacity** — more back end ports can be installed and more expansion units can be connected to these back end ports.

- A significantly **larger amount of cache** to service host I/O optimally.

- The ability to deliver **high performance in multi-thread processing** — it can handle much higher number of I/O requests from multiple hosts.

- **Higher throughput** — the internal buses and interface are able to handle more data faster than midrange storage system. Throughput is measured in GB/sec.

- **Fault tolerance architecture** to improve data availability — there are more means for hardware and software tools to provide undisrupted access to data.

- **Connectivity to mainframe computers** and open system hosts.

- Often, the ability to manage other storage systems via the process of **storage space virtualization** to consolidate a heterogeneous infrastructure.

- **Support of automated dynamic tiering**.

- Sophisticated support of data migration.

Mainframe computers are the most powerful computer systems that have evolved from the first powerful computers created in late 1950s. These computers used to occupy entire rooms and even now consist of several racks. Mainframe computers are extremely expensive and extremely powerful. They are used largely in government institutions and research facilities, such as NASA.

Storage space virtualization of a heterogeneous infrastructure means that you can use the enterprise storage system for controlling other storage systems (modular and enterprise) and creating a single unified virtualized storage area that can be further divided into logical units. This is especially useful for companies that have storage systems from different vendors because they must pay for software licenses, maintenance and employee training for each system, which becomes costly. With one virtualized storage area, companies can manage all their storage systems from different vendors with one software tool, and pay only for one kind of license software, maintenance and employee training on a single product.

Automated dynamic tiering is a storage system functionality that automatically moves data to hard drives of different performance according to frequency of access. This is closely related to data lifecycle and archiving. For now, it is important to know that in storage systems terminology, a *tier* is defined as a storage area based on a single technology. Therefore, you can have a fast tier for frequently accessed data based on SSD drives. Then you can have a tier based on SAS or SATA drives or an archiving tier with tape backup technology. Automated dynamic tiering is very useful and will be discussed later when we talk about archiving.

In Figure 2.25, we can see the Hitachi Virtual Storage Platform, which is an enterprise storage system that brings state-of-the-art technology and many innovative features. One of them is *3D scaling*, which allows you to expand the storage system into three dimensions — you can add performance and storage space, and you can connect other vendors' storage systems and virtualize them.

Figure 2.25 — Hitachi Virtual Storage Platform is an example of an enterprise storage system. In this picture, we have two VSP systems with expansion units installed in additional racks.

This chapter provided you with detailed information on the design and architecture of midrange storage systems. Now you should be able to:

- Name all individual components and explain their function.

- Explain basic concepts of achieving and improving performance.

- Explain basic concepts that ensure data redundancy.

In addition, we compared midrange and enterprise storage systems. Both are based on very similar concepts and architectures — the main differences are in performance and application.

3

Storage networking and security

What are you going to learn in this chapter?

- How to describe basic networking concepts
- How common network devices operate
- What possibilities we have in storage system networking
- How devices communicate with each other through a network
- How to secure storage area networks

Introduction to networks

Nowadays, a standalone piece of IT equipment is of little use. It is the ability to communicate with other devices that makes technology so powerful. People would hardly spend so much time in front of their computers if they could not share the outcome of their work with other people. When we say the ability to communicate with other devices is important, we especially mean the ability to transmit and receive information encoded in the form of data to and from other members of a network. A *network*, therefore, describes an infrastructure of technical means that facilitate this interchange of information. These means are both hardware and software based. Among the hardware network components, there are cables, network adaptors installed in personal computers, servers, storage systems or other devices, and components dedicated for routing the stream of data to its destination. The software layer of networking consists mainly of protocols that contain sets of instructions that govern the process of communication among the network members. Each protocol supports a specific area of application (i.e., type of network) and type of network adaptor. For each type of network, we need a dedicated solution through a particular set of cables, network adaptors and protocols. Storage systems are highly sophisticated devices that must be able to provide extremely high performance. As a result, storage systems require a different type of networking than regular workgroup computers. In this chapter, we will focus primarily on storage system networking.

Why do we need networks?

There are several reasons we use networks. Before we get to the technical descriptions of individual component designs and functions, it is good to clear up what motivation people have to use a network.

- A network interconnects electronic devices to **establish communication**. People can use many tools to communicate: email, instant messaging, telephone and video.

- A network enables people to **share information in the form of data**. It is possible to access files stored on the other side of globe within seconds.

- Thanks to networking, we can **share technological resources**. For example, one office printer can be used by multiple users. This feature is also very important when we talk about cloud solutions, when end users access and take advantage of remote computing means. This means we can have common computers connected to a cloud computing service that does all the calculations. In this way, the end user with a common computer can use applications that require performance beyond possibilities of personal equipment. We can also employ distributed computing that allows us to merge the performance of several network devices to complete the task.

This is the motivation behind network implementation. But networks also have several **inherited properties** that need to be taken into consideration. The major threat of networking is its potential **security risks**. Each network can be the subject of cyber attacks and unauthorized access. Computer viruses and worms use networks to spread. Therefore, networks must be secured. To secure a network, we have a range of hardware and software means, such as firewalls and antivirus programs. A network infrastructure may also interfere with other technologies. This applies especially for wireless networks where data is transmitted over air. Networks are also very complex in terms of implementation, configuration and maintenance. Careful infrastructure planning is important because networking can be costly and require highly professional personnel.

Network cables

Network cables are the basic building block of any wired network. They serve as the medium through which data flows from one network device to another. The type of cable chosen for a network is closely related to the network's type, topology, protocol and size. Each cable type has its characteristics that influence network performance and determine the area of application. The two basic kinds of cables used in networking are *twisted pair* and *fiber optic*.

Figure 3.1 — Twisted pair cable structure, RJ45 connectors.

In Figure 3.1, you can see an example of a **twisted pair cable**. A twisted pair cable is usually made of copper and has pairs of insulated wires twisted together. The twisting reduces electromagnetic interference and cross-talk from neighboring wires. Twisted pair is the least expensive type of cabling used in networks. However, it provides limited distance connectivity. This means that you cannot use twisted pair cables in a wide area network (WAN). The maximum available throughput depends on the cable quality and construction. The tighter the twisting, the higher supported transmission rate. The cables allowing higher speeds are also more expensive. The common throughput ranges from 10Mb/sec to 1Gb/sec. The maximum cable length reaches only 100m. Twisted pair cable usually use RJ45 standardized connectors well known from common network adaptors installed in personal computers and laptops.

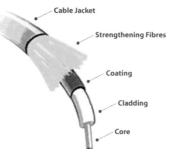

Cable Jacket

Strengthening Fibres

Coating

Cladding

Core

Figure 3.2 — Fibre Optic Cable.

Fiber optics is a technology that uses glass or plastic fibers to transmit data as light impulses. A fibre optic cable consists of a bundle of fibers; each fiber can transmit millions of messages modulated onto light waves. Usage of glass or plastic materials makes the cable resistant to electromagnetic interference. However, these materials also make the cable fragile. That is why additional cladding and strengthening fibers are added. Fiber optic cables have the following advantages over twisted pair cables:

- Provide a greater bandwidth

- Allow data to be transmitted digitally

- Can carry data over long distances

All these advantages make fiber optic cables ideal for WANs. The main disadvantage of fiber optic cables is that they are expensive to install. The decision to use a twisted pair or a fiber optic cable in a network depends on the protocol used. It is possible to distinguish between **multi-mode optical fiber** and **single-mode optical fiber**. Multi-mode optical fiber is suitable for communication over short distances, up to 600m. This points to the area of application in an organization's infrastructure. Single-mode optical fiber is suitable for long-distance communication. The difference in technology is that multi-mode optical fiber is cheaper, since it has a larger and more robust core that allows cheaper implementation of light emitting diodes (LEDs) and vertical-cavity surface-emitting lasers (VCSELs). In simple terms, the manipulation with multi-mode optical fiber is easier and less expensive to implement. Fiber optical cables are color coded to easily show the type. **Single-mode optical fiber cables are yellow, and multi-mode optical fiber cables are orange.** However, purely for practical reasons, sometimes we use different colored cables of a single type to distinguish among paths in a network and simplify cable management.

As for the connectors that are used with fiber optic cables, the situation is more complex than with twisted pair. There are many standards of fiber optic connectors depending on the area of application. Optic cables are used not only in networking, but also for transmission of audio signal and other purposes. The common connector for fiber optic cables used with networking of storage systems is called LC, which stands for Lucent connector (name of manufacturer), little connector or local connector. Fiber optic cable connection to a port also requires a special device able to convert optical signals into electrical signals and vice versa. This device is called a transceiver. Sometimes the transceiver is built-in as part of a port, but more often it is a standalone component. There are two types of transceivers commonly used in storage system networking:

- Gigabit interface converter **(GBIC)**

- Small form-factor pluggable **(SFP)**

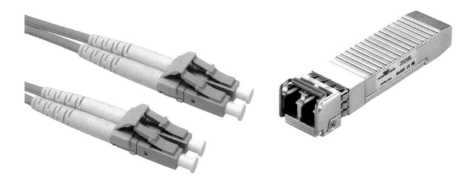

Figure 3.3 — Fiber optic cable LC connector and SFP transceiver.

It is possible to say that both GBIC and SFP do the same work, while the GBIC solution is older and becoming obsolete. SFP transceivers are smaller and offer higher speeds. Both types of transceivers are highly reliable and hot swappable. There are several sub-types of SFP transceivers that are implemented according to the area of application.

For multi-mode fiber with orange color coded cable coating:

- **SX** — 850nm, maximum 4.25Gb/sec over 150m

For single-mode fiber with yellow color coded cable coating:

- **LX** — 1310nm, distance up to 10km

- **BX** — 1490nm, two paired cables for uplink and downlink (BS-U and **BS**-D respectively) for distances up to 10km

- **EX** — 1550nm for distances up to 120km

In storage systems networking you will be mostly dealing with or-ange color coded multi-mode optical fiber cables with LC connectors and SFP SX transceivers that are marked as 850nm and support 4.25Gb/sec and a 150m distance.

Network members — nodes

A node transmits or receives data over a network. Nodes are there-fore any devices that participate in mutual communication among all network members. A node can operate as a communication end point: personal computer, tablet, server, storage system. A node can also op-erate as a redistribution point, when the device redirects a stream of data from the communication originator to the communication target. Each node has its unique identification, which serves for addressing purposes in the network. We will look at the most important means of network identification.

An Internet Protocol (IP) address is a numerical identifier assigned to each device connected to a computer network that uses Internet Protocol for communication. Addressing based on IP identifiers is com-mon in local area networks (LANs). In other words, you can encounter an IP address at your home network. An IP address looks something like this: 192.168.1.1.

A media access control (MAC) address is a worldwide unique identifier assigned to a network interface card (NIC). This identifier is not dependent on protocol, such as IP addressing, because a MAC address is built into the device by its manufacturer. This is why MAC addresses are sometimes referred to as **physical addresses**. A MAC address looks something like this: 01:2F:45:67:AB:5E. As you can see, hexadecimal digits separated by colons or hyphens are used. The hexadecimal digits represent a 48b binary code.

A World Wide Name (WWN) is a unique label, which identifies a particular device in a Fibre Channel network. To be more precise, it is used for addressing Fibre Channel communication targets or serial attached SCSI (SAS) targets. As you may guess, WWN addresses are used in storage area networks (SANs), the primary focus of this chapter. Later we will discuss the structure and usage of WWN addressing.

Except for such nodes as computers, printers or even storage systems, which we call endpoint network members, we have network devices that serve primarily as data stream redistribution points. To understand how data is transmitted and distributed, it is necessary to get familiar with the Open Systems Interconnection (OSI) model definition of network communication layers.

The lowest communication layer, the physical layer, is represented by **a stream of bits** and their transport over a network. On this level of communication we deal just with ones and zeros.

The second layer is called the data link layer, in which data frames are transported over a network. A frame consists of three basic elements: a header, payload field and trailer. A payload field contains the usable data we want to transfer — the data that conveys information. The header and the trailer carry metadata that notify the beginning of a frame, the end of a frame and, most importantly, the originating device and target device physical addresses (i.e., MAC or WWN). The primary function of the second OSI layer is, therefore, physical addressing. Thanks to this metadata, we know exactly where the frame is coming from and where it is heading. Another defining feature of a frame is that it has fixed size, i.e., the number of bits dedicated to the header, payload field and trailer. The size of a frame depends on the type of network and protocol used.

The third layer, which is the last one that's important for us at the moment, is the network layer. On this level, we are dealing with **packet transfer**. The packet determining feature is the use of logical addressing to allow network routing. In network devices, packets are encapsulated into frames that are then sent over a network.

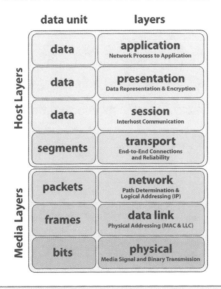

Figure 3.4 — The OSI model.

Communication over a network is a very complex process that works on several layers represented by the OSI model. The highest layer is the application level. When an application wants to communicate over a network, it passes data to a lower layer of processing, e.g., an operating system, network protocols and drivers or network interface cards, while the lowest level is binary code. The layer system is implemented because of work division — an application itself cannot work directly with frames, and frames alone are of no use to an application. The process of passing data to a lower layer is called *encapsulation*. The process of encapsulation can be understood as putting a sheet of paper into envelope. The sheet of paper contains data, the envelope address, a stamp, and so on.

When we talk about network data stream redistribution nodes, we mean particularly network hubs, switches and routers. Each of these devices has its own area of application. For different types of networks and network cables, we need different types of hubs, switches and routers.

- **Hubs** — a hub is a simple device that allows interconnection and communication among nodes. A network hub works on the first, physical, OSI level. It accepts the stream of data from one port and simply distributes it to all other ports, which increases network traffic and reduces network performance. A hub therefore cannot direct the stream of data to the particular destination and it does not provide any network security features. Network hubs have no intelligence and almost no possibilities for configuration. A hub is inexpensive but not scalable.

- **Switches** — a switch also allows interconnection and communication among nodes within one network. Unlike hubs, network switches are working on the second layer of OSI model. They use physical addressing and they work with frames. When a frame arrives at the switch, the switch reads its header, retrieves the MAC or WWN identification number and then sends the frame directly to its destination. Switches are therefore much more efficient in network communication than hubs. Switches are possible to configure and can provide network security features, such as zoning (discussed later).

- **Routers** — a router provides an interface between two different networks, for example, between a WAN and LAN. A router works on the third layer of the OSI model and uses logical addressing. Logical addressing is represented by IP addresses. A router receives and transmits packets according to their IP addresses. Routers can be used at home to share Internet connectivity. A router is assigned an IP address for communication with the provider's gateway. The router then assigns local IP addresses to all the computers connected in the LAN, enabling them to access the Internet. Routers are configurable.

Except for these network redistribution points, you can encounter other devices such as repeaters, which amplify the network signal, or bridges, which can enhance the effectiveness of network communications over a LAN.

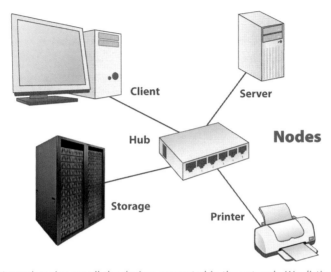

3.5 — Network nodes are all the devices connected in the network. We distinguish between endpoint communication nodes and data redistribution nodes.

Storage networking topologies

As we already know, storage system networking is based on Fibre Channel technology. In Fibre Channel, we have several possibilities of interconnecting the individual nodes. The way in which are nodes connected to each other is commonly called *network topology*. The main Fibre Channel topologies are:

- **Point-to-point or FC-P2P**

- **Arbitrated loop or FC-AL**

- **Switched fabric or FC-SW**

A point-to-point topology is considered the simplest topology, in which two devices are directly connected using Fibre Channel. It has fixed bandwidth, and data is transmitted serially over a single cable. This topology can be implemented as direct attached storage (DAS). Point-to-point topology supports legacy products and can be used for tape backups.

Arbitrated Loop (AL) is an FC topology we already know from storage system back end architecture. FC-AL networking works on very similar principles. All devices are part of a loop, and only one device can communicate with another device at a time. In AL, devices use an access request mechanism called a TOKEN, or arbitrate (ARB), which circles the loop. A device can use ARB depending on its priority and access rights; the device with the highest priority gets first access. Arbitrated loop topology is designed for mass storage devices and other peripheral devices that require very high bandwidth. Arbitrated Loop is usually deployed in small environments and in tape drives because it is inexpensive and easy to implement, and it supports legacy products. The main disadvantage is that adding and removing a device from the loop interrupts all activity on that loop.

The hardware that connects workstations and servers to storage devices in a SAN is referred to as a *fabric*. The SAN fabric enables any-server-to-any-storage device connectivity through the use of Fibre Channel switches or network directors. In **switched fabric topology**, bandwidth is not shared between devices, enabling devices to transmit and receive data at full speed at all times. Switched fabric is, therefore, the most powerful and complex topology and it is also the preferred Fibre Channel network topology implementation. It supports multiple concurrent point-to-point connections; it is a highly reliable, available and scalable solution. The main disadvantage of switched fabric topology is cost — it requires at least one switch to establish connections between devices, ideally two for redundancy.

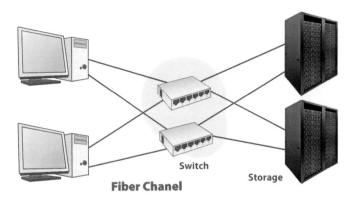

Figure 3.6 — Switched fabric topology. All the devices in the network can communicate with each other any time at full speed.

Direct attached storage (DAS)

Storage systems offer high performance. To take advantage of this performance and inherited redundancy features, storage systems require specific networking solutions. The easiest way to connect a storage system into a network infrastructure is through direct attached storage. In direct attached storage, a storage device is directly connected to an individual server equipped with a host bus adaptor card (Fibre Channel interface). A DAS device is not shared, so no other network device can access the data without first accessing the server.

DAS is mainly used in a configuration where primary data access is required by the applications that run on the directly connected server. The advantages of this solution are lower initial costs. You do not need Fibre Channel switches to build a DAS network. The concept of DAS also does not mean that you can connect only one server to the particular storage system. Any storage system is equipped with more than one front end Fibre Channel port. In midrange storage systems it is usually four front end Fibre Channel ports. This effectively means that you can connect up to four servers in DAS. In the event that you would want to maintain no single point of failure, you would use two paths from the server connected to two front end ports in a storage system. It is also possible to connect clustered servers.

The disadvantages are that one or two servers usually do not use the full potential of a storage system, which is achieved by sharing the hardware means across the network.

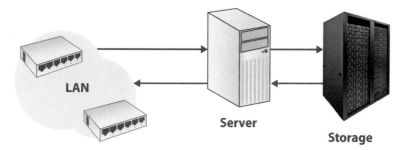

Figure 3.7 — Direct attached storage infrastructure. Server is directly connected to a storage system. Storage system can be accessed only through the server. Server can be accessed from LAN.

Storage area network (SAN)

To meet high performance requirements and use all possibilities storage systems offer, we can create network infrastructure dedicated to storage systems. Because this network type is dedicated to implementation only with storage systems, it has features tailored to ensure a high level of redundancy, fault tolerance and high availability. A storage area network is a high-speed network of shared storage devices. Servers attached to a SAN can access any SAN attached storage devices. The components in a SAN are storage devices and switches. A SAN is designed to connect computer storage devices, such as disk array controllers and tape libraries, to multiple servers or hosts.

In a SAN, the processing power of a production server is reserved for applications. Therefore, a SAN implementation ensures faster processing of the applications running on this server (i.e., there is no overhead). In DAS, the processing performance of the attached servers can be diminished because it must provide part of its resources for requests from hosts connected in the LAN. Therefore a communication overhead exists due to accessing the storage system through the server.

In addition, SAN has the following advantages:

- Effective disaster recovery

- Redundancy and fault tolerance

- High-speed access

- High security

The main function of a SAN is to transfer data between computer systems and storage elements, such as storage devices and switches. A SAN moves all data storage to a separate network, used only for data. A SAN is ideal for complex data centers, multiple data centers or when applications and departments need access to shared data. A SAN meets requirements on high availability, scalability, reliability and performance.

Disaster recovery is a formal plan that describes how an organization will deal with potential disasters, including precautions to maintain or quickly resume mission-critical functions.

Fault tolerance is the ability of a system to continue to perform its function at a reduced performance level, when one or more of its components have failed. Fault tolerance in disk subsystems includes redundant instances of components whose failure would make the system inoperable, where redundant components assume the function of the failed ones.

High availability is the ability of a system to perform its function continuously for a significantly longer period than the reliabilities of its individual components would allow.

Scalability is the ability to grow or support growth so all capabilities of the system remain balanced. For example, a storage system whose data transfer capacity increases by the addition of channels as its storage capacity increases by the addition of disks is said to scale.

Reliability is an attribute of any computer component (software, hardware or network) that consistently performs according to its specifications.

Storage area network components

Storage area networks use Fibre Channel infrastructure, which in-cludes host bus adaptors installed in servers, Fibre Channel cables and switches, and Fibre Channel ports installed in the storage system front end and proprietary network protocols.

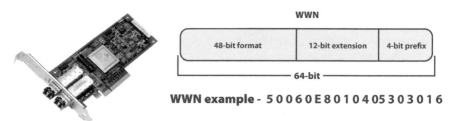

Figure 3.8 — Host bus adaptor and an example of WWN.

In a storage system, **an HBA** is a Fibre Channel interface card installed in a server. It connects a computer and storage devices on a network. HBAs can offer one or two Fibre Channel ports for connecting optical cables via SFP transceivers. Each HBA has a unique WWN, which serves as a physical address, similar to MAC addresses used in LAN interface cards. There are two types of WWNs on an HBA:

- Node WWN: Shared by all ports on an HBA

- Port WWN: Unique to each port on the HBA

As you should already know, a World Wide Name is a unique built-in identification used to address each element on a Fibre Channel stor-age network. Each WWN is a 64b number derived from the Institute of Electrical and Electronics Engineers (IEEE) standard. The 64b number includes a 48b format, a 12b extension and a 4b prefix.

Fibre Channel switches are different from those used in LAN. They are used in small to midsized SANs. They allow the creation of a **Fibre Channel fabric**, which is the shortened name of Fibre Channel switched fabric topology **(FC-SW)**. In FC-SW, devices are connected to each other through one or more Fibre Channel switches. This topology allows the connection of up to the theoretical maximum of 16 million devices, limited only by the available address space (2^{24}). Multiple switches in a fabric usually form a fully connected mesh network, with devices being on the edges of the mesh.

Fibre Channel switches are not highly reliable or scalable. To ensure high availability and no single point of failure, each node needs duplicate paths across the SAN via independent Fibre Channel switches.

A Fibre Channel director is a large and complex switch designed for application in large storage area networks such as enterprises or data centers. It is highly available, reliable, scalable and manageable. It is designed with redundant hardware components, which provide the ability to recover from a non-fatal error. Fibre Channel directors are capable of supporting mainframe connection via FICON protocol. FICON protocol will be described in detail later in this chapter.

Storage area network over iSCSI interface

SAN can be implemented by using a network protocol standard called iSCSI, which uses the SCSI protocol to transmit data over TCP/IP networks. iSCSI allows organizations to utilize their existing TCP/IP network infrastructure without investing in expensive Fibre Channel switches. iSCSI uses TCP/IP as an alternative to Fibre Channel to overcome the limitations of Fibre Channel, such as high expense and distance limitation. iSCSI has the following advantages:

- Facilitates data transfers over intranets

- Manages storage over long distances

- Is inexpensive to implement

- Provides high availability

- Is robust and reliable

iSCSI is best suited for web server, email and departmental applications. iSCSI ports can be found in a storage system front end interface board. Storage systems usually support both Fibre Channel ports and iSCSI ports.

Network attached storage (NAS)

Network attached storage is a highly specific solution that differs from common SAN storage systems in many ways. The main difference between storage systems and NAS systems is that NAS can be defined as a file-level data storage device that provides file access over a network to heterogeneous clients. We know that SAN storage systems are operating on the data block level and that the file system layer is installed in connected servers. A SAN storage system therefore needs a server with running applications that can use a mapped LUN capacity that appears to the server as a physical hard drive. Compared to this, NAS is very different.

NAS operates not on the block level but on the file level. This means that a NAS device has a file system installed. A NAS device does not provide LUNs that need to be mapped — it provides network locations where it is possible to store and read data in the form of files. A NAS device is attached directly to LAN infrastructure enabling all hosts to access the files stored in NAS. The host computer cannot see volumes as physical installed hard drives, because there is no LUN mapping. The host computer sees the network location volumes. These volumes can be accessed from any device in the LAN. A NAS device can be a specialized storage system that supports NAS functionality (NAS appliance), a server equipped with one or more hard drives connected in RAID, a server with a NAS application connected to a midrange storage system, or an enterprise storage system equipped additionally with a NAS option (or NAS blade). Large and powerful NAS storage systems allow virtually thousands of client connections to access a single file simultaneously. See Figure 3.9 to get a general idea of how NAS solutions actually look.

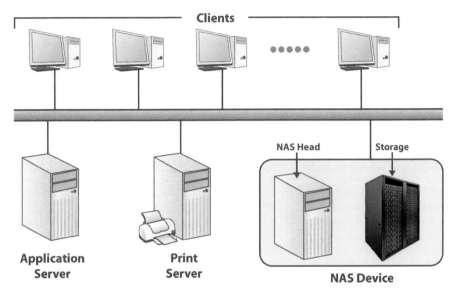

*Figure 3.9 — Network attached storage. The NAS device is represented by the server that functions as the NAS head and common storage system. There are solutions that integrate both these functionalities in one package (NAS appliances). NAS devices work relatively independently; they do not require servers with applications. All clients, application and other servers can access **files** stored in a NAS device.*

A NAS device is sometimes called a "filer" because the focus of its processing power is file services and file storage. Supported file access protocols are Network File Protocol (NFS), Common Internet File Protocol (CIFS) and protocols from the Internet environment (HTTP, secured HTTPS and FTP). NAS devices support Fibre Channel and iSCSI connections between the NAS head and a storage system. The NAS head is always connected to a LAN using standard RJ45 connectors. A NAS system moves the overhead of file system processing and serving off the host to a dedicated device or devices optimized for these tasks. NAS devices are made up of the following components:

- Network interface using one or more interface cards (NIC), typically 10Gb Ethernet

- Network file system protocols (NFS, CIFS)

- Internal or external RAID storage

- File system

- Cache

- Industry standard storage protocols to connect to and manage physical disk storage resources

The advantages of a NAS solution are that it offers storage to computers running different operating systems over a LAN. It can be implemented within the common network infrastructure with no requirements for SAN Fibre Channel technology. It solves the problem of isolating data behind servers typical for DAS and even SAN block-level storage systems. NAS devices are optimized for sharing files between many users. Implementation to current infrastructure is easy.

The disadvantages are that a NAS solution relies on the client-server model for communication and data transport, which creates network overhead. Compared to SAN, NAS provides lower performance. Furthermore, NAS provides only file sharing — no other traditional file server applications, such as email, database or printing servers, are supported.

The mentioned advantages and disadvantages suggest the area of application to be midsized organizations with remote departments, or branch offices of large organizations, with networks that have a mix of clients, servers and operations. It is ideal for collaborative environments with file sharing between departments. NAS solutions are successfully implemented where there are requirements for easy file sharing, software development, computer-aided design and computer-aided manufacturing (CAD/CAM), audio-video streaming, publishing, broadcasting, etc.

NAS implementation and converged infrastructure

There are several methods of NAS implementation. NAS can be implemented using a NAS appliance or filer, NAS blade or NAS gateway. A **NAS appliance** combines a front end file server and back end storage system in a single unit. This approach is sometimes referred to as a closed-box approach. In one device you get the file server and the storage array. This solution is highly reliable and provides efficient performance. It enables easy installation, management and use. It is also the least expensive NAS implementation. The downside is that NAS appliance is not scalable and does not provide pool storage, which makes it difficult to achieve high utilization.

A NAS blade allows multi-protocol data storage in a large disk array. The NAS blade is basically an option that is installed to enterprise level storage systems. It adds ports that make it possible to connect the storage system to a local area network, and it has a built-in file server. You can add more than one NAS blade option into your enterprise disk array, which means that this solution is scalable. It also provides the full functionalities of an enterprise storage system — high performance, security, availability and redundancy (data can be replicated in addition to RAID redundancy features).

In a **NAS gateway**, all devices communicate directly with the file system. A NAS gateway overcomes the limitations of a NAS appliance. It separates the file server from the storage device, it offers better utilization rates and, most importantly, it allows creation of a converged NAS and SAN infrastructure by providing NAS functionalities to SAN storage. Combination of NAS with SAN capacity enables you to meet growing storage requirements. A NAS gateway controller uses Fibre Channel protocol to connect to external storage.

There are three types of storage networking architecture: DAS, NAS and SAN. In DAS, a storage device is directly attached to an individual server. SAN is a high-speed network of shared storage devices. SAN implementation uses Fibre Channel technology or iSCSI and operates on block level. In NAS, data is presented at file level and the storage device directly connects to the LAN.

See Figure 3.11 for comparison.

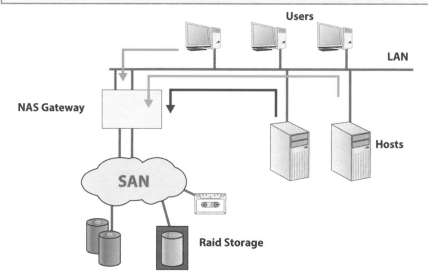

Figure 3.10 — Converged SAN and NAS infrastructure. NAS head with storage connected over SAN. NAS scales to the limits of SAN, which is limited by the NAS file system's capacity. Implementation of several NAS gateways is possible; this type of solution is scalable. Converged solution can coexist with application servers, and it can be centrally managed.

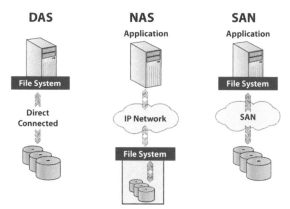

Figure 3.11 — Storage networking architecture overview.

Network protocols

A protocol is a set of rules that governs communication between computers on a network. It regulates network characteristics in terms of access method, physical topologies allowed in the network, types of cable that can be used in the network and speed of data transfer. The different types of protocols that can be used in a network are:

- Ethernet

- Fibre Channel Protocol (FCP)

- Fiber connectivity (FICON)

- Internet Protocol (IP)

- Internet small computer system interface (iSCSI)

- Fibre Channel over IP (FCIP)

- Internet Fibre Channel Protocol (iFCP)

- Fibre Channel over Ethernet (FCoE)

Ethernet protocol uses an access method called carrier sense multiple access/collision detection (CSMA/CD). Before transmitting, a node checks whether any other node is using the network. If clear, the node begins to transmit. Ethernet allows data transmission over twisted pair or fiber optic cables and is mainly used in LANs. There are various versions of Ethernet with various speed specifications.

The **Fibre Channel protocol** defines a multi-layered architecture for moving data. FCP packages SCSI commands into Fibre Channel frames ready for transmission. FCP also allows data transmission over twisted pair and over fibre optic cables. It is mainly used in large data centers for applications requiring high availability, such as transaction processing and databases.

FICON is a protocol that connects a mainframe to its peripheral devices and disk array. FICON is based on FCP and has evolved from IBM's implementation of Enterprise Systems Connection (ESCON).

Internet protocol is used to transfer data across a network. Each device on the network has a unique IP address that identifies it. IP works in conjunction with the TCP, iSCSI and FCIP protocols. When you transfer messages over a network by using IP, IP breaks the message into smaller units called packets (third layer in OSI model). Each packet is treated as an individual unit. IP delivers the packets to the destination. **Transmission control protocol** (TCP) is the protocol that combines the packets into the correct order to reform the message that was sent from the source.

iSCSI establishes and manages connection between IP-based storage devices, and it hosts and enables deployment of IP-based storage area networks. It facilitates data transfers over intranets, manages storage over long distances and is cost-effective, robust and reliable. As we already mentioned, iSCSI is best-suited for web server, email and departmental business applications in small to medium sized businesses.

Fibre Channel over IP is a TCP/IP based tunneling protocol that connects geographically distributed Fibre Channel SANs. FCIP encapsulates Fibre Channel frames into frames that comply with TCP/IP standards. It can be useful when connecting two SAN networks over the Internet tunnel, in a similar fashion to virtual private networks (VPNs) allowing connection to a distant LAN over the Internet.

iFCP is again TCP/IP based. It is basically an adaptation of FCIP using routing instead of tunneling. It interconnects Fibre Channel storage devices or SANs by using an IP infrastructure. iFCP moves Fibre Channel data over IP networks by using iSCSI protocols. Both FCIP and iFCP provide means to extend Fibre Channel networks over distance. Both these protocols are highly reliable and scalable. They are best suited for connecting two data centers for centralized data management or disaster recovery.

Fibre Channel over Ethernet is an encapsulation of Fibre Channel frames over Ethernet networks. This allows Fibre Channel to use 10Gb Ethernet networks while preserving the Fibre Channel protocol. FCoE provides these advantages:

- Network (IP) and storage (SAN) data traffic can be consolidated using a single network switch.

- It reduces the number of network interface cards required to connect disparate storage and IP networks.

- It reduces the number of cables and switches.

- FCoE reduces power and cooling costs.

To put this into simple words, you can build your SAN using Ethernet cables (mostly twisted pair). You can use one switch for your IP based network traffic (LAN) and for creating SAN infrastructure. Even though the switch and cabling are the same, LAN will run on TCP/IP while SAN runs on FCP.

Storage area network security

SAN networks benefit from inherited security features over IP-based networks. These features are determined by a smaller number of nodes in the network and isolation from local area and wide area networks. However, with the emergence of converged network solutions and cloud computing solutions, it is necessary to employ some additional techniques to ensure integrity and security of SAN infrastructure.

LUN mapping, which is sometimes also called *LUN masking*, provides the means for permitting access to the particular logical unit from hosts based on their physical address. Usually only one server can access one LUN, either through one or two paths. In a server cluster (server re-dundancy, where a clustered server is ready to take over if the primary server fails) it can be two servers accessing a single LUN. It is possible to provide access to a LUN from more servers, but this is not usually implemented in order to maintain consistency of data stored on a LUN. In other words, when a server stores a database on a LUN, this database is constantly changing because there are ongoing transactions. Furthermore, a LUN operates on the block level — the file system is installed on the server. These are the reasons data on this particular LUN with a database cannot be read on another server — from the perspective of another server, the data is inconsistent and thus unusable. The LUN is mapped on a disk array controller level using disk array management software. The particular LUN can be accessed from servers, whose HBA's WWN addresses are listed in disk array configuration software. Access to the LUN is denied to all other WWNs.

LUN mapping is the feature fully managed on storage systems. Fibre Channel switches also provide a feature that helps to create a secure SAN environment. On the level of Fibre Channel switches, we employ **zoning**. Zoning is one of the most important mechanisms within a switched fabric network that helps to achieve a higher level of security. Zones are defined in order to establish rules that govern mutual communication of network devices. A Fibre Channel switch allows frame forwarding only within the configured zone. Imagine that you have a SAN infrastructure that consists of a disk array, tape library, five servers and one backup server. Zoning can be designed in such a way that all the servers are able to communicate with the disk array, while the tape library is able to communicate only with the backup server. Zoning is automatically propagated to all FC switches within the network, so it is enough to configure just one switch.

Zoning can be configured as **zoning based on WWN addresses**, port zoning or mixed zoning. Zoning based on WWN addresses allows communication between a particular disk array front end port and a server host bus adaptor based on the WWN address. This type of zoning is sometimes called soft zoning. It allows great flexibility because it is resistant to changes in cable infrastructure. This means that if you need to add a new node and change cabling (e.g., which cable is connected to what port in a switch) you do not have to reconfigure zoning. The WWN address is a physical address, which means it is built-in and does not change. On the other hand, in **port based zoning**, we do not use WWN addresses; we define which ports of a switch allow mutual communication instead. This is sometimes called hard zoning. Compared to WWN zoning, port zoning is more secure. But if you want to change cabling, you have to reconfigure hard zoning.

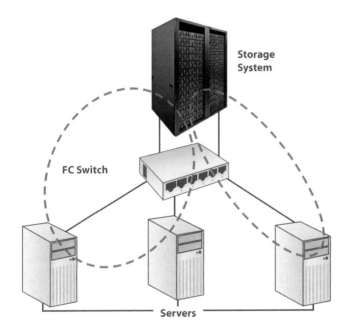

Figure 3.12 — An example of WWN based zoning.

Mixed zoning combines both port zoning and WWN based addressing. When we set up a mixed zone, we define which ports located on the FC switch can communicate, and then, using WWN, we authorize the particular host bus adaptor to access the zone. Mixed zoning is the most secure. Implementation of certain types of zoning depends on security requirements and the number of installed nodes.

Additional tools that can help us make SANs more secure include the definition of policies and standards and regular auditing. It is a matter of course that all node microcode and firmware are updated regularly, access to all node configuration tools is secured by using strong passwords and event logs are stored in a secure location.

Both LUN masking and fabric zoning should ensure that SAN resources are accessed only on a "need to access" basis. This means that a server can access only its own assigned LUNs even though the switched fabric allows practically all servers to 'see' all storage device connections. LUN mapping and fabric zoning cannot be configured from the production servers, eliminating possible intrusion threats. In LUN masking, a logical unit is paired with the server's host bus adaptor WWN address. LUN masking is configured on the storage system controller. In zoning, we can apply soft zoning, hard zoning or a combination of both. Zoning is configured on Fibre Channel switches and prevents frame forwarding to nodes that are not members of the particular zone.

Network Attached Storage Security

Unlike SAN, which is to a certain degree isolated from LAN and WAN environments, NAS is directly connected to the existing LAN infrastructure, which makes it more exposed to possible threats. Since NAS devices contain a file system and allow direct access to the files, NAS security is based on the definition of **access policies and authentication**. Authentication services can be provided by NAS device management software. However, in a business environment application, authentication is usually provided by the server with an installed directory service, such as openLDAP or Microsoft Active Directory®. The server must make the authentication service available on the network and it must be powerful enough to handle authentication load. Users who are not assigned necessary privileges are denied access to the particular folder or file. Another way to enhance the security of a NAS device is to create a **virtual local area network** (VLAN), which is a physical switched LAN (or more LANs) divided into logical segments according to usage. We can create a virtual network that will use only those local area network resources that are needed by a certain group of users. For example, you can create VLANs for company departments, project teams, subsidiaries, etc. To a certain extent, VLAN segmenting can resemble fabric zoning used in SAN because both are configured on the switch level. Access to a particular VLAN is granted according to which switch port is used or according to MAC address. Joining a VLAN can also be governed by a special server that can grant access based on authentication.

This chapter provided you with a technological description of networking. Now, you should be familiar with storage system networking possibilities. Remember that modern storage systems are usually implemented in a SAN environment, i.e., they are connected to Fibre Channel switches and HBAs installed in servers. NAS devices connected directly to a LAN are also increasingly popular. On the other hand, DAS and iSCSI connection implementation is increasingly marginal. The most important protocols are FC, TCP/IP, iFCP and FCIP. FICON protocols are used only with mainframes.

Business continuity and replication

What are you going to learn in this chapter?

- How to describe the concepts of business continuity
- How to describe business impact analysis and risk assessment
- What common backup strategies are and how they are implemented
- How business continuity and disaster recovery are connected to IT
- The meaning of replication and the kind of replication possibilities we have
- How to describe concepts of clusters and geoclusters

Business continuity concepts

The major focus of this chapter will be on protection of our critical data. We will discuss the techniques and tools we can use to ensure we do not lose data that plays a crucial role in our business. However, even before that, we will start with business continuity principles that create a functional framework that encompasses not only securing data and IT infrastructure, but continuity of the mission critical business processes in non-standard and potentially destructive situations.

We all hope that our organization will not be affected by a cyber attack or theft. However, these things happen and it is better to be prepared for them. Imagine there is a fire in your company that destroys half the building — your IT equipment and offices. To be prepared for such a situation means that you have an alternative location, which can be temporarily used as offices. It means that you need to know what equipment is the most important and you have to be able to contact your suppliers and order this new replacement equipment as soon as possible. It also means that you must have employees trained and prepared for handling such situations. In the event that your servers and storage systems are out of order, your applications do not work. These applications may be responsible for accounting, ordering goods or shipping goods. If you are unable to process orders from your customers, you could face significant financial loss. However, it is not only immediate financial loss; the whole incident, depending on its severity, could seriously damage the reputation and image of your organization and affect your future revenue.

Business continuity management identifies critical business processes and establishes rules and procedures that should prevent interruption of these key processes in the event of unexpected situations that could negatively impact an organization. The goal is to reduce the negative impact of crisis situations on the organization and to mitigate the risk involved in your area of business. The implementation of business continuity management is governed by regulations and standards. In most countries, it is a legal requirement to have a plan for handling crisis situations. The standards provide methodology that helps to create a functional business continuity plan.

The best known standard is the **British Standard for Business Continuity Management** (BS25999), which provides terminology, as well as guidance for the determination of business processes and their importance. Training based on this standard also provides you with best practices that can significantly simplify business continuity management implementation in your organization. When you meet all the criteria represented by BS25999, you can receive certification from an independent external auditing company, which proves that your organization is well prepared for handling the most probable incidents. This can bring you an advantage over your competitors, not only through an improved response to times of distress, but also through increased credibility and trustworthiness. Business continuity management also helps you protect your trademark, shows you how to make your investments and can grant you lower insurance prices.

There are other well known and commonly used standards in addition to BS25999, such as the North American Business Continuity Standard (NFPA1600) and BS ISO/IEC 27001-2:2005 International Information Security Standard. It is important to note that, according to these standards, business continuity principles are applicable to any organization, regardless of its business area and size.

Business continuity planning

Business continuity (BC) planning is the implementation of business continuity concepts with respect to the particular organization. It's obvious that the business continuity plan of an international airport will be very different from the business continuity plan of a supermarket since the processes of both companies are completely different. However, to prepare a functional BC plan, both organizations need to undergo certain procedures based mainly on analysis of their inner and outer environments. The output of these procedures is then represented by several documents that are all part of the BC plan. The functional business continuity plan includes:

- **A business impact analysis** is the assessment of crucial business processes of a particular organization.

- **A risk assessment** is the determination of possible risks and the attitude an organization assumes towards these risks.

- **The definition of policies and roles is** based on the risk assessment output. A BC policy should define the focus of the BC plan with respect to the organization's business strategy and the current market state. The definition of roles provides transparent and clear division of responsibilities among BC team members.

- **A recovery resources description** is also a vital part of the BC plan. An organization can have its own resources in several locations or these resources can be provided by suppliers and contractors.

- **A business recovery plan is a** step-by-step plan, or script, that defines procedures to be taken when a particular situation occurs.

- **A disaster recovery plan** is a recovery plan for IT infrastructure and equipment. It describes how to get the critical applications working again after an incident takes place.

- **A testing and training schedule and maintenance plan** provide methodology and a timeline for business continuity plan testing. It should also include the name of a person responsible for keeping the BC plan updated.

The first step is to set up a business continuity team, which usually includes business processes owners and upper management. This team must translate the business requirements into an overall business continuity plan that includes **technology, people and business processes** for recovery. The major considerations are requirements for data restoration (such as whether the business requires restoration up to the point of the disaster or can restore from a previous data backup) and recovery time requirements. These considerations determine the technologies and method used to support the disaster recovery plan. For example, if the business requires near-continuous recovery of data (with no lost transactions), it will likely use remote mirroring of data and wide-area clusters that enable a "hot" standby application environment. The shorter the recovery time and the less transaction loss, the higher the cost of the recovery solution. As more and more businesses rely on critical applications to generate revenue, the requirement increases for shorter recovery time (less than 1hr) or even continuous recovery (within minutes).

We have described a business recovery plan, which includes scripts that provide step-by-step instructions on how to handle particular situations. There can be anywhere from two or three scripts to dozens of scripts prepared for different possible scenarios, depending on the size of an organization. Scripts are prepared for handling events such as fire, burglary or sabotage. When such an event occurs, the business continuity team **activates** the right script and simply follows the instructions divided into tasks. A well prepared BC plan significantly increases an organization's resistance to unexpected situations. All BC documentation needs to be regularly updated and audited to ensure that the business continuity plan reflects the current state of inner and outer environments for the particular organization.

Business impact analysis

A business impact analysis (BIA) is part of the planning phase that identifies which business processes, users and applications are critical to the survival of the business. This process feeds into the next planning step for business continuity. Performing a BIA can help identify "cost of data unavailability" (downtime), which can be used to support decisions for various recovery solutions.

A BIA provides information necessary for creating BC strategies. Its extent is determined by the scope of products and services the organization provides. Business processes can be divided into operation processes (such as production, sales, customer support, distribution and billing), support processes (such as IT, human resources and external services) and strategic processes (such as management, project management and planning). If the importance of a process changes over time (e.g., accounting at the end of financial year), assessment is made according to the busiest period. The mutual relationship and dependencies of the processes also need to be considered.

The output of a business impact analysis is expressed through the following values: maximum tolerable period of disruption (MTDP), recovery time objective (RTO) and recovery point objective (RPO). These values are attributed to each process and process support layers. These values are very important and basically tell us what level of redundancy and availability we need and how costly it will be to meet these requirements. RTO and RPO are major concerns when deciding what backup or replication strategy we must use.

The recovery time objective value tells us what the tolerable duration of the process disruption is. In other words, how soon we have to resume the process to avoid significant negative consequences. RTO is usually determined in cooperation with the business process owner. We can also set RTO for process dependencies; in this case we are talking about RTO layers, which can be, for example, resumption of power supply, air conditioning in the server room, resumption of server operation, network or storage system, RTO of installed application.

The recovery point objective, on the other hand, tells what data loss we can afford for the particular business process. In other words, it tells us how old our backup data can be. If the last backup is at 7:00 PM and our storage system is destroyed at 10:00 PM by fire, it means we lose all the data that was stored in those 3hrs.

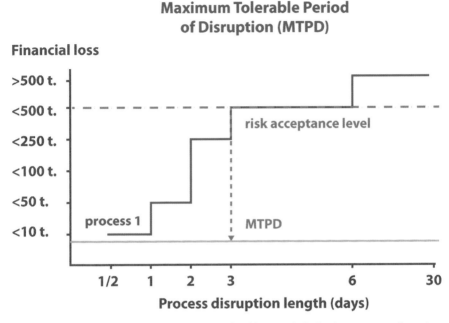

Figure 4.1 — Maximum tolerable period of a business process disruption.

The maximum tolerable period of disruption is output of the business impact analysis, but risk management also plays a role when determining MTPD values. The MTPD value shows us the length of a business process disruption after which the viability of this particular process, or organization as whole, is seriously threatened. In other words, once the time marked by MTPD value passes, it is practically impossible to restore the business process because the damage caused by the disruption is too severe. The MTPD is determined on the basis of financial loss incured because the business process was interrupted, and the risk acceptance level, which marks the amount of financial loss an organization is capable of handling. To avoid reaching the MTPD boundary, an organization must take precautions. The best option would be to take such precautions that the financial loss is near to negligible. However, high availability and failure resistant systems are so expensive that it is necessary to determine the risk acceptance level. Up to this level, financial loss can be significant, but it does not endanger the business as whole. Accepted possible financial loss is still significantly lower than the cost of implementing precaution measures. Remember, that the first letter of MTPD stands for maximum. This makes the MTPD values highly hypothetical because no company will set its recovery time objectives as high as MTPD. Process disruption time allowed by recovery time objective values will always be significantly lower than values determined by MTPD.

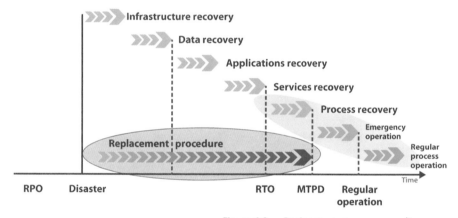

Figure 4.2 — Business process recovery diagram.

In Figure 4.2, you can see that the RPO is always lower than the RTO. We also know that the RTO is lower than the MTPD. The resumption of a disrupted business process is achieved by completing individual recovery steps. First, it is important to recover the infrastructure to have power and cooling for servers and disk arrays. Then we can recover the data from backup. The technology nowadays **allows us to set the RPO value to zero and the RTO to seconds or minutes**. This can be achieved by redundant duplicate infrastructure (servers and disk arrays) placed in a separate location, which is ready to take over when the first location fails. This type of solution is called geoclustering, and it is by far the most expensive solution available. We will discuss geoclusters in detail when we talk about cluster solutions and remote replication. If the business process is not critical and it's not necessary to invest large amounts of money into geoclusters, we can set **RPO and RTO values to minutes and hours**. This setting is allowed through several means, such as synchronous remote data replication and an alternative location. The cheapest solutions based on tape backup allow **RPO and RTO to be set to hours and days**.

When we design an IT infrastructure, we need to consider RPO and RTO values. RPO and RTO values are concerned with business processes that are dependent on hardware availability, software functionality, human intervention and non-standard situations (sabotage, natural disaster, theft, etc.). When everything is working as it should work, we say that the system is available, meaning users can access applications running on servers and servers can access data stored on disk arrays. **Availability** is expressed in a percentage that shows us how much time a year the system is operable. Availability takes into account unexpected incidents causing disruptions, as well as planned maintenance procedures. If we have **99.9% availability**, it actually means the system will be out of order for a maximum of 9hrs a year. Other commonly used figures include 99.95% availability, which represents a total outage of 5hrs a year; 99.99% availability, which makes 1hr a year; and 99.999% which allows disruption for only 5min a year. The availability reaching higher values than 99.9% is commonly called **high availability**.

Midrange and especially enterprise level storage systems are designed to provide high availability. High availability is achieved by redundant dual controller architecture and by hot-swappable components that can be replaced without disruption. Storage systems usually also allow nondisruptive maintenance, which includes microcode upgrade and other procedures, such as migration and logical unit expansion.

Risk assessment

Risk assessment is another part that constitutes the proper business continuity plan. It provides important data that amends business impact analysis and helps to make the right choice of means when designing failure resistant IT environment. Risk assessment determines the probability of threats that can lead to disruption of an organization, and it also determines the impact of these threats. The difference between BIA and RA is that BIA determines the impact of business process disruption on the operation of an organization, while RA measures and evaluates the possibility of threat occurrence and its impact on the business processes.

The major concerns are the probability of threat and the impact of this threat. Threats can be represented by a human factor failure, a natural disaster, a technological failure, an economic situation or political instability. Another categorization divides threats into random and intentional — threats that are possible to prevent and threats that are not possible to prevent. Some threats can be recognized before they strike, which buys us some time to prepare for them, and other threats have no prior notice. It is also necessary to determine whether the particular threat can strike locally (e.g., fire) or regionally (e.g., earthquake). All these factors need to be accounted for, and this information, in cooperation with a business impact analysis, helps us choose a functional business continuity strategy.

The impact of a threat can lead to financial loss, unavailability of employees, limited or no access to a building and premises, hardware failure, data unavailability, infrastructure outages and unavailability of critical documentation. If you took classes in risk management, you probably know there are many methods that help us assess and evaluate the risks. Among the most important are the what-if analysis, the cause-consequence analysis, the brainstorming approach and the event tree analysis. For the purpose of this book, all you need to know is that some of these methods are more sophisticated and scientific than others, and good risk management usually makes use of a combination of different methodologies.

The purpose of risk assessment is to help an organization assume the right attitude towards a risk based on its probability and the severity of its impact. The possible threats and calculated probability constitute a risk quartile matrix, which looks something like this:

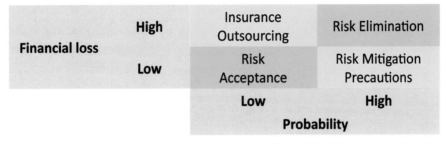

Figure 4.3 — Risk assessment matrix.

If the threat is unlikely to happen and would cause low financial loss, an organization usually accepts the risk. The threats that are unlikely to happen but would cause high financial loss (e.g., a fire or flood) are usually treated with the proper insurance. If the threat is likely to occur and cause low financial loss, an organization will try to mitigate the risk by taking precautions. When the threat is likely to take place and the financial loss that would be incurred is high (e.g., your organization is set up on a river bank that floods every spring), the risk needs to be eliminated.

From the perspective of the IT infrastructure and the continuity of its operation, we are mostly concerned with threats with impact that can be avoided by taking precautions. The precautions to be taken are summed up in a risk treatment plan, which is part of risk assessment documentation. The risk treatment plan determines clearly what precautions and actions will be taken to prevent the threat or to mitigate the threat impact.

RPO and RTO are major considerations when designing a failure resistant IT environment. Remember that RPO stands for recovery point
objective, and it tells us what amount of data transactions we are allowed to lose in the event of disaster. It determines how old our backup
data can be. RTO, which stands for recovery time objective, tells us what
the maximum desirable period of disruption is. After the RTO time passes, the application should work properly. The MTPD, or maximum tolerable period of disruption, is purely hypothetical and it defines the "point
of no return." The RTO will always be significantly lower than the MTPD.

All these values are outputs of the business impact analysis. The risk
assessment complements and amends the BIA.

Business continuity vs. disaster recovery

The business continuity plan focuses on all business processes important for a particular organization. Imagine you need to prepare a BC
plan for an airport. This BC plan will include a description of actions that
need to be taken, for example, when it's freezing outside and the supplier failed to deliver fluid for defrosting the aircraft. As you can see, this
has little to do with IT infrastructure and its operations, yet it definitely
needs to be accounted for. BC planning is a large-scale process that ex-
plores how a particular organization is operating. A BC plan can be tailored even for companies that do not use IT equipment at all, although
there would be very few of them nowadays.

Now it's time to stress that disaster recovery **is not** business continuity. Sometimes these terms are mistakenly confused and their use
is not interchangeable. **Disaster recovery** is the part of business continuity that **focuses only on IT infrastructure** and business processes
that depend on IT equipment. Some organizations have all their business processes depend on IT infrastructure, for example, data centers,
mobile network operators and banks. For these organizations, disaster
recovery is crucial. However, even these organizations need a business

continuity plan that considers supplier and employee availability in times of crisis.

Some storage system manufacturers see business continuity as the equivalent of disaster recovery. You can see this in the name of their management software or in their marketing. We should now understand that while this can be true from their perspective, in a broader context, business continuity will always stand above disaster recovery.

Disaster recovery plan

Business continuity should prepare your organization for a disaster that can cause disruption of vitally important business processes. It allows you to learn a lot about your own company, and it allows you to recognize possible threats before they even happen. A disaster recovery plan, together with a business recovery plan, will help you most when a threat strikes. A business recovery plan generally focuses on the business processes. It provides solutions in situations when the building with your offices is inaccessible, your employees cannot get to work because of harsh weather conditions, and other disruptive events. A disaster recovery plan focuses only on the continuity of business processes that are dependent on IT infrastructure. By IT infrastructure, we mean servers, switches, disk arrays, connectivity to the WAN (Internet), etc. We can also include power supply and air conditioning. In a situation of distress, when your IT equipment is stolen, destroyed by fire or malfunctioning, you will use your DR plan, which contains a description of all IT related processes together with step-by-step guidance for their recovery.

A disaster recovery plan contains:

- **Basic information:** purpose, area of application, requirements, log of DR plan modifications, members of DR team and their roles and responsibilities

- **Notification/activation phase:** notification procedure, call tree, damage assessment, activation criteria, plan activation

- **Recovery procedures:** succession of recovery procedures according to their importance, logging, escalation

- **Standard operation resumption:** checking whether all systems work properly, termination of DR plan

- **Amendments:** call book, vendor SLA, RTO of processes

Let's start by talking about the notification/activation phase, which is especially interesting. When something happens, let's say, part of your equipment gets stolen, you need to notify the people responsible for recovery of processes dependent on IT equipment and IT infrastructure. You would use a call tree list, which tells you who should be notified first. Together with the members of the DR team, you would assess the extent of damage and the expected recovery time. This assessment must be done quickly because the clock is already running.

To help you with damage assessment, the DR plan provides individual IT equipment locations in the building and a checklist that guides you through the procedure. The checklist is usually designed so that even employees with no IT experience can assess the damage. The checklist typically uses simple directions, such as: "Check switch x located in room y. Are the green lights glowing?" The instructions and questions are this simple so that unqualified personnel can perform the assessment before qualified personnel arrive. Once you have analyzed the extent of the damage, you can check whether the damage is serious enough to qualify for DR plan activation. If yes, the plan can be activated. Once the DR plan is activated, all members of the DR team, or their delegates, must be present and ready to perform their part of the recovery procedures.

Recovery procedures are followed in a logical order, where the most important processes need to be recovered first. The importance of a procedure is usually assessed based on prerequisites — if you have not restored Internet connectivity, then it is useless that your email server works seamlessly. You should also consider which procedures can be done simultaneously.

The order of recovery procedures in a small company can look similar to this example:

LAN recovery ➡ WAN recovery ➡ SAN recovery ➡ Backup server ➡ Domain controller ➡ Email server ➡ Microsoft SharePoint° server ➡ Accounting software and databases, etc.

Each procedure has its own recovery time estimate, checklist, and supplier and maintenance provider contact details (escalation). Once all the procedures are complete, the functionality of all systems can be tested. When everything is operational, the DR plan is terminated.

Speed of individual process recovery is determined especially by technological means. The performance of disaster recovery planning depends highly on backup strategies, data replication strategies and cluster solutions. Some solutions are less resistant to failure than others, but they are usually less expensive.

Disaster recovery support in storage systems

Disk arrays store our data, which makes them the most vulnerable part of our IT infrastructure. In the event of a disaster, you can always buy new hardware, and you can install your application from a DVD or some other media, but you cannot recover your data if you did not have it protected effectively enough. That's why storage system manufacturers offer a wide range of services and software solutions and best practice guidance to make storage systems even more resistant to data loss.

We can say that storage systems are inherently redundant. This means that they provide no single point of failure architecture, where all important hardware is installed twice (remember, CTL0 and CTL1). No vendor would sell storage without these capabilities. Nor would a vendor sell a storage system without RAID support. This is what makes storage systems reliable and powerful. However, software also plays an important role. Software can help you employ and optimize data replication. Software agents can also enable close cooperation between applications running on production servers and disk arrays. The supplied software will also help you to maintain data consistency and integrity, which is especially important for DR procedures. If your data is not consistent, it cannot be read and is, therefore, useless. It is essential to maintain consistency, especially with databases. Databases are living data, changing every second due to a high number of ongoing transactions. Software supplied by a storage system manufacturer can help you simplify management of very complex operations. Remember that if you purchase a storage system, the actual hardware may cost less than the software licenses. This should give you some idea of how important software supplied by a storage system manufacturer is.

Backup and replication

By now you probably understand that both data backup and data replication are key words in disaster recovery planning. Before we get to the description of the individual techniques and solutions, it's necessary to understand what we mean when we talk about backup and data replication. In other words, we'll discuss what the difference is between these two.

In broad terms, a backup means we create duplicates of data, either in the form of files or raw data blocks. Data replication can be seen as part of data backup. From home computer use, you know it's good to keep a copy of your important files in another location, such as another hard drive, a USB flash drive or a CD. If your computer breaks and you lose your data, you can restore it from your backups. This is the basic idea. In an enterprise environment, there is so much data that it's impossible to manually back up all the files. With a server application, it's even more complicated because you have to back up very complex databases. That is why there are many dedicated hardware devices and software products to handle the process in an effective and reliable way.

In technical terms, data replication is very different from data backup. When we **back up** data, it means that if we need to access this data, we have to **restore** it. The backup restoration, therefore, takes time. Depending on the media that contains our backed up data and depending on our backup strategy, the process of data recovery can take from hours to days. On the other hand, data replication does not need any recovery; replicated data can be used instantly, or nearly instantly.

When you back up data on an enterprise level, you use dedicated software and equipment. When we want to restore this data, we must use this software and equipment to make the data accessible to an application that is running on your production servers. The data replica can be accessed directly by applications running on your servers; there is no need to use backup servers and software.

You may wonder why we back up our data, when data replication is clearly better. It is all about cost and capacity. You can back up your data to a tape library, which is quite a cheap solution and very reliable. Tapes can hold terabytes of data. For data replication you need to have a storage system and enough disk capacity installed in this storage system. Imagine that you create a LUN on a disk array. You want to replicate the data on this LUN. To do that, you need to create another LUN with exactly the same size as the production LUN. Then you create a replication pair out of these two LUNs. The source LUN becomes a P-VOL (stands for production, or primary, volume) and the LUN that contains the replica becomes an S-VOL (secondary volume).

In the context of storage systems, data replication is controlled solely by a disk array. An S-VOL contains exactly the same raw data blocks as a P-VOL. The consequence of this can be understood in another example: imagine you create a LUN of 10GB. This LUN may contain only 1GB of data. You will create a replication pair, the source LUN will become a P-VOL and the target LUN will become an S-VOL. Both volumes will have the size of 10GB and both volumes will contain only 1GB of actual data. This means that data replication also copies the empty blocks that contain no real data. This is what makes replication more expensive than data backup. The major downside of data replication is that it merely mirrors the data on the P-VOL. If the P-VOL becomes corrupted or part of the data is accidentally deleted, data replication will mirror this corrupted data.

Both data backup and data replication play important roles in data loss prevention. Whether we employ backup or replication depends on the data lifecycle and the importance of a business process that uses the data. Less critical data can be backed up because if there is trouble, we do not need to restore it in 10min. Important data will be replicated to make it accessible under any circumstances. Note that when we employ data replication, we usually back up this data as well. If a server fails, replicated data is used. If a disk array containing both a P-VOL and an S-VOL fails, we need to restore data from a back up. In an enterprise environment, tape libraries are standard for data backup.

Backup concepts

We have been talking about backup for a while and now it is time to learn how it is actually done. In your organization, you have several production servers that run important applications. To back up the data from these servers, you need:

- **A backup device:** In an enterprise environment it will most likely be a tape library, but it can also be a storage system with a LUN dedicated for backup. (Do not confuse this with a replication pair!)

- **A backup server:** In most cases, you need a backup server that is communicating directly with the backup device and controls backup from all the servers.

- **Backup software:** This software runs on a backup server and allows you to make configurations according to your needs.

- **Backup agents:** These agents are small applications installed on all your production servers. They are part of backup software and they allow communication between a backup server and production servers with applications and databases.

The backup server can be part of your LAN or SAN environment, depending on your requirements. **LAN based backup topology** does allow you to use either a tape library or NAS device as a backup location. The advantages are easy implementation and low cost. The disadvantage is that backup creates extra traffic, which can slow down your LAN performance. **SAN based backup topology** uses a backup server that is installed in a SAN environment, which enables it to take advantage of its features — fast Fibre Channel data transfer and inherited security.

A backup server then **pulls** the data scheduled for backup from production servers. It is also possible to configure backup agents to **push** the data from a production server to a backup server. However, this is not recommended because it is less secure. If an agent pushes data to the backup server that means it has permission to do write operations. The pull strategy is more secure because it eliminates the risk that the backed up data will be overwritten, either accidentally or on purpose.

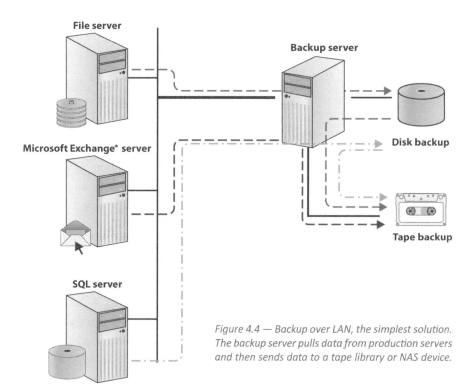

Figure 4.4 — Backup over LAN, the simplest solution. The backup server pulls data from production servers and then sends data to a tape library or NAS device.

To choose our backup topology and the proper software, we have to decide when and how we want to back up our data. We have to prepare a **backup schedule** and define the time of a **backup window**. A backup window is a time of day when we make our regular scheduled backup. It is usually set at night when the systems are not under high load and backup traffic will not result in decreased performance of production servers and network.

In addition, we also have to choose to what extent the data is going to be backed up. We can decide to create a **full backup**, which means that every time a backup is scheduled, all data is stored in exact copies. This can be slow and demanding in terms of capacity needed for backup.

Sometimes a full backup is understood as **system imaging**, meaning that you create an image of the hard drive installed in the server, which contains production data. This image can then be used for recovering the server to the exact state it was in at the time of backup. This technique is often used for recording known good configurations after a clean install and for distribution of this configuration to other servers. A system image can be useful for backing up employee desktops and notebooks, but it is not likely to be used as a tool for making ongoing backups of all the server applications and their databases. Other backup models are by:

- **Incremental backup** — at the beginning, a full backup is made. Then at every scheduled backup, only the data that was changed or added since last time backup is recorded. The disadvantage is that when you need to recover data, you need to combine the initial full backup with all incremental backups which is demanding in terms of time and capacity.

- **Differential backup** — at the beginning, a full backup is made. At every scheduled backup, only the data that differs from the initial full backup is recorded. This technique delivers good recovery times — you need to combine only the initial full backup with the most recent differential backup.

- **Reverse delta backup** — at the beginning, a full backup is made. At every scheduled backup, the initial full backup image is synchronized so that it mirrors the current state of data on servers. During the reverse delta backup, a differential file is created that allows you to go back and restore previous versions of data if they are needed. This is probably the best option to choose, because it allows you to achieve the fastest recovery times since you always have the most recent full backup ready to use.

The last thing that remains to be considered is backup validation. No matter what backup model you choose, it will always be a structured backup, meaning that backed up data contains additional information, such as when the data was recorded, where, and what the extent of the backup was. Backup validation is a functionality presented by backup management software. It checks whether all data was backed up successfully with no error occurrence. It is a self-check mechanism that provides feedback to IT administrators. Backup management software also offers plenty of other features, such as backup data encryption that enhances the security of your data.

 We didn't mention one backup concept closely connected with storage systems — **serverless data backup**. This technique is sometimes called extended copy and is based on SCSI commands that allows you to backup data from LUNs directly onto a tape library, without the participation of any backup server. A serverless backup environment is therefore SAN based.

Backup based on tape libraries

Magnetic tape backup is the cheap and safe way of depositing your data for recovery in case of primary data loss. The tape library used in midsized organizations usually costs a bit less than a midrange storage system. The individual tapes offer capacity in terabytes and they are much cheaper than hard drives. The important limitation is that data stored on tapes is **accessed sequentially**. It is similar to old VHS video tapes — you need to rewind or fast forward the tape to get to the place where your data is. Despite this drawback, magnetic tapes are still used, not only because of their price, but also for their reliability. Magnetic tapes can store data for many years. Another specific feature of tapes is **WORM functionality**. WORM stands for "write once read many," and this functionality should ensure that backed up data cannot be altered or modified once it is written.

When we back up on tapes, we need to determine how many copies we need to meet our business continuity policy. Usually we create one onsite copy and one offsite copy. The advantage of tapes is that they are easily moved to another location. An offsite backup repository can be located at another building owned by a particular organization or at specialized data center that offers disaster recovery services. In the event of a disaster, the first thing to do is restore servers — you need to either install OS or restore it from an image. After that, you can restore your data from onsite or offsite tapes. Data recovery from tapes can take hours or even days.

Backup strategies

When deciding what backup strategy to employ, we need to sum up all our requirements and make sure these requirements are met. We have to be sure we are protected against:

- **Disk failure** — if we use a storage system, then RAID redundancy should provide a good level of security. In addition, we can employ a storage-to-tape backup strategy.

- **Accidental file deletion** — backup software running on a backup server should take care of this problem. It is also possible to restore files from tapes.

- **Complete machine destruction** — we need a backup machine, system image that will restore known and used configuration, storage system, tapes, etc.

- **Destruction of any onsite backups** — we would need remote replication and offsite tapes.

We also need to decide to what extent we will back up. A business impact analysis lets us know the importance of business processes. This, together with RPO and RTO values, is the key to determining our backup strategy. You need to work with many variables — how much storage capacity is possible to dedicate to backups, time and money available for backup software and technology, human resources allocation on backups, and performance impact on production servers and network bandwidth. The backup strategy needs to be designed as scalable to continue meeting the backup requirements as the business grows. The most important thing is to know what dangers you want to protect against and how you will handle restoration procedures for each item you backup, such as files, databases and system configurations. It is also likely that you will employ different backup strategies for production servers and workstations. Regular backup testing and validating helps to determine whether the currently used backup strategy is working sufficiently or whether it would be advantageous to make adjustments.

Another thing to consider is the **backup data retention** plan. You need to define how long you will keep individual versions of backup data. If your backup server creates backups every 2hrs, you need to set the number of copies to be retained. When the limit is reached, the oldest backup is automatically deleted. Data retention has a lot to do with both legal requirements (e.g., those set by accounting, hospitals and government institutions) and with the data lifecycle. As we know from the first chapter, the data **lifecycle** represents the changing value of data over time. It is necessary to make such backup settings that take data lifecycle into consideration, because, otherwise, you may not realize the data you are backing up intensively every two hours is not so important anymore and you are wasting money and resources. Your backup strategy, therefore, needs to be updated regularly.

Backup optimization

Every organization has limited resources, especially in terms of capacity that can be used for backup and the cost of backup hardware and software. It is therefore important to use resources carefully to maximize the utilization of your equipment. There are several techniques that can make backup more effective. The desirable backup solution is fast, does not have much influence on production server performance and network bandwidth, and offers good value for money. The techniques that allow you to achieve better utilization are data compression, deduplication, multiplexing and staging.

Compression is well known from personal computers. Most users have already encountered .zip or .rar files that represent a package of files encapsulated into one archive to provide easier manipulation and compression — the output archive file is smaller than the total of the original files. The efficiency of compression is expressed as a ratio. For example if you have a compression ratio of 1:2, the compressed file will be half the size of the original file. The compression is achieved by coding the files with a special algorithm. The efficiency of the algorithm is based on the level of information entropy presented in the source file. Simply said, information entropy is represented by sequence of numbers in code and their randomness. The higher the level of randomness, the higher the entropy. If we had code represented by totally random numbers with no hidden pattern, then compression is not possible. This, however, does not happen very often, and usually it is possible to achieve at least some compression ratio. Lossless data compression can be compressed to an extent allowed by the data entropy. A lower amount of randomness allows the algorithm to find underlying patterns that are logged. If the pattern occurs more than twice, the second occurrence is replaced by a reference to the first occurrence. Compression is employed in tape libraries without exception. Processing compression algorithms may affect backup performance. In tape libraries, this problem is eliminated by adding extra hardware processors that take care only of calculating data compression and decompression. Compression therefore does not affect read and write speed in tape drives.

Deduplication is the technique that eliminates duplicities in data. Thanks to this technique, it is possible to save disk space. Unlike compression, deduplication searches for a larger string of identical data. If we backup our email database, it is likely there will be dozens of instances of the same email. If the duplicate data is found, it is replaced by reference to the original data. Deduplicated backup data can occupy up to 90% less disk space than data that contains duplicities. We can employ inline deduplication, which takes place in real time when we back up data. If the backup device recognizes a chunk of data that has already been stored, it makes reference to this previously stored data without storing the new chunk of data. As opposed to inline deduplication, we can employ post-process deduplication, which takes place after the backup is finished. First, backup data is stored and then it is analyzed for duplicities. The post-process deduplication is more effective than inline deduplication, but it requires more disk space. The extra disk space is required because, during the analysis of backup data, deduplication software creates large temporary files. Deduplication is very popular and often implemented. Note that deduplication cannot be used with tape libraries. The data stored on tapes is accessed sequentially, which disables the possibility of easy manipulation with previously stored data (rewinding and fast forwarding). Data deduplication can be used when we back up our data on hard drives or storage system LUNs.

Multiplexing in the context of data backups expresses the ability of software and equipment to back up data from several sources simultaneously. In broader terms, multiplexing is a method that combines multiple digital data streams into one signal that can be transferred over one medium (wire). Similarly, in relevance to backup optimization, multiplexing allows you to backup all your IT infrastructure on a single backup device, providing it has enough capacity and it supports this functionality.

Disk staging is a key part of the disk-to-disk-to-tape backup procedure (D2D2T). When we want to back up our data to a tape library, we have to consider whether the data processing speed of the particular tape device is sufficient. To speed up the backup process, we can set the software to back up to a hard drive (or LUN) first and then transfer the data from this hard drive to tape. The hard drive therefore works as a temporary storage area on a similar principle to cache. Disk staging can increase performance of frequent and small random access restores, because the disk has much faster random access than tape (no rewinding and seeking on the tape). If we need to restore data, it can still be present on the staging disk, ready for fast restore (depending on the backup software configuration).

All these techniques can be employed together, and they often are. Remember that you cannot employ deduplication when using a tape library as a primary backup device. Deduplication is, however, possible when we also employ disk staging. Data is deduplicated on the hard drive and then transferred to a tape library. This, however, adds an extra step when restoring the data — data is loaded from the tape and then it must be restored one more time by reversing the deduplication process. Multiplexing and compression are common features offered by most backup software manufacturers.

Replication objectives

In this chapter, we are describing techniques that ensure high availability of data and business continuity with a focus on disaster recovery and data loss prevention. There is a large number of solutions that help to accomplish these objectives. Their efficiency goes hand-in-hand with their cost. The backup solutions we have discussed so far are among the cheaper solutions. However, even backup solutions are scalable and can deliver high performance. As you know, all backup techniques require some time for restoration, which will always be their limitations. For critical applications that need to be online all the time, backup itself is not sufficient, because recovery time from backup does not meet RPO and RTO requirements. For this case, we have data replication. On the following pages, we will not be dealing with database replication or replication done on the application level. We will focus mainly on replication possibilities offered by storage system manufacturers. **Remember that all the replication techniques we describe in detail happen on the controller level, without participation of production servers. We are talking about array-based replication.**

The reason we use data replication is to achieve lower RPO and RTO of key business processes. When the data replication is employed together with server redundancy (server clusters) we can reach zero RPO and RTO in minutes. When we add a hot standby site in another location, we can reach zero RPO and RTO in a few seconds. The data replica contains the same data blocks as a source volume, which enables immediate usage of data by application with no restore procedures. Data replicas are also useful for application testing and data migration. We are going to start with in-system replication and and snapshots, which can also be considered as a replication technique. We will see how replication works with server clusters. Towards the end of this chapter we will get to solutions that can offer 99.999% availability. These solutions are based on remote replication and geocluster technology. As the chapter progresses, the solutions presented are going to get more technical, sophisticated and costly.

The replication strategy depends on the importance of data and its availability. Bank institutions that offer Internet banking services or mobile service providers need the highest availability possible because banking transactions and call logging are ongoing processes that will always have zero RPO and RTO in seconds. Imagine a bank that loses data on user accounts or a mobile service provider that cannot store information about customer calls. Even a minute of disruption can pose an unacceptable threat and can lead to devastating consequences. Data backup is not powerful enough to prevent data loss on such a level. That is why we employ more sophisticated and costly solutions — data replication and geographically diversified IT infrastructure.

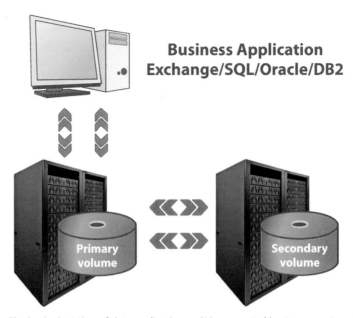

Figure 4.5 — The basic depiction of data replication as it is supported in storage systems. The Primary Volume (P-VOL) is a LUN mapped to a server. Data from the P-VOL is replicated to an S-VOL that can be located in the same storage system as the P-VOL or in a storage system located elsewhere. The P-VOL and S-VOL must be the same size.

Overview of replication commands

When we decide to employ data replication on the storage system level, we usually use software supplied by the storage system manufacturer. Individual replication functionalities are usually subject to licensing, so you usually have to pay to enable a particular replication feature. Replication management software typically offers both a graphical user interface (GUI) and command line interface (CLI). A command line interface is very useful for replication procedure automation because it allows you to write your own scripts. Commands that are used to control data replication differ from manufacturer to manufacturer. To learn how to create a replication pair, you usually need to go through storage system documentation or attend a specialized training. However, there are few commands that are common with most storage system manufacturers. Among these commands, or replication functionalities, are:

- **Pair create and initial copy**

- **Pair split**

- **Pair resynchronization**

- **Reverse synchronization/restore**

When we create a replication pair, the source LUN becomes a P-VOL and the target LUN becomes an S-VOL. Immediately after the pair is created, initial copy takes place. Initial copy creates an exact replica of all data blocks on the P-VOL, including empty blocks. During initial copy, the P-VOL is accessible for I/O operations, but the performance can be affected. Some storage systems allow you to select the priority of the initial copy process when creating replication pairs. The slower pace minimizes the impact of the initial copy operations on system I/O, while the faster pace completes the initial copy operations as quickly as possible. The best timing is based on the amount of write activity on the P-VOL and the amount of time elapsed between up-date copies. Under all circumstances, it is better to create replication pairs when the system is not under high load.

Write operations performed on the P-VOL during the initial copy op-erations will always be duplicated to the S-VOL after the initial copy is complete. The status of the pair is **COPY** while the initial copy operation is in progress. The pair status changes to **PAIR** when the initial copy is complete. Once the initial copy is finished, differential data is synchro-nized to the S-VOL. See Figure 4.6 for reference.

Note that it's impossible to perform read or write operations on the S-VOL while the replication status is PAIR. To make use of the S-VOL, you need to stop the continuous volume synchronization by splitting the pair.

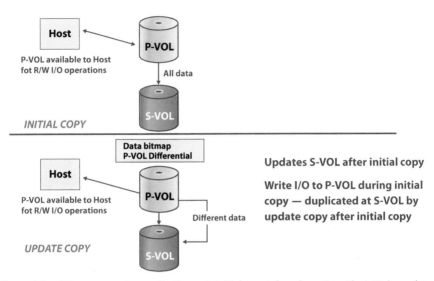

*Figure 4.6 — When we create a replication pair, initial copy takes place. Once the initial copy has been completed, the content of the S-VOL is synchronized with the P-VOL regularly. When the S-VOL status is **PAIR**, it's not possible to read or write from the S-VOL.*

Pair split operation performs all pending S-VOL updates (those issued prior to the split command and recorded in the P-VOL differential bitmap) to make the S-VOL identical to the state of the P-VOL when the suspend command was issued and then provides full read/write access to the split S-VOL. While the pair is split, the system establishes a bitmap for the split P-VOL and S-VOL and records all updates to both volumes. The P-VOL remains fully accessible during the pair split operation.

Once the P-VOL and S-VOL replication pair is split, you can access the data on the S-VOL for testing, data mining, performance test or backup. When you want to resynchronize the suspended pairs, you start the pair synchronization operation. During this operation, the S-VOL becomes unavailable for I/O operations. The regular pair synchronization procedure resynchronizes the S-VOL with the P-VOL. It is also possible to use reverse synchronization with the copy direction from the S-VOL to the P-VOL. When a pair synchronization is performed on a suspended (split) pair, the storage system merges the S-VOL differential bitmap into the P-VOL differential bitmap and then copies all flagged data from the P-VOL to the S-VOL. When reverse pair synchronization takes place, the process goes the other way. This ensures that the P-VOL and S-VOL are properly resynchronized in the desired direction.

Another common operation that can be performed on a replication pair is pair status transition. If necessary, it is possible to swap P-VOL and S-VOL labels. S-VOL then becomes P-VOL and P-VOL becomes S-VOL.

When you want to use the data replication feature, you need to create a target LUN that has the exactly same size (measured in blocks) as the source LUN. You should create the target LUN in a RAID group different from the one that contains the source LUN to avoid performance bottlenecks. You can also create the target LUN on slower hard drives, depending on your requirements. Then you can start pair create operation. The result of this operation is a replication pair. The replication pair consists of a P-VOL (source volume) and an S-VOL (target volume). When the replication pair is active, data on S-VOL is updated from the P-VOL. It is not possible to perform read or write operations on a paired S-VOL. To be able to use the S-VOL, you need to split the pair. To resynchronize the P-VOL and S-VOL, issue a pair synchronization command. The synchronization can work in both directions according to your needs.

In-system replication: logical unit cloning

In-system replication allows creating a single, local replica of any active application volume while benefiting from full RAID protection. The result of this procedure is a volume clone that can be used by another application or system for a variety of purposes. Depending on the type of storage system, you can create several S-VOLs per P-VOL within the same system to maintain redundancy of the primary volume. In-system replication allows you to split and combine duplex volumes and provides you the contents of static LUNs without stopping the access. It is nondisruptive and allows the primary volume of each volume pair to remain online for all hosts for both read and write I/O operations. When the replication pair is established and the initial copy procedure is completed, replication operations continue unattended to provide an internal data backup.

In-system replication automatically creates a differential management logical unit (DM-LU), which is an exclusive volume used for storing replication management information when the storage system is powered down. For redundancy purposes, it is usually possible to configure two DM-LUs. The data stored on the differential management logical unit is used only during shutdown and startup of the system. Note that the DM-LU does not store the actual changed data; it just has the metadata for the differential data.

When we split the replication pair, we stop the ongoing synchronization and we make the S-VOL accessible for other applications. The S-VOL created through in-system replication can then be used for **backup purposes**. This enables IT administrators to:

- Execute logical backups faster and with less effort than previously possible

- Easily configure backups to execute across a SAN

- Manage backups from a central location

- Increase the speed of applications

- Ensure data availability

To use in-system replication to produce full logical unit clones for backup purposes makes sense because it works on the volume level. There is no need for a backup server, and the traffic does not lower network performance. The storage system management software controls the whole procedure. Data from the S-VOL can be used for serverless backup to tape library. Aside from high-performance serverless backup, the replicated volume can be used for data mining, data warehousing and full volume batch cycle testing.

Data mining is a thorough analysis of structured data stored in databases. It uncovers and extracts meaningful and potentially useful information. The data mining methodology is based on statistics functions, interpretation and generalization of mutual relationships among the data stored in a database. Data mining can provide highly valuable information for marketing purposes. Data mining is conducted by specialized software that is programmed with some degree of artificial intelligence to be able to deliver relevant results.

A data warehouse is a specialized database used for data reporting and analysis. The data stored in a warehouse is uploaded from production servers and their databases. This could affect the performance of the server and the mapped LUN. This effect can be avoided by implementing in-system replication and using an S-VOL for feeding the data warehouse database. The data warehouse database provides powerful search capabilities conducted by queries.

Testing and benchmarks can be conducted using an S-VOL to determine database performance and suggest changes in configuration. It is risky to test new procedures and configuration on a P-VOL because it can potentially lead to data loss and it can affect performance. An S-VOL provides the ideal testing environment.

The S-VOL replica also provides hot backup for instantaneous data recovery if the P-VOL fails. If this happens, the P-VOL and S-VOL statuses are swapped, which makes the S-VOL immediately available to the production server.

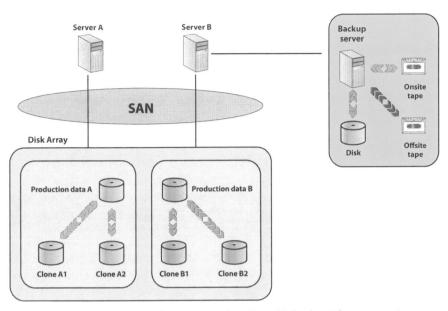

Figure 4.7 — In-system data replication in combination with backup infrastructure. In-system replication mirrors the source volumes and creates its exact replica or clone.

Copy-on-write snapshots

Copy-on-write snapshot software is a storage-based functionality for point-in-time, read-only backups. Point-in-time backups capture the state of production volume at a particular time. With in-system replication, the whole LUN is mirrored or cloned. On the other hand, snapshots store only differential data into a data pool. The data pool consists of allocated physical storage and is used only for storing differential data. One data pool can store differential data from several P-VOLs. A snapshot pair consists of a P-VOL and a virtual volume (V-VOL). The V-VOL does not physically exist but represents a set of pointers that refer to the data's physical location, partially in the pool and partially in the P-VOL. Since only part of the data belonging to the V-VOL is located in the pool (and the other part is still on P-VOL), copy-on-write snapshot software does not require twice the disk space to establish a pair in the way in-system replication creates full volume clones. However, a host will recognize the P-VOL and the V-VOL as a pair of volumes with identical capacity. The copy-on-write snapshot internally retains a logical duplication of the primary volume data at the time of command instruction. This software is used for restoration; it allows data to be restored back to the time of snapshot instruction. This means that if a logical error occurs in the P-VOL, the snapshot can be used to return the P-VOL to the state it was in at time the snapshot was taken. The duplicated volume of the copy-on-write snapshot function consists of physical data stored in the P-VOL and differential data stored in the data pool. Although the capacity of the used data pool is smaller than that of the primary volume, a duplicated volume can be created logically when the instruction is given. The data pool can share two or more primary volumes and the differential data of two or more duplicated volumes. Copy-on-write means that whenever the data in the P-VOL is modified, the modified blocks are transferred to the pool to maintain the V-VOL relevance to the point-in-time the snapshot was created.

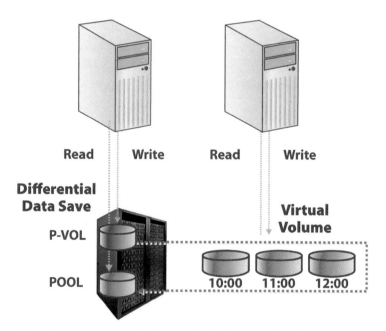

Figure 4.8 — Copy-on-write snapshot. Notice that both the P-VOL and V-VOL are accessible for I/O operations. Snapshots can be created instantly.

When a production server needs to write to its mapped LUN that is part of a snapshot pair, the request to perform a write operation on the P-VOL is sent to the storage system. Before the write is executed, the block is copied to the pool area. The set of pointers that represents the V-VOL is updated, and all the requests going through the V-VOL for the original block are physically taken from the pool. From the perspective of the host, the V-VOL (snapshot image) has not changed.

Snapshots are usually taken regularly, and they are part of a backup strategy. The snapshots can be taken every hour for LUNs that contain very important data, or every day. There is no need to schedule backup windows, since snapshot creation does not affect network traffic or storage system performance.

We use copy-on-write snapshots because they require less capacity to maintain virtual copies. In-system replication that produces volume clones for backup solutions raises the entire system price, as the storage requirement grows based on the number of copies required.

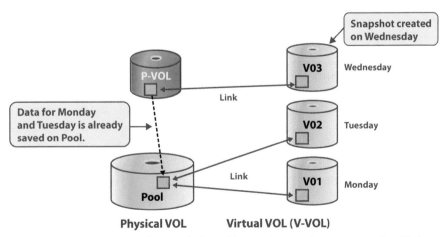

Figure 4.9 — Snapshots are taken regularly. In this case the snapshot was created on Wednesday. The new snapshot image will refer to the data on the P-VOL. As the data is modified on the P-VOL, the set of pointers in V-VOL 03 will change to point to the data stored in the pool.

	Copy-on-write snapshot	In-system replication
Features	Provides a very quick copy since it is a virtual volume	Offers superior protection because it is a complete copy; immediate restore if P-VOL becomes corrupted
Time to create	Instantaneous	From minutes to hours, depending on the size of the P-VOL
Disk space used	Size will vary depending on rate of data change but will be far less than the P-VOL	Exactly the same amount as P-VOL (measured in data blocks)
Data recovery time after P-VOL is corrupted	Two stage restore: 1. V-VOL verify, data not available to host 2. Copy back from a tape library	Instantaneous
Size of physical volume	P-VOL is larger than pool for one V-VOL	P-VOL = S-VOL
Pair configuration	Generally speaking, storage systems support a higher number of snapshots than data clones	
Restore	P-VOL can be restored from any V-VOL	P-VOL can be restored from S-VOL

Figure 4.10 — Copy-on-write snapshot and in-system replication comparison

Server clusters

To create completely failure resistant IT environments with zero RPO and nearly zero RTO, it is not enough to employ data replication and backup. Data backup requires time for data restore. Data replication provides instantly available data if the P-VOL becomes corrupted and fails. Neither of these solutions ensures high availability and redundancy of other IT infrastructure components, such as SAN Fibre Channel switches and especially servers. Fibre Channel switches can be made redundant easily by installing another switch. The first path from the server to a storage system goes through the primary Fibre Channel switch; the second path goes through the secondary Fibre Channel switch. With servers, the problem is more complex. Storage systems and tape libraries ensure that we do not lose data stored on a storage system's LUN. Except for a mapped LUN that is used for databases and shared files, servers use internal hard drives to store operating system and application installation instance. We can create a disk image that will serve as a backup of this server drive, but then again, we will need time to restore the copy, which increases the time for recovery. It is also possible to load the operation system and applications over a LAN or SAN from a storage system. However, this solution is not suitable for all applications. There is always a time lag when the server hardware failure occurs because we need to replace one physical server with another that is not broken. To prevent this lag, we need to make even servers redundant. The technique that allows us to achieve this is called *server clustering*.

Server clustering allows us to interconnect servers and their operations on the application level. There are computing clusters that combine the computing performance of all individual servers. The cluster solution then provides the sum of the servers' performance. However, for the purposes of this book, we will be most interested in **high-availability server clusters**. You can see how such a cluster works in Figure 4.11.

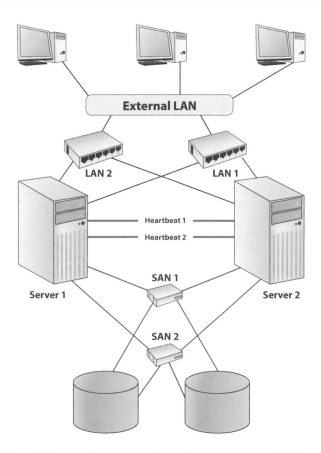

Figure 4.11 — A failure resistant server cluster. Servers are connected to a storage system through two Fibre Channel switches to meet redundancy requirements. The servers are also interconnected by a LAN that allows communication with external users and between servers. Notice the line between servers that is labeled as the "heartbeat." The heartbeat is a clustering software monitoring process. If Server 1 fails, Server 2 does not receive a heartbeat response from Server 1, so it takes over the tasks Server 1 was working on.

To enable cluster functionality, you need to install a specialized clustering software layer on the servers. Servers then share the same tasks. It is possible to implement an active-active cluster connection, which provides load balancing. In this case, both servers are working together, performing the tasks of one application. When we implement an active-passive cluster connection, only one server is processing the application request and the second is in stand-by mode, ready to take over in case the active server fails. The application status and configuration is synchronized constantly. The clustering software allows you to set the conditions for processing takeover. Usually, the servers are communicating their updated statuses in defined periods of time — this is called the heartbeat. If one server does not receive a response for a status update request, it determines that the server on the other side is broken, and it takes over immediately with no noticeable lag. This allows us to achieve zero RPO and RTO.

The cluster protection can work within one location (organization building). In this case, the IT infrastructure is completely resistant to hardware failure and, to an extent, is resistant to power failure (depending on power source redundancy). It is also resistant to minor security incidents, such as theft and sabotage. To make your IT infrastructure resistant to natural disasters such as flood, fire or destruction of the building, you need to geographically diversify your IT infrastructure. This means that you need to replicate data to another location or create geoclusters — clusters over a WAN.

Remote replication: logical unit mirroring

Storage system based remote replication is the first step to geographically diversified IT infrastructure. It allows connecting a local disk array to another storage system and to a remote storage system. The remote storage system can be located either in another building that belongs to the particular organization or in professional disaster recovery data center. Remote replication is a nondisruptive, host-independent solution for disaster recovery or data migration over any distance. The key parameter that determines seamless remote replication is the type of network connection to the secondary location. The connection can be established using FCIP or iFCP protocols over the WAN (basically the Internet), public line or dark fiber.

The public line that allows asynchronous transfer mode (ATM) represents a standard of unified network that serves both for transmission of telecommunication services (landline) and data. It was designed to achieve low latency and high speed. It requires a dedicated infrastructure. This technology is declining in favor of transmitting data over IP networks.

Dark fiber is a specific technology based on dense wavelength-division multiplexing (DWDM). At your primary location, you have several storage systems that need to replicate data over distance. Fibre Channel cables from every storage system are plugged into a special multiplexing device that merges signals from multiple Fibre Channel cables into one optical cable that connects both locations — primary and secondary. At the secondary location, the multiplexing device transforms the signal from one optical cable into more Fibre Channel cables connected to each storage system. Dark fiber optical cable is capable of transmission over 100km. To enable data transmission over longer distances, it is necessary to implement a signal amplification device — a repeater. Dark fiber technology requires an optical cable infrastructure that connects both sites. Nowadays, it is possible to rent the dark fiber bandwidth from a telecommunication company that owns optical wiring infrastructure. Dark fiber technology ensures high performance and reliability.

Once we have successfully interconnected storage systems at both sites, we can perform standard replication procedures — create, split and resynchronize replication pairs. The only thing different from in-system replication is that we always have some network limitations, because the bandwidth and reliability of local networking is always higher than the bandwidth and reliability of solutions designed to carry data over significant distances. To overcome these limitations, we need to optimize remote replication. We need to consider network performance, especially latency, and decide whether we want to employ synchronous or asynchronous remote replication. Both solutions are highly reliable, and their function will be further described.

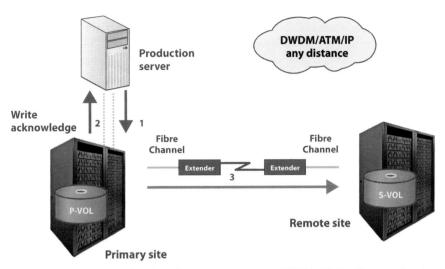

Figure 4.12 — Remote replication scheme. As you can see, DWDM, ATM or IP connections to a remote site are possible.

Synchronous remote replication

Synchronous remote replication can be implemented when we have a very good connection to the secondary site. It is especially important to reach high transfer speeds and a very short response time (latency). The key element that distinguishes synchronous remote replication from asynchronous remote replication is write acknowledgement reporting. When a production server wants to perform a write operation on a storage system, it needs to receive acknowledgement that the write operation was successful. When we employ synchronous replication, data is written to both storage systems at both sites simultaneously. The primary site storage system needs to wait to receive acknowledgement from the secondary site. The primary site storage system can send acknowledgement to the production server only if the second write is successful. No sooner than when the data is written at both sites can the server move on and request another write operation. This is why we need such a good network connection to the remote site — if the latency is too high, performance of the production server is affected because it has to wait for the remote site to send acknowledgement of the successfully completed write operation.

The advantage of synchronous remote replication is obvious — the S-VOL located at the remote site contains exactly the same data as the P-VOL at any point-in-time. This provides the smallest exposure to data loss and fast disaster recovery. The high requirements on network performance and latency means that the distance between the primary site and the remote site is somewhat limited. Synchronous replication could hardly be employed between sites located in different countries or even continents. Synchronous replication is likely to be implemented if the remote site is located within the same city or region. The maximum theoretical distance for synchronous remote replication is 300km. However, best practices recommend not implementing synchronous replication if the distance between the sites is greater than 100km.

The strictly synchronous replication performs atomic write operations — this means that the write operation either completes at both sites or not at all. It also means that if connection to the remote site is lost, the local system freezes and is unable to perform any operations until the connection to the remote site is restored. This behavior guarantees zero data loss. However, it is usually preferred to continue write operations to the local system if the connection to the remote site fails. This provides continuous operation of the local site, but it can lead to losing the desired RPO values.

Synchronous remote replication always affects the performance of local production servers. The limitation is not technology, but rather the speed of light. For a 20km distance, even when we use an Fibre Channel connection, the roundtrip takes 134µs, whereas nowadays cached in-system writes are completed in 10-20µs. Deciding whether or not to employ synchronous remote replication, therefore, requires careful consideration. If the remote site is located in the same city as the primary site, the performance impact is usually not serious and allows synchronous remote replication. The low distance between the sites, however, does not protect our data from regional natural disasters such as earthquakes.

Asynchronous remote replication

In asynchronous remote replication, production servers do not wait for write acknowledgement from the remote site. The write operation is considered completed as soon as the local storage system sends a write acknowledgement. Data from the local storage system is then replicated to the remote site with a time lag. This enables long-distance replication to a site located in another country or even another continent. This type of remote replication also provides the least impact to host performance. The disadvantage is that data at the remote location can lag a number of seconds behind the primary image. This means that the most recent data can be lost if the primary locality fails completely.

When a production server requests to perform a write operation, the local storage system sends a write acknowledgement to the host. The host then considers the write operation successfully completed. The local storage system then stores the differential data for a remote site update into a log file. The log file is then sent to the remote site. The remote site updates the S-VOL with data from the log.

Frequency with which the remote site is updated depends on network latency and bandwidth. The remote site can be updated nearly instantaneously or in minutes, or even in hours in the most extreme cases. Asynchronous data replication helps you ensure IT infrastructure resistance to regional natural disasters. When implemented correctly, asynchronous remote replication ensures that you lose a maximum of a few seconds of the most recent data if the primary location fails completely.

Remote replication, both synchronous and asynchronous, is very costly, and it represents the highend of data loss prevention solutions. Another step that would ensure an even higher level of data protection and data availability is to implement remote replication together with geoclusters. We'll discuss this step on the following pages.

The log of changes that is exchanged between sites during asynchronous replication is called a *journal*. Journal data is stored in a dedicated journal volume (pool).

Dynamic replication appliance

Storage system based replication does not require the participation of host servers; it merely mirrors the data stored on one LUN to another LUN within the same storage system or to another storage system over a distance. This solution is effective as long as you have homogenous IT architecture (i.e., your infrastructure consists of storage systems from one manufacturer). To manage disk array based replication, you would use the software provided by the particular storage system manufacturer. If you use several storage systems from several storage system manufacturers, then you also need to use several management tools to implement replication. This is costly and inefficient. You need to unify the replication management to simplify the procedures and save money that you would otherwise have to spend on extra staff, training and management software licenses.

Essentially, you have two options:

- **Virtualization of storage systems** — you can buy an enterprise level storage system with virtualization capabilities. This storage system will virtualize all the storage systems you have, regardless of their manufacturers. You can then perform all administration procedures, including replication, with the software supplied with this enterprise level storage system.

- **Replication appliance implementation** — you can also purchase a dedicated device that takes care of replication. The replication then does not take place on the storage system level, but on the network level. The replication appliance, therefore, represents **network based replication**.

A replication appliance is connected into a SAN, between hosts and storage systems. The replication appliance then presents the storage array LUNs to the host. As all I/O operations pass through the appliance, the write I/Os are detected and replicated to a storage system. The configuration of the replication appliance is much more difficult and complicated than storage system based replication because you need to make adjustments for each server and LUN. It is also necessary to consider the operations of the multipath software layer installed on the server (two paths per server and LUN for redundancy and load balancing). This is called **pass-through replication appliance implementation**. In this implementation, the replication appliance needs to provide sufficient performance when processing all I/O coming from servers so that it does not slow down the entire SAN environment.

The replication appliance can be also implemented using **agents** running on production servers. The agents are small programs that split write I/O into single copies. This happens on the production server. One copy then goes directly to a mapped LUN on a storage system over the SAN as if there were no appliance at all. In other words, the replication appliance does not stand in the way of data; it doesn't even need to be implemented in the SAN. The second copy is then sent to the replication appliance, which routes the data to the replica volume. The replica volume is presented to the replication appliance either as a TCP/IP target (replication over LAN or remote replication over WAN) or a Fibre Channel target (LUNs located in SAN require individual paths for replication). These modes are called *split write over TCP/IP and split write to Fibre Channel target.*

Implementation of a replication appliance can be complicated, but it provides the best performance for large institutions with a heterogeneous IT infrastructure. The key features of this solution are:

- Network based local or remote recovery and continuous backup to disk

- Continuous data protection (CDP) for optimal RPO/RTO — ideal for remote or branch offices (see Figure 4.13)

- Rapid recovery

- Support of disk-to-disk-to-tape storage for backup and activation

- Single site or remote site data center support

- Heterogeneous storage and server environment support

- Application integration with Microsoft Exchange, Microsoft SQL Server, Microsoft SharePoint, Oracle®, etc. (dedicated agents designed to run on server)

The replication appliance is usually implemented in split write over TCP/IP mode as depicted in Figure 4.13. Pass-through implementation is possible but usually avoided because the replication appliance can decrease the performance of data processing over the SAN.

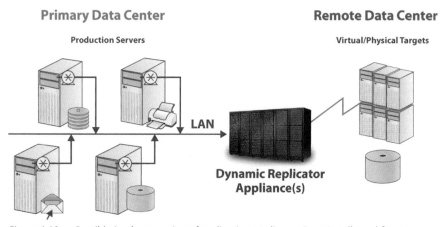

Figure 4.13 — Possible implementation of replication appliance. Data is collected from servers over the LAN and then sent to a storage system. Each server is running an agent that splits the data.

Remote replication and geoclusters

For array-based remote replication, we need at least two storage systems, usually from the same manufacturer. One is installed locally, and the other is installed in a professional data center or another building that belongs to the organization. A local storage system is used by local servers, while a remote storage system is used solely for replication purposes and can be installed without production servers. We know that local high availability clusters add server redundancy that allows immediate data traffic takeover in the event of one server failure. Geoclusters operate in a very similar fashion. The prerequisite for geoclusters is that we have duplicated a fully redundant remote location. In this remote location we not only have a storage system for remote data replication, but also servers that are clustered together with the servers at the local site.

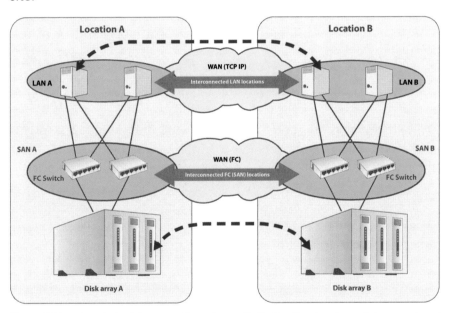

Figure 4.14 — Geocluster interconnection scheme. Both sites (local and remote) are equipped with the same nodes. Data from Disk Array A is synchronously replicated to Disk Array B over iFCP, FCIP or dark fiber technology. Both SANs are interconnected. Servers in both locations are also interconnected, usually using TCP/IP protocol.

Note that geoclustering, or long-distance clustering, as depicted in Figure 4.14, looks quite simple. However, the whole problem gets more complex when we have to mirror dozens or even hundreds of servers.

You can imagine that the configuration and installation is rather complicated. Crucial parameters that determine the overall performance of geoclusters are again the network transfer rate and response time. Geoclustering with synchronous replication can be deployed to a remote site located no more than 50km from the primary location.

When we talk about geoclustering, we are usually talking about high availability clustering, not computing clustering, which would be extremely demanding on network performance. The key words here are *cold site* and *hot site*. A cold site is a remote site with hardware that is powered down and consists only of the most important components. This solution is cheaper, but it takes time to resume all the business processes if the primary site fails. For large institutions that are highly dependent on data availability, hot site geoclustering is the right solution. The whole IT infrastructure is mirrored. The heartbeat between servers is checked regularly and specialized geoclustering software is used. Complicated algorithms that are part of geoclustering software need to decide when to forward the traffic to the remote location. In other words, it needs to evaluate whether the situation in the primary location is critical enough to perform a swap operation.

A swap operation is usually performed by a tailored script that switches the S-VOL status of the remote replica to the P-VOL and makes it accessible for production servers. This script also restores database consistency, usually by issuing a rollback command. Maintaining database consistency is of major importance and will be discussed later.

Three data center multi-target replication

Two data center replication strategies are viable for most in region recovery — for example, serving as a hot site for a campus level or metropolitan level server cluster or for out-of-region recovery sites where propagation delays are not an issue. Synchronous replication provides very fast recovery time (low RTO) and good data currency (low RPO).

However, asynchronous replication provides better protection against regional disasters, albeit with a less favorable RPO. A three data center strategy offers the best of both worlds: a combination of in-system and remote replication that enables fast recovery and excellent data currency for local site failures, combined with advanced protection from regional disasters.

Three data center multi-target replication therefore is the most advanced and secure solution that can be implemented to ensure uninterrupted operation of business processes. This solution can be extremely expensive and it is suitable only for the organizations that are most sensitive to operation disruptions. See Figure 4.15.

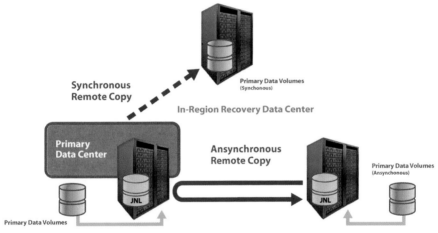

JNL = Journal Volume
Primary JNL — Data is stored before transmission.
Secondary/Remote JNL — Correct record sequence is re-established after transmission.

Figure 4.15 — Three data center multi-target replication. The maximum possible data protection is ensured by using two remote sites for data replication.

Replicated data consistency

In the first chapter, we described what data consistency is. For data replication, data consistency is of major concern, especially when we are replicating volumes that contain large databases. In this case, it's very important to maintain transactional consistency. Let's say an application is running on the production server. This application stores its data in the form of a database. Items in the database are being updated constantly; we are talking about **live data**. One update of one item is one transaction. An application can use the database only when it is consistent, (i.e., when there are no pending and incomplete transactions). In the context of storage systems, data (especially database) consistency is something that needs to be carefully considered when we replicate the volume that contains a live database.

When we have a replication pair, the P-VOL is continuously synchronized with the S-VOL. During the synchronization, we cannot access data on the S-VOL. When we need to access the data on the S-VOL, we need to split the pair. If we split the pair without considering data consistency, it can easily happen that data on the S-VOL will contain incomplete transactions and thus be unusable for an application and for testing or recovery. That is why we either need to stop the database operations (transaction update on the P-VOL) on the production server before splitting the replication pair, or we need to use an agent installed on the production server that communicates with the storage system. When the agent determines the database is consistent, it allows the storage system to perform pair split operations. Then both the P-VOL and S-VOL are consistent and can be accessed by an application. Note that it is the data on the P-VOL that needs to be consistent before the pair split. This does not necessarily mean that we need to completely stop the production server. Transactions can be still handled — they are just not stored to the P-VOL during the time of pair split operation; they are stored in the storage system's cache. Once the pair split operation is complete, data from the cache can be flushed to the P-VOL again.

When we replicate data with asynchronous replication to a remote location, we could lose a few transactions or parts of transactions because of synchronization delay. The remote replica then contains corrupted and inconsistent data. An application that uses the particular database then cannot work with the database until the consistency is somehow restored. Consistency is usually restored by issuing a *rollback* command (SQL), which restores the last known consistent state of the database by erasing the incomplete transactions.

Continuous data protection (CDP)

The term *continuous data protection* denotes a data loss prevention strategy that is different from conventional backup and data replication strategies in several ways. Continuous data protection is sometimes also called continuous backup or real time backup. Continuous data protection is usually provided as a functionality of advanced backup software that allows backup of every single change made to data.

In a traditional backup, we need to determine backup windows and backup scheduling. We can schedule backup once a day or even every hour. If there is a problem, we can restore the system to the previous state as it was captured during the last backup. Unlike traditional backup, no scheduling is necessary in CDP, simply because the procedure is ongoing. Every change in data is traced and backed up.

There also is a difference between data replication and continuous data protection. Data replication only protects one copy of data, the most recent, because it mirrors the current state of the P-VOL. If the data stored on the P-VOL becomes corrupted or is purposefully deleted, these changes will be automatically propagated to the secondary volume without the possibility of restoring the data to the previous state before the data corruption or deletion occurred. CDP, on the other hand, allows you to restore any version of data at any point of time. You can go back step by step, reversing all individual changes that have been made. **Continuous data protection works on the block level,** not the file level. This means that if we have a Microsoft Word document and you change one letter, the backup software does not save a copy of the whole file. It saves only the changed bytes. Traditional backup usually make copies of entire files. The CDP technique is therefore more disk space efficient.

The downside is that continuous data protection can be expensive to implement, and it can also heavily affect LAN performance, especially if the data changes are too frequent and extensive. CDP is, therefore, not very suitable for backup of large multimedia files. Small changes in databases or documents can be handled efficiently because we are talking about relatively small amounts of data. In the case of multimedia processing, changes in data can be too large (gigabytes of data). The whole backup procedure is then slow, and LAN performance is highly affected.

If the CDP functionality is supported by your backup software, it can usually be implemented using your existing backup infrastructure. CDP functionality requires the presence of agents on the production servers.

Redundancy in basic infrastructure

The concept of redundancy has been accompanying us from the very beginning of this book. Data management as a whole is mainly about three things: what data we need to keep, where we keep it and how can we prevent its loss. Business continuity management adds requirements on high availability of data that is vitally important for operation of critical business processes. This all leads us to fully redundant architecture. We need to have redundant copies of data through RAID implementation, data replication, data backup and data archiving. To ensure these techniques work seamlessly, we need redundant hardware: dual controller architecture in a storage system, redundant SAN components (switches, HBAs, NICs) and also redundant servers (clusters). We have even discussed location redundancy issues: remote replication and geo-clustering. The trick is that you need to have everything at least twice. The last thing to take care of is a redundant basic infrastructure.

By basic infrastructure we mean especially power supply, air conditioning of server rooms and Internet (WAN) connectivity. When there is a power outage, a storage system powers down immediately. Installed batteries keep data in cache alive for at least 24hrs, which allows operation resumption with no data loss once we have power back on. In some storage systems, large batteries are installed that allow flushing the data from the cache to the designated hard drive. Once this operation is completed, the whole system powers down, including the cache.

To overcome short power outages that last for seconds or minutes, we can install **uninterrupted power supply** (UPS) units. A UPS device is equipped with extremely powerful batteries that are able to provide electricity to servers usually for several minutes. There is a large scale of UPS products that can be used with home computers as well as with whole server rooms. UPS devices able to support whole server rooms are very expensive. If a power outage occurs, the UPS provides electricity stored in batteries. UPS batteries can last for several minutes, which is enough to overcome short power outages or cover the time necessary for switching to an alternate source of electricity, such as a power generator. If the UPS batteries are nearly depleted and the electricity supply has not been resumed, the UPS unit starts a controlled shutdown procedure, safely shutting down all servers, preventing a cold/hard shutdown. Large companies and especially data centers have redundant power sources such as connection to two separate grid circuits or a diesel engine based power generator.

IT equipment produces a lot of heat. That is why server rooms are equipped with air conditioning. If there is a disruption of air conditioning, the threat of IT equipment overheating becomes imminent and all the servers and disk arrays must be powered down to prevent hardware damage. That is why air conditioning must also be made redundant. Regular air conditioning maintenance is necessary as well.

Internet connectivity and access to public data circuits based on optical cables are another threat of operation disruption. An organization should ensure connectivity availability by contracting at least two connectivity providers.

Tests and drills of disaster recovery procedures

Business priorities of organizations are changing rapidly as new technologies emerge and the market demands these new technologies. That is why any business continuity documentation needs regular maintenance to reflect these changes and to ensure currency of the plans. A disaster recovery (DR) plan is part of a business continuity plan that deals with securing IT infrastructure operations and preventing data loss. To make sure the disaster recovery plan is effective, extensive testing and drills must be conducted.

DR plan efficiency can be tested in a virtualized testing environment that simulates real applications and equipment the company uses for its business. A virtualized testing environment is a very safe way to test the efficiency of disaster recovery plans, as it is completely risk free. However, it can be difficult to simulate all the processes in a virtualized environment. That is why testing is also conducted with production equipment.

Every particular threat that is dealt with in the DR plan can be simulated. The drill then involves all members of the DR team and IT equipment necessary for operation of the particular process that can by disrupted by the threat. For example, we can conduct a drill based on the scenario that the organization's building has been destroyed or rendered inaccessible. The DR team then activates the DR plan as if the situation were real. Personnel then proceed with the plan's individual steps — meeting at emergency location (offices), restoring data from the remote replica, switching the traffic to a remote location geocluster, etc. These drills are very effective and help to discover weaknesses of the documentation. Tests and drills are an essential part of business continuity documentation, and their importance should not be underestimated.

Disaster treatment overview

In this chapter we have mentioned the most important techniques of securing data and preventing its loss. Before we close this chapter and move to virtualization concepts, we can review the most common threats an organization can face and suggest relevant technical solutions. Remember that none of the techniques mentioned in this chapter will save us on their own. To design appropriate solutions, we need to employ a combination of functionalities tailor-made to measure an organization's particular infrastructure.

Disaster	RTO	Disaster Impact Prevention
Power cut	Delayed RTO	UPS, storage system equipped with batteries to support cache
	Immediate RTO	Power generator, redundancy connection to different power grid circuit
Stolen equipment	Delayed RTO	Disaster recovery plan activation, ordering new replacement equipment, local server cluster data recovery from onsite or offsite tapes
	Immediate RTO	Data recovery from remote replication site, hot site geoclusters, CDP
Fire incident, minor	Delayed RTO	Disaster recovery plan activation, ordering new replacement equipment, data recovery from offsite tapes
	Immediate RTO	Local server cluster, local replication, local tapes, remote replication, geoclusters, CDP
Flood	Delayed RTO	Emergency location (offices), remote cold site, ordering new replacement procedure, offsite tapes
	Immediate RTO	Geocluster solution, synchronous replication
Earthquake	Delayed RTO	Emergency location in another region, offsite tapes, asynchronous remote replication to distant datacenter
	Immediate RTO	Geoclustering, three datacenter multi-target replication

Figure 4.16 — Disaster treatment overview table.

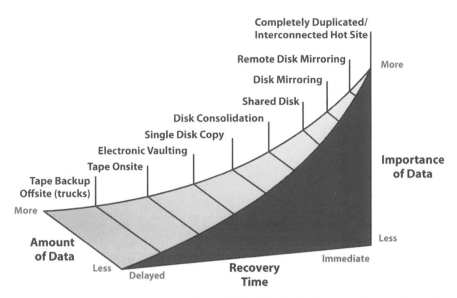

Figure 4.17 — Diversity in data protection requirements.

All data is not created equal. It is likely that only a portion of data is critical to the basic operation of a company. The key is to think through the data protection requirements for different classes of data. It's quite likely that in most scenarios you will have some subset of data that would warrant remote disk mirroring. Refer to Figure 4.17 to see appropriate solutions depending on the data importance, recovery time objective and amount of data.

Fibre Channel offers the best performance for both short and long distances, but it has the highest cost. NAS and iSCSI are at the low end of the cost spectrum, but they sacrifice performance for both short and long distances. FCIP, iFCP and DWDM are solutions that perform better than NAS and iSCSI but at a higher cost. However, they are cheaper when compared to Fibre Channel. See Figure 4.18 for reference.

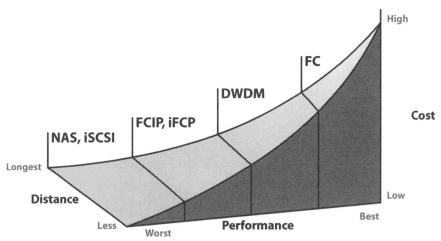

Figure 4.18 — Solution area of cost, performance and distance.

This chapter provided you with the most important aspects of business continuity planning and solutions that enable disaster recovery. Remember that the final design of failure resistant IT infrastructure is always a combination of the techniques mentioned, and it must reflect the needs of the particular organization.

Virtualization of storage systems

5

What are you going to learn in this chapter?

- How to describe virtualization and its benefits
- What layers of virtualization there are and what is possible to virtualize
- How we can virtualize servers and why we do it
- What virtualization possibilities we have in storage systems
- The difference between fat and thin provisioning
- Virtualization concepts in a SAN

What is virtualization?

When we take a look at trends in information technology, we can observe several important facts. For example, we can agree that hardware is getting more and more powerful. You have probably heard about Moore's law, which says that every two years the processing of computers is doubled. At the same time, the price of hardware is decreasing. It means that, for less money, you can get more performance. This is more or less applicable in every area of IT. Powerful enterprise level storage systems used to be so expensive that only a few organizations could afford them. Nowadays, a midsized organization can afford to purchase IT equipment that was too expensive for government institutions and banks about ten years ago. As hardware gets more and more powerful and costs less and less, we can observe another phenomenon — software becomes the most expensive item on the shopping list.

In the past few years the hardware became so powerful that it was nearly impossible to achieve good utilization of all the performance it could provide. The traditional model is based on a one server per one application scheme. (Refer to Figure 5.1.) If your company uses 10 applications, then you need to have 10 physical servers. Let's say that out of these 10 applications, only three are mission critical and can use all the performance of a server. The remaining applications are not used so intensively and thus require only about 25% of the actual computing power of a server. Yet all 10 servers consume power, have high cooling requirements, occupy some space and need to be backed up or clustered. This leads to inefficiency because you have 10 servers and you pay for their operations, but you actually use less than 50% of their computing capacity.

Virtualization addresses this problem. If you looked up the definition of the word *virtualization* you would probably find that virtualization is an abstraction of hardware. This is true, but it can be hard to imagine what actually lies behind this definition. Virtualization takes all the hardware resources, such as processor performance, RAM size and disk space, and creates a resource pool. This resource pool can then be sliced into several logical a resources, which we call virtual machines. If you virtualize a server, you get several logical servers. Each of these logical servers can then be used for operating system installation and for applications. The operating system works on a virtual machine without knowing it is a virtual machine; the operating system does not communicate directly with hardware but with the virtualization layer, which provides an interface between the hardware and a virtual machine. The virtualization layer allows you to configure how much physical resources the virtual machine can use. Virtualization is achieved through implementation of specialized software. Alternatively, it can be provided as an inbuilt capability of a particular device (such as a storage system). If the virtualization functionality is inbuilt, configuration is made through a microcode interface, which can be either a CLI or GUI.

If we get back to our 10 applications and 10 servers example, we can see that with virtualization we need only one or two powerful servers to run 10 virtual machines, each with its own instance of operating system. This allows you to save money and achieve good utilization of all the physical hardware you buy.

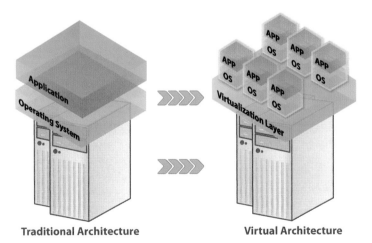

Traditional Architecture   **Virtual Architecture**

Figure 5.1 – Server virtualization. The traditional architecture model requires one physical server per operating system and application. A virtualized server is able to run several virtual machines that all share the physical hardware.

Virtualization is the abstraction of computer resources. It hides the physical characteristics of computing resources from the way other systems, applications or end users interact with those resources. Once virtualization takes place, a single physical resource appears to function as multiple logical resources. It is also possible to virtualize multiple physical resources so that they appear as a single logical resource. In personal computers and servers, logical resources are called *virtual machines*.

Virtualization: area of application

Virtualization can be implemented at least to some extent in all devices used in information technology. Nowadays, virtualization is often employed in:

- Personal computers

- Servers

- Storage systems and their components

If you do not have much experience with servers and storage systems, you can take a look at several examples well known from personal computers. We have already mentioned **hard drive partitioning**. If you have a single hard drive installed in your computer, you can divide it into two logical units. In a Microsoft Windows environment, they appear as "C:" and "D:" volumes. Both these logical volumes can be accessed and used as if they were two separate physical hard drives installed in your computer. Disk partitioning or disk concatenation can be seen as virtualization because the operating system is accessing the hard drive through the two logical units. Widely used **virtual CD/DVD drives** are another example of virtualization in personal computers. A specialized software will create a virtual CD/DVD drive, which is able to open images (or clones) of actual CD or DVD medium. Virtual CD/DVD drives are very popular because there are lot of CD/DVD images available on the Internet. Usage of virtual drive eliminates the need to burn these images on physical media before usage. CD/DVD imaging is also often used for backup of purchased film DVDs or audio CDs.

Some operating systems also natively allow you to run another operating system. We can take Windows 7 Ultimate® as an example. This operating system allows you to run older Windows XP® as a virtual machine to enhance compatibility of user application with operating system. If you have an old application that does not run in a Windows 7 environment, you can set up a virtualized Windows XP environment in which the application runs without problems. It is also possible to purchase specialized virtualization software, such as VMware® Workstation, that allows you to run several instances of an operating system. This can be useful for setting up a **testing environment**. Information technology students, software developers or IT administrators can set up several virtual machines while running an ordinary computer with regular client version of operating system. There they can perform application development or testing without the interference with other installed applications and operating systems. VMware Workstation is installed within the operating system. Thanks to encapsulation, all virtual machines are then saved on the hard drive in the form of files that can be copied or easily transferred to another computer. Virtual machines are then accessed in a similar fashion as remote desktops — you can open a full screen window with an OS instance.

VMware Workstation and similar virtualization applications usually require a CPU that natively supports virtualization. Nowadays, most processors in personal computers offer virtualization capabilities. Hardware support of virtualization is sometimes referred to as *virtualization acceleration*. Virtualization support in a CPU allows virtual machines to effectively access hardware means through the virtualization layer without performance overhead. This leads to very good virtual machine performance.

In servers, virtualization is becoming a standard for several reasons. Virtualization in servers allows you to achieve a higher level of hardware resource utilization. Virtual machines are also much easier to manage because of unified and consolidated environment. If you have several physical servers, they are likely to contain different hardware components. This requires additional configuration of different device drivers. In virtual machines, you always have a unified environment. The operating systems see the virtualization layer as a set of physical components. This means that if you open the operating system's device manager, you can see virtual processors, virtual RAM, virtual network interface cards and virtual host bus adaptors as if they were real. The virtualization layer takes care of linking these virtual components to their physical counterparts. Virtual components are the same on all physical servers. Therefore, the manageability of servers is increased — you do not have to take care of updating different component's with different drivers.

Virtual machines use encapsulation. Each virtual machine, with all its components — operating system, applications, user data, etc. — is represented by a single file. This allows very simple migration. You can actually copy a virtual machine on an external hard drive and run it on another server without any modifications. Virtualization software that runs on servers is more sophisticated than virtualization software designed for personal computers and is mainly for testing purposes. It must provide enhanced capabilities for virtual machine backup, migration, redundancy, high availability and high performance. The possibilities we have with server virtualization will be described later in this chapter.

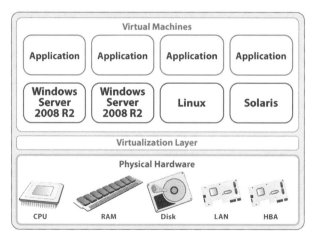

Figure 5.2 — The virtualization layer provides interface between physically installed components and virtual machines. Virtual machines see unified virtual components that are linked to their physical counterparts.

Server virtualization has been implemented for quite some time and it is becoming standard in most larger institutions. **Storage system virtualization**, on the other hand, is more complex. The very basic virtualization technique that takes place in a storage system is RAID. A single parity group consists of several hard drives linked together by RAID functionality to provide a logical storage area, which can then be further partitioned. RAID is implemented for redundancy and performance reasons because data striping allows us to achieve faster read and write transfer rates. Every storage system offers RAID functionality. RAID, similarly to partitioning, represents virtualization of physical hardware resources. However, inclusion of RAID functionality in a disk array does not qualify as a virtual storage system.

When we talk about the virtualization of a storage system, we usually do not mean RAID functionality because it is somehow considered as a given. We typically mean techniques that allow virtualizing a single storage system by partitioning its resources, such as cache, ports and hard drives. One storage system then appears as two or more. Other virtualization capabilities make it possible to virtualize several storage systems by various vendors. A storage system equipped with such virtualization capabilities consolidates other storage systems and unifies their management. Among other virtualization capabilities of a storage system are pooling and functionalities based on it, such as thin provisioning. In pooling, we put several parity groups together and we create a pool that can be further used for thin provisioning. Thin provisioning allows us to allocate more storage capacity to the host than is actually physically installed on a storage system. We'll describe how this is done and why we do this later in this chapter.

Storage based virtualization is always managed in the storage system without the participation of a host. The functionality is included in the storage system's microcode and is usually subject to additional licensing. In other words, you have to pay to enable these functionalities. Storage system virtualization is configured directly in the storage system's microcode using a CLI or GUI.

Layers of virtualization

We can virtualize personal computers, servers, storage systems and even networks. We can picture this as horizontal virtualization. However virtualization can also be vertical, implemented in layers. When we have a storage system, we get the first layer of virtualization when we create a parity group, or RAID array. When we take several parity groups and create a storage pool, we take already virtualized logical storage and virtualize it even further. Out of this pool we can create several virtual volumes that will be dynamically allocated the storage space; this is yet another layer of virtualization. We usually deal with several layers of virtualization, which are implemented to provide enhanced functionality. The host will then access the highest layer of virtualization — in this case a virtual volume — without knowing about other virtualization layers. Only virtualization software knows where the data is physically located, because data is striped within a single parity group across several physical hard drives and then over several parity groups within one storage pool.

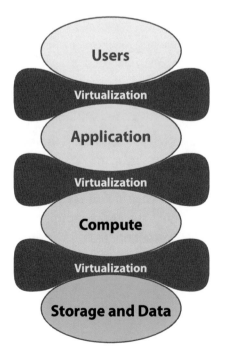

Layers of virtualization can also be seen when we look at our IT infrastructure as a whole — the host is accessing a virtualized storage area, either a LUN or, in the case of thin provisioning, a virtual volume. The server can also be virtualized. Applications can run on several virtual machines that share one physical server. Users can then access the application from yet another virtual environment, such as a virtual desktop.

Figure 5.3 — Virtualization layers in IT infrastructure.

Virtualization benefits

Let's review a summary of the virtualization benefits we have mentioned in this chapter. The most important motivation that leads us to virtualization implementation is management simplification. Virtualization is implemented to simplify management of heterogeneous IT infrastructure. The individual benefits of virtualization are:

- **Migration** — virtual machines and LUNs can be easily transferred from one physical device to another. In some cases this is possible without disruption of operation. This means that we can transfer a running virtual machine with OS and applications to another hardware environment without impacting its operations. Users can still access the application during the migration. This is achieved by encapsulation of a virtual machine into a single file.

- **Backup** — encapsulation also makes it easier to back up the whole virtual machine. Virtualization software usually provides backup functionalities.

- **Hardware platform independence** — physical servers can be of different configurations, yet the virtualization layer ensures unified environment for virtual machines. This means that within one virtualization platform, you can transfer virtual machines from one physical server to another regardless of their physical configuration. There are no issues with drivers.

- **Enhanced utilization** — virtualization allows effective use of resources. A virtual machine is allocated the exact amount of computing performance, RAM and storage space it requires, and no more. If it requires more, other resources are provided dynamically and nondisruptively. Imagine you are running a virtual server that is under high load. The high load is detected by the virtualization platform and the virtual server is allocated another processor that would support its performance.

- **Unification** — unification of infrastructure allows you to save money. You can manage several storage systems by different vendors with only one piece of software. Functionalities that require additional licensing are enabled (purchased) only for the storage system that takes care of virtualization. The functionalities enabled in the virtualizer are automatically propagated to another storage system. Imagine you want to employ remote replication. Without virtualization, you would have to purchase a license for each storage system, which is costly. With virtualization, you purchase a license only for the virtualizing storage system. Remote replication is then available for all storage systems.

- Virtualization enables you to run several virtual machines on one physical server. This means you do not need to invest too much in physical equipment. This leads to **lower consumption of electricity** and lower cooling requirements.

- Virtualization helps you achieve **lower RPO and RTO.** It is much easier to conduct disaster recovery procedures in a virtual environment, especially thanks to unification, encapsulation and detachment from physical hardware. The virtualization layer can run on several servers. When one server fails, other physical servers provide sufficient means to support all virtual machines.

- **Physical resources can be added without disruption.** You can add memory, processors or even whole servers to increase performance of virtual machines without actually disrupting their operations.

VMware based server virtualization

VMware is one of the best known providers of virtualization solutions for servers. We have already mentioned VMware Workstation, which is well suited for use in personal computers, mainly for testing purposes and application development. For server virtualization, VMware offers two essential products — VMware Server and VMware ESX Server.

VMware Server is installed into an existing operating system in the same manner as any other application. The operating system can be either Microsoft Windows Server or a server version of Linux. VMware Server then runs as operating systems services and provides tools and management for virtualized environment. When you start the control console you can immediately begin to create and configure virtual machines. Each virtual machine is allocated virtual resources, such as processors, memory, hard drives, network interface cards and graphical adaptors. Once you have your virtual machines configured, you may proceed with installation of individual operating systems. These operating systems run independently and can be different types. At the end you have several virtual machines with instances of operating systems running on a single physical server. In addition, the originally installed operating system with VMware Server is still available and running together with virtual machines. This type of solution is very easy to implement and provides a good level of performance and reliability. However, the limitation is that VMware Server does not have direct access to hardware means; it can only use resources provided by the underlying operating system. VMware Server has to communicate with hardware through an interface offered by the originally installed operating system. This does not have to be an issue, but you need to accept at least slightly diminished virtual machine performance. A problem in the original instance of the operating system can result in instability of all virtual machines. The maximum possible stability of a virtualized environment and the best usage of hardware resources can be delivered when you use another VMware product — VMware ESX server.

In VMware ESX implementation, you do not need any underlying, previously installed, operating system. ESX Server contains its own dedicated and thin operating system and can therefore be installed directly on a physical server. This ensures direct access of the virtualization layer to hardware resources, delivering the best possible performance. Once you have ESX Server installed, management and configuration of virtual machines is practically the same as in VMware Server. The major advantage of ESX Server is stability and performance. In addition, ESX Server provides a range of advanced functionalities for efficient clustering, backup, disaster recovery and virtual machine migration. In ESX Server, a virtual machine can be transferred nondisruptively to another physical server. If we upgrade our hardware or simply purchase a new server, existing virtual machines can be easily transferred to this new server while on and running. Virtual machines can be easily updated, too. You can allocate processors, memory and other virtual components without the need to reboot the virtual machine. You can also configure these resources to be allocated automatically when needed.

Thanks to its flexibility and performance, VMware ESX Server is well suited for implementation in enterprises.

Microsoft Hyper-V™ based server virtualization

Hyper-V is a virtualization solution developed by Microsoft. It is included in the Microsoft Windows 2008 Server operating system, but it can also be purchased as a standalone product called Microsoft Hyper-V Server.

In Windows 2008 Server, you can enable Hyper-V as a server role. This means that you need to have an installed instance of Windows 2008 Server, and virtual machines are then configured similarly as in VMware Server. If you choose a Hyper-V Server role, other functionalities of Windows 2008 Server can be limited and certain services may be unavailable. Through integration with an operating system, you achieve high performance and reliability.

Hyper-V is a hypervisor based virtualization solution. Hypervisor is another, more specific, name for the virtualization layer. The Windows 2008 Server instance is installed as a *parent partition*. Virtual machines are then located in *child partitions*. Operating systems installed on virtual machines are presented with virtual resources. These virtual resources are linked to hardware resources through VM buses (VM stands for *virtual machine)*. Here we can see a difference between VMware Server and Hyper-V. VMware Server can access only resources presented by the operating system. VM buses are native to Windows 2008 Server and they facilitate direct access to hardware means in Hyper-V based virtualization. The Hyper-V Server solution then works similarly to VMware ESX Server — neither of them requires an underlying operating system instance.

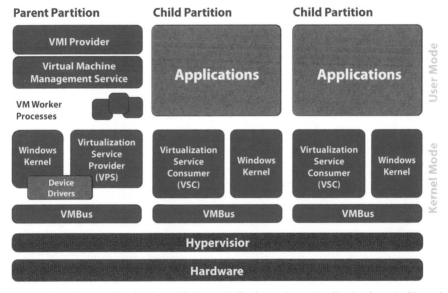

Figure 5.4 — *Server virtualization with Hyper-V. The hypervisor virtualization layer is thin and optimized for direct access to hardware resources. Virtual machines in child partitions access the virtualization layer through the VMBus interface. Device drivers for virtual machines are loaded from the parent partition with the original instance of Windows 2008 Server. Virtual machine configuration and management are also done in the parent partition operating system.*

Virtualization with blade servers

Before we get to advantages of blade server virtualization, perhaps we should consolidate our server knowledge. A server is a computer that provides services to other computers on a network. Basically, any desktop computer or even notebook can assume the role of a server.

Due to high requirements on reliability, availability and performance, we use computers that differ from those you have at your home or office. The computers designed to work as servers are equipped with high performance processors, more durable and reliable hard drives, motherboards that can bear significantly more RAM modules and specialized interface cards such as HBA for Fibre Channel connection. A server computer can look exactly the same as any other personal computer; it can be a rack server or it can be a very modern blade server.

Computers that are modified so they can be installed in a rack are called *rack servers*. These are the most common. A rack is a standardized chassis that can be equipped with many IT components such as rack servers, switches, hubs, tape libraries and midrange storage systems. Rack servers are more space efficient than standalone servers.

The most modern type of server design is the blade server. A blade server has a specialized chassis that provides shared powering, cooling, storage and networking resources. Individual servers then look like computer cards that are simply plugged into the chassis. A blade server's chassis is then installed into a standard rack. Individual blades then contain processors and memory modules. Blade servers represent a highly scalable solution that saves a lot of rack space. Blade servers also provide simplified cable management. Aside from these characteristics, blade servers provide additional functionalities that can differ from vendor to vendor. Because of their robustness and complexity, blade servers are well suited for clustering and virtualization. Some vendors provide built-in virtualization capabilities based on logical partitioning of the installed hardware resources. This functionality is similar to mainframe management, where you have one super computer further partitioned into logical computing units.

The logical partitioning of hardware resources is a functionality available in microcode stored in components that are part of a blade server's chassis. Through the management console, you can create logical servers (basically virtual machines) and allocate them directly with physical resources. The number of physical resources depends on the number of blades with CPUs and memory installed in the chassis. Individual blades are hot swappable. This is a powerful solution that does not require the participation of any third party virtualization software. Logical partitioning functionality sometimes hides behind the abbreviation *LPAR*.

Figure 5.5 — Blade servers are installed in a blade server chassis. The chassis is then placed in a standard rack. In this picture we see Hitachi Data Systems blade servers that are an essential part of Hitachi Content Platform. These blade servers offer logical partitioning, which is a highly sophisticated form of server virtualization.

VM hardware requirements and networking

All virtualization strategies based either on third party virtualization software or virtualization capabilities built-in microcode allocate virtual machines with computing and memory resources. The virtualization implementer or administrator has to decide how many physical resources will be allocated to a particular virtual machine. The minimum hardware requirements are usually determined by the operating system requirements to be installed on the virtual machine. The most important resources are computing power represented by the number of processors or processor cores and the size of RAM. For small dedicated servers, we usually need at least one virtual processor and 2GB of RAM. With robust solutions and servers that run mission critical applications under high load, we have up to 64 processor cores and 256GB of RAM per virtual machine. These are rough numbers to give you a general idea of virtual machine hardware requirements.

A standalone virtual machine would hardly be of any use with no connection to a network. Virtual machine networking is configured from a virtualization software management console by allocating a network interface card (NIC) and HBA cards. Once you add an NIC, you may configure it in the traditional way using common protocols, usually meaning TCP/IP protocol for LAN networks and Fibre Chanel Protocol for SAN networks. When we connect a virtual machine to physical network, we say we *bridge the connection*. Virtualization software also provides the functionalities of a virtual switch by enabling mutual communication among virtual machines.

Memory overcommitment in server virtualization

When we create a virtual machine, we allocate it with hardware resources. Common sense would suggest that you can allocate only as much hardware resource to virtual machines as you have physically installed in a server. To achieve the best possible utilization of your hardware, you can, in certain situation, allocate more hardware resources to virtual machines than you have physically installed in your server. We are talking about RAM in particular. This can be especially helpful when you have several virtual machines that are not under high load and are not showing good utilization. One example is desktop virtualization. In desktop virtualization, you have a server that is running dozens or even hundreds of client operating systems instances. The reason for this approach is to use one powerful server with high computing performance instead of dozens of expensive and powerful client computers or laptops. Employees of the company then use thin clients, for example, less powerful, inexpensive computers that serve only for connection to a virtualized client operating system running on a server. This is similar to a remote desktop connection, only the performance and stability of this solution is much higher. Desktop virtualization also simplifies management and backup of client workstations. The example of memory overcommitment is based on two assumptions. The first is that not all employees are using their computers simultaneously. In other words, there is always a certain number of virtual machines that are turned off. The second assumption is that the client operating system is not using the allocated memory completely. If you cleverly allocate more hardware resources than physically available, you save money and increase utilization, because you can install more virtual machines per server. Memory overcommitment is not limited to desktop virtualization; there are other areas of application. The IT administrator must decide how much memory to overcommit. If the overcommitment were too high, running virtual machines could potentially use all the physically installed memory, and on the attempt to use memory beyond what is physically available, the virtual machines would crash.

Memory overcommitment is another example of a virtualization technique. Even though it may seem illogical and potentially dangerous, it can increase utilization of hardware and save costs when skillfully implemented. In the context of storage systems, memory overcommitment is similar to thin provisioning.

Thin provisioning

Provisioning is the process of allocating storage resources and assigning storage capacity for an application, usually in the form of server disk drive space. The storage administrator has to determine the application's need for storage and allocate adequate resources on a storage system. These resources are then mapped to a server as a logical unit (LUN) and made available for an application. Nowadays, we differentiate between the traditional model of provisioning (also called *fat provisioning*) and *thin provisioning*.

When you deploy a new application, you need to assign it a storage area. To avoid future service interruption, it is common to overallocate storage by 75% or more. This is called fat provisioning. Imagine that your application requires a storage area of 100GB. You expect that application requirements on storage will rise in future. To ensure that the application always has enough storage, you allocate 200GB. To allocate 200GB you need to have this capacity installed in your storage system. If you do not, you need to purchase additional hard drives. Remember that with RAID implementation and possible employment of in-system replication you may need about 1TB of physically installed capacity to be able to provide 200GB of storage for this particular application. This can be costly, especially if you have dozens of applications. To achieve higher utilization, you can implement thin provisioning functionality.

In thin provisioning, whenever there is a new application, its entire storage allocation is not required initially, so the application is allocated virtual storage. This is similar to memory overcommitment in server virtualization.

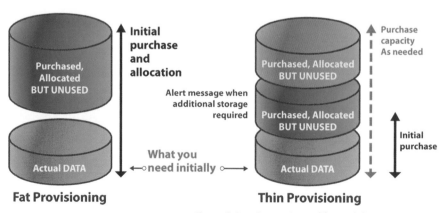

Figure 5.6 — Comparison of fat and thin provisioning.

To enable thin provisioning, you need to set up parity groups that are configured in the desired RAID level. Several parity groups are then virtualized into one storage pool. The servers and their applications are then allocated virtual volumes. Virtual volumes themselves do not represent any physically installed capacity. Virtual volumes are mapped as LUNs, and servers cannot see the difference between a traditional LUN and a LUN that hides a virtual volume. Virtual volume size can be configured without concerns about the physically installed capacity. When a server needs to write data on an allocated virtual volume, storage is automatically provided from the storage pool. Similar to copy-on-write snapshots, a virtual volume contains only pointers that point to the actual location of data in a storage pool.

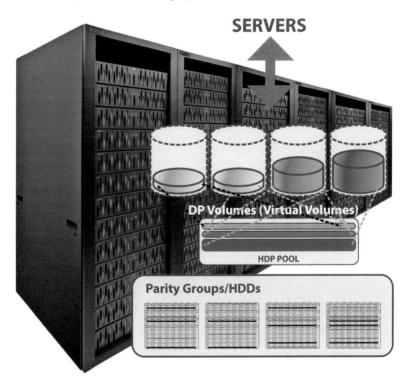

Figure 5.7 — Thin provisioning. Parity groups are added to a thin provisioning pool. Virtual volumes are mapped to servers. Virtual volumes do not contain any actual data. Data is stored in the storage pool. Virtual volumes contain pointers that point to the location of data in the pool.

Thin provisioning is a modern trend that reaches both enterprise level storage systems and midrange storage systems. It is the most common virtualization technique used in storage systems.

Take a look at the list of thin provisioning benefits:

Storage performance

- Storage pools allow increased physical disk striping. Data is striped within RAID implementation and then again over parity groups. This helps to avoid bottlenecks.

- Increased physical disk striping evenly spreads I/O activity across all available physical disk resources.

- Thin provisioning reduces the need for performance expertise and analysis. It is simple, and thanks to added performance, you may not need to employ complicated performance tuning.

Storage administration

- Thin provisioning simplifies application storage capacity planning and administration.

- It increases storage utilization and reduces wasted storage capacity.

- Thin provisioning eliminates downtime for application storage capacity expansion.

- It improves application uptime and SLAs.

We can see that thin provisioning not only saves money, but it also delivers increased performance and simplified management. In traditional (fat) provisioning, you need to determine what requirements the particular application will have in the future, and you overallocate the storage using physically installed capacity. If you happen to run out of space on an allocated volume, you need to extend the mapped LUN. This is fairly simple from the perspective of a storage system, but it can be tricky from the perspective of the server. Remember that additional reconfiguration must be done in the server. If you extend a LUN on a storage system, the host will not be able to see the added space until you reconfigure the file system to spread over the added storage. In thin provisioning, you can create a virtual volume without limitations in size. If your application needs 100GB, in fat provisioning you would allocate at least 175GB. In thin provisioning you can overallocate much more, without paying for physical storage.

Thin provisioning is a functionality that provides virtual storage capacity. It simplifies application storage provisioning by allowing administrators to draw from a central virtual pool without immediately adding physical disks. When an application requires more storage capacity, the storage system automatically allocates the necessary physical storage. This just-in-time method of provisioning decouples the provisioning of storage to an application from the physical addition of capacity to the storage system. In addition to simplified management, thin provisioning delivers better performance and higher utilization of physically installed storage system capacity.

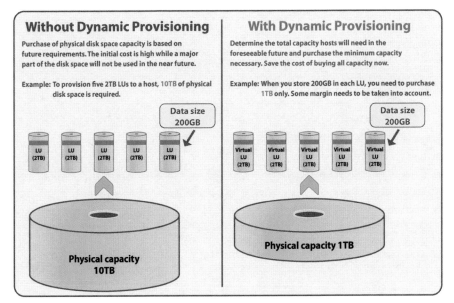

Figure 5.8 — An example of how thin provisioning can help you save the cost of buying all the capacity in advance. Thin provisioning is sometimes called dynamic provisioning.

To add physical capacity at a later time, you should analyze the actual data consumption for each thin provisioning storage pool in the past. With this data you can plan the schedule to add physical capacity to the storage pool. Also, when the actual data consumption increases rapidly, you can get notification through alerts sent from the storage system.

Thin provisioning limitations

We implement thin provisioning to avoid future administrative tasks connected with the extension of LUN capacity and an installed file system. The extension of a file system can be especially tricky and time consuming. With thin provisioning implementation, the file system will be installed to cover the capacity of the virtual volume, which is overal-located and does not correspond with the installed capacity. When we add capacity, we do not have to extend the file system. In thin provi-sioning implementation, the data path is as follows:

Application <-> file system <-> virtual volume <-> storage pool <-> parity groups <-> HDDs

When we format the storage area with a particular file system, this file system writes metadata. Depending on the architecture and fre-quency of metadata writes, we can distinguish among file systems that are suitable for application of thin provisioning and file systems that are not suitable for thin provisioning. This is because the metadata itself can occupy significant storage pool space. With implementation of file systems such as UFS, JFS or HFS, the file system formatting occupies the same capacity as the virtual volume. This effectively means that we cannot overallocate the installed capacity. Suitable systems are, for ex-ample, New Technology File System (NTFS), VMware, XFS and VxFS.

Another problem that can occur in thin provisioning implementa-tion is connected with data deletion. When we delete data stored on a mapped virtual volume, this data should be removed from the storage pool and the space it occupied should be freed for other virtual volumes. This does not happen. When you delete data, the space in the storage pool is not automatically freed. The file system usually does not delete data — it just marks it as empty and allows overwriting. The storage system does not know this and therefore cannot free the storage space in the storage pool.

The file system can be tuned for performance or for effective data management. NTFS is performance oriented. That is why it does not remove deleted data completely; it just marks it as deleted instead. NTFS also performs write operations where the actuator arm and I/O head are at the moment. With frequent delete and write operations, more and more storage pool capacity is taken and almost none is freed. This is not very effective when using thin provisioning.

On the other hand, certain file systems prefer more effective usage of storage space. For example, the VMware file system overwrites deleted data, which does not consume additional capacity from the storage pool.

The issues connected with deleted data and cleaned storage pool are caused by the independent nature of the relationship between thin provisioning functionality and the file system. When we are not using thin provisioning, the file system operations do not cause trouble. However, customers often demand thin provisioning implementation, so the choice of file system needs careful consideration. To ensure optimized utilization of the storage pool, storage system vendors implement **zero page reclaim** functionality. The storage system scans the storage pool for used data blocks that contain only zeros. These blocks are then erased and freed automatically. The problem is that zero page reclaim is hardware functionality, which is again independent from the file system. A file system usually does not overwrite deleted data blocks with zeros. To make zero page reclaim functionality work, we have to interconnect its logic with file system logic by choosing the suitable file system and configuring it properly.

Because of its advantages, thin provisioning is very often implemented. To ensure good utilization of a storage pool that provides capacity to virtual volumes, we need to choose a suitable file system. The file system should support effective deletion of once used data blocks and it should perform write operations by overwriting data blocks that were marked as empty instead of using unused capacity. Storage systems offer zero page reclaim functionality, which helps to solve issues connected with freeing up deleted data blocks in a storage pool. The file system must support zero page reclaim functionality.

Fat provisioning occurs on traditional storage arrays where large pools of storage capacity are allocated to individual applications but remain unused (not written to) with storage utilization often as low as 50%

Thin provisioning is a mechanism that applies to large scale centralized computer disk storage systems. Thin provisioning allows space to be easily allocated to servers, on a just-enough and just-in-time basis.

Overallocation is a mechanism that allows server applications to allocate more storage capacity than has been physically reserved on the storage array itself. This allows leeway in growth of application storage volumes without the need to accurately predict which volumes will grow and by how much. Physical storage capacity on the array is only dedicated when data is actually written by the application — not when the storage volume is initially allocated.

Virtualization in storage system controller

Controller based virtualization is a functionality we have briefly discussed in previous chapters. Now it's time to look at this technology in detail. Controller based virtualization functionality is supported mainly by robust enterprise level storage systems. This enterprise storage system allows configuring one or more of its front end Fibre Channel ports as external. This Fibre Channel port then serves for connecting other storage systems, midrange or enterprise, of various vendors. Management and advanced configuration is then provided by the virtualizing storage system. This can be especially useful when we have many storage systems from different vendors. Management of such infrastructure is very demanding and expensive because you have to pay for more storage systems administrators, their training and their licenses for advanced functionalities such as data replication. Controller based virtualization unifies the management of heterogeneous storage system infrastructure and enables you to use functionalities available on the virtualizing enterprise level storage system on all your virtualized external storage systems. External storage systems provide their LUNs to the virtualizing storage system. The virtualizing storage system then sees these LUNs as if they were internal.

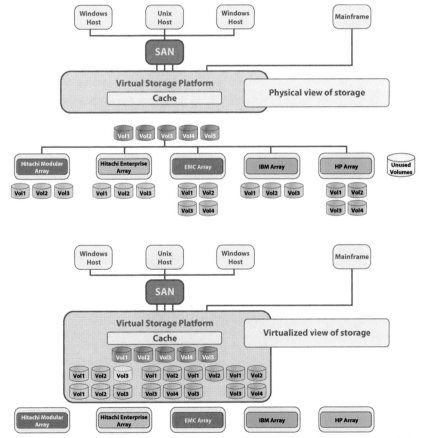

Figure 5.9 — Controller based virtualization of external storage, the physical and logical view. Hitachi Virtual Storage Platform (VSP) is an example of an enterprise level storage system that supports virtualization of external storage.

To illustrate how the virtualization of external storage system is done, we will use the example of HDS Virtual Storage Platform, which is an enterprise level storage system that supports controller based virtualization.

First you need to set one or more ports as external. An external port is used for discovering volumes presented from the external storage system. The external storage system cannot be connected to ports other than the external port. In order to set the port attribute to external, you need to release the paths set to the port. The attribute of the port where the paths are set cannot be changed to external. Before starting the management operations, you need to know the ports whose attributes can be changed to external. Remember that we have already learned that front end Fibre Channel ports can be set as initiator, target, replication and external.

To use an external volume with Virtual Storage Platform, you first prepare the volumes in the external system connected to the systems. The volume in the external system should be between 64MB and 4TB. If LUN security is enabled on the port, you need to add the WWN of the external port on the VSP system to the host group with the volumes that need to be set as external volumes.

The external storage system and Virtual Storage Platform external ports are cabled to the SAN. You need to configure zoning to enable the external ports to connect to the external storage system. Fibre Channel Arbitrated Loop and direct connections are also supported. Externally, storage can be attached directly via Fibre Channel or attached through a Fibre Channel switch. Data can be copied or moved between internal and external storage over Fibre Channel distances.

The external storage is then ready to be discovered by Virtual Storage Platform. The VSP system will see the LUNs on the external storage system after the external storage discovery. Once the external storage systems are discovered and the LUNs available, you can map volumes in the external storage system as volumes in the local storage system.

Now the LUNs of an external storage are ready to be propagated to hosts through the VSP systems. You only need to configure additional parameters such as cache mode and inflow control.

Cache mode specifies whether the write data from the host to the external storage system is propagated synchronously or asynchronously (with or without waiting for successful write acknowledgement). All I/O to and from the local storage system always uses cache. Write operation are always backed up in duplex cache (Chapter 2, Cache Mirroring).

Inflow control specifies whether the write operation to the cache memory is stopped or continued when the write operation to the external volume is impossible. If you enable inflow control, the write operation to cache is stopped and the I/O from the host is not accepted when the write operation to the external volume is impossible. If you select Disable, the I/O from the host during the retry operation is written to the cache memory even after the write operation to the external volume is impossible. Once the write operation to the external volume becomes normal, all the data in the cache memory is written to the external volume (all the data is destaged).

Improper configuration of cache mode and inflow control attributes can negatively impact performance.

Virtualization of external storage enables you to view an entire SAN as one storage pool, independent from its physical location. It masks the differences between heterogeneous devices, and it allows you to use common storage management, data replication, data migration and lifecycle management tools.

These benefits may sound intriguing, but remember that all the data from external storage to the hosts go through one cache — the cache that belongs to the virtualizing enterprise system. A few external storages will have negligible impact on cache performance, but there are certain limitations that need to be considered. Note that this functionality is often subject to licensing, which can be very expensive.

Virtualization of a storage system: logical partitioning

You have already been introduced to logical partitioning of blade servers. Logical partitioning offers the possibility to divide one physical piece of hardware into many logical resources. This functionality is also available in some storage systems.

Logical partitioning in storage systems enables data center administrators to perform logical partitioning of cache, ports and disk capacity, including external storage, on the storage system to create independently managed virtual storage machines. The private virtual storage machines help to maintain quality of service by acting as dedicated resources that are independently managed and reserved for specific applications. The crucial capabilities of this functionality are:

- Logical partitioning of a storage system restricts access to data and resources from users and storage administrators to the elements of a single partition.

- It also restricts access from users and administrators to data and resources outside of their authorized partition.

- It dedicates resources for exclusive use by specific applications to maintain priority and QoS for business-critical application.

These capabilities result in advantages, such as data security improvement, application performance optimization, management and utilization based on business requirements.

Logical partitioning is a storage system microcode based capability. It is usually possible to dynamically reconfigure logical partition (virtual storage machines) without disruption of service.

Logical partitioning can be particularly useful in large data centers that provide services to companies that need storage. A virtual storage machine can be configured to exactly match the customer's storage performance and capacity requirements.

When implemented within one organization, logical partitioning of a storage system provides enhanced security (administrators can access and configure only the assigned partition) and QoS management.

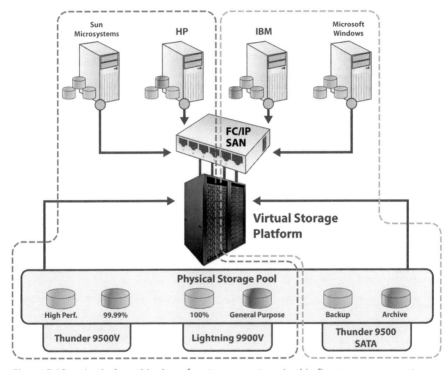

Figure 5.10 — Logical partitioning of a storage system. In this figure we see one storage system (Hitachi Virtual Storage Platform®) with three external storage systems that create a virtualized storage pool. USP is then virtualized to provide two logical partitions — private virtual storage machines. Hosts are then able to access and use only the resources (cache, ports and disks) assigned to the respective partition.

Automated tiered storage

At the beginning of this book we mentioned the data lifecycle and how it relates to data tiering. By now you should know that frequently used data is stored in high performance SAS or SSD drives, while archived data is stored on cheaper and less powerful SATA or tape drives. Data tiers are groups of hard drives with the same performance characteristics. With tiering we can move data from a LUN that is created of high performance drives to another LUN that consists of low performance drives. Some storage systems allow automation of this process.

You may ask, "What does this have to do with virtualization?" Automated tiering uses virtualized disk space — a storage pool. This storage pool is spread over several parity groups, each group containing hard drives of one type — we can have SSD parity groups, SAS parity groups and SATA parity groups. Once we have a storage pool, we assign the hosts with virtual volumes. Automated tiering is often implemented together with thin provisioning because of shared prerequisites (storage pool). To remember the basics of data lifecycle management that represent motivation for automated tiering implementation, let's take a look at what kind of data we have according to availability requirements:

Mission-critical data

- This is the most important data; its loss will stop the business from functioning.

- Storage infrastructure for mission-critical data must provide high performance, high availability and almost zero downtime.

Business-critical data

- This data is still important, but its loss will not stop the business from functioning.

- Storage infrastructure must provide reasonable performance and availability.

- In the event of failure, the system must recover within 8hrs.

Accessible online data

- This data is cost sensitive, in a large volume, with a low access rate.
- Storage system must provide online performance and high availability.
- In the event of failure, the system must recover within 8hrs.

Nearline data

- This type of data is cost sensitive and has a low access rate, and large volumes.
- The storage infrastructure must provide automated retrieval in less than one hour.

Offline data

- This data is usually archived data related to backup or compliance.
- The storage infrastructure provides limited access and is cost sensitive.
- It can take up to 72hrs to retrieve from the storage infrastructure.

Once created, most data is rarely or never accessed. It should be moved off your most expensive storage tier to lower, less expensive tiers. This is the premise and promise of data lifecycle management methodologies and tools. But how do you determine what can be moved and how to move it efficiently? Automated tiering functionality solves this problem.

With automated (or dynamic) tiering, the complexities and over-head of implementing data lifecycle management and optimizing use of tiered storage are solved. Dynamic tiering automatically moves data on fine grained pages within virtual volumes to the most appropriate media according to workload, maximizing service levels and minimizing the total cost of storage system ownership.

For example, a database index that is frequently read and written will migrate to high performance flash technology, while older data that has not been touched for a while will move to slower, cheaper media. No elaborate decision criteria are needed; data is automatically moved according to simple rules. One, two or three tiers of storage can be defined and used within a single virtual volume using any of the stor-age media types available for the particular storage system. Tier crea-tion is automatic based on user configuration policies, including media type and speed, RAID level and sustained I/O level requirements. Us-ing ongoing embedded performance monitoring and periodic analysis, the data is moved at the sub-LUN level to the most appropriate tier. The most active data moves to the highest tier. During the process, the system automatically maximizes the use of storage, keeping the higher tiers fully utilized. Automated tiering functionality is usually available only on enterprise level storage systems.

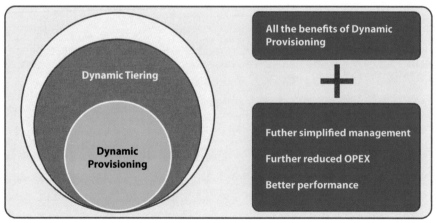

Figure 5.11 — Dynamic tiering (also automated tiering) uses dynamic provisioning technology and thus inherits its advantages of simplified provisioning, capital savings and self-optimizing performance maximization. OPEX is an abbreviation of operational expenses.

Automated tiering traditionally supports a maximum of three tiers in a pool. The SSD-SAS-SATA hierarchical model is the most common. The capacity of any tier can be added to the pool. Capacity can also be removed from a pool. Automated tiering functionality fills top tiers as much as possible while monitoring I/O references. The data is moved from one tier to another in chunks called *pages*. In Virtual Storage Platform systems, one page has a fixed size of 42MB. Page placement is adjusted according to cyclical trailing of the 24hr heat map. I/O reference monitoring essentially operates on a 24/7 basis. Following a cycle, we begin a background operation to move or relocate pages to better fit the I/O pattern. The average sustainable I/O rate of the tier is also monitored and calculated. The system avoids overdriving a tier. Sometimes a tier may not be able to handle all the most heavily used pages, so it may elect to keep some in a lower tier. This is unlikely to be a real problem in most cases, but nevertheless, the system watches for this.

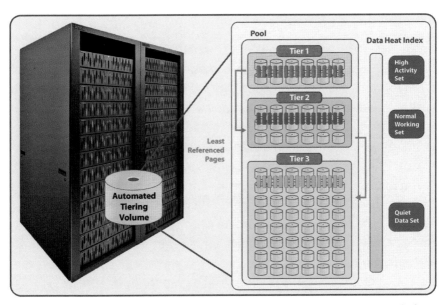

Figure 5.12 — Dynamic tiering in Hitachi Virtual Storage Platform.

Automated tiering works on the storage level, without the participation of hosts. It does not recognize files; instead it divides raw data blocks into chunks called pages. This is often called page level tiering.

20% of data accounts for 80% of the activity — this is why automated tiering increases utilization and optimizes costs. It moves active, frequently accessed data to high performance and expensive tiers, while storing cold data in cheaper volumes.

Automated tiering is often implemented with thin provisioning. Both technologies use virtual volumes that draw capacity from virtualized storage space — storage pools.

Network based virtualization

Virtualization of servers can be implemented by using third party software products or as inbuilt microcode functionality. Storage system virtualization is again a functionality that is part of the microcode. To virtualize external storage systems, we need an enterprise level storage system that supports this functionality. We know that this type of virtualization has certain limitations. The major disadvantage is that we have to purchase an expensive storage system capable of provisioning virtualization services. In addition, we also need to purchase expensive licenses to enable this functionality. Performance limitation is determined by the fact that data from all connected external storages flows through one cache. If we connect a high number of external storage systems, we can observe more or less significant performance reduction. To avoid this issue, we can consolidate our heterogeneous storage system infrastructure by virtualizing it with a dedicated appliance.

A virtualization appliance can be connected in-band or out-of-band. In-band virtualization is also called *synchronous* virtualization and out-of-band virtualization is sometimes referred to as *asynchronous*. We'll look at the difference between the two shortly. First, let's look at the similarities.

Both in-band and out-of-band virtualization controllers add intelligence to provide functionality available only in high-end enterprise level storage systems. These functionalities include mirroring, replication and leveraging the connectivity of the SAN. Storage and SAN vendors argue that intelligence and storage functionality belongs in the SAN (it should be controlled by a dedicated appliance), and storage should be a commodity. Both in-band and out-of-band solutions have no relevance to the controller-based storage virtualization implemented in some enterprise storage system. These solutions are thought to have an advantage over storage controllers since they map common functionality across heterogeneous storage systems.

The general concept of in-band is that the mapping of virtual to physical is done in an appliance that sits in the data path between the host application and the target device. With out-of-band, the virtual to physical mapping is done in an appliance that sits outside the data path and the mapping is communicated over a control path to SAN switches (or HBAs) that sit in the data path between the host application and the target device.

In-band virtualization refers to its location in the storage network path, between the application host servers and the storage systems. An appliance or blade intercepts the I/O from the host, cracks open the data packets to examine the original content directory blocks and remaps them to another storage address. It provides both control and data along the same connection path.

Out-of-band virtualization describes products where the controller is located outside of the SAN data path. The virtualization appliance communicates over a separate network with agents installed on the hosts, intercepting and redirecting the I/O across the SAN. This type of solution separates control and data on different connection paths.

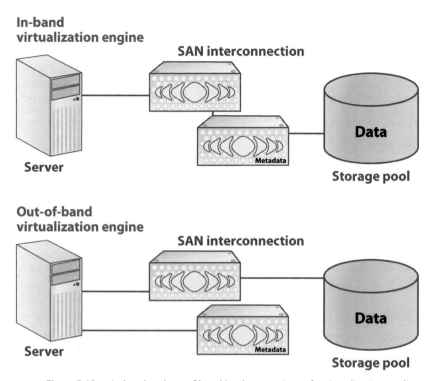

Figure 5.13 — In-band and out-of band implementations of a virtualization appliance.

Cloud computing and storage

Virtualization establishes strong justification for transition to the cloud model of service provisioning. In cloud computing, a large data center offers a lease of infrastructure. In the data center, there is a large number of servers (typically blades) and storage systems. Thanks to virtualization, these resources can be sliced into many virtual machines that exactly match a customer's requirements. The customer can rent a number of virtual machines with clearly defined characteristics, such as the number of processors, RAM, storage capacity and throughput. This model of service provisioning is very flexible. The customer pays only for the computing and storage capacity needed. Furthermore, the customer does not need to worry about maintenance.

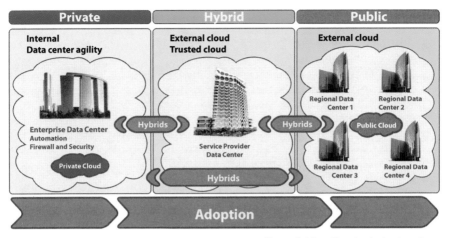

Figure 5.14 — Cloud solution topology.

We differentiate among private, hybrid and public clouds. The private cloud is located within a customer's data center and provides greater flexibility and faster time to value. **Time to value** (TTV) includes, for example, the effort, barriers, time, resources, planning and change that a customer experiences before first seeing a tangible business value from a product or service.

In a hybrid cloud, certain data or applications are extended outside a customer's firewall and moved to a trusted provider, stored either on a shared infrastructure with multitenant capabilities or a dedicated infrastructure for each customer. The provider would have security practices and auditable processes.

A public cloud is a publicly hosted facility that offers general access to data. Generally, SLAs, security, and data availability and durability cannot be guaranteed. Additionally, you may not have visibility or the ability to audit your data once it's inside the cloud. From an adoption perspective (Figure 5.14), enterprise customers are adopting from left to right even though a private cloud is more expensive than a public cloud. As cost goes down, risk goes up, and vice versa.

The provisioning of cloud based solutions can be divided into three distribution models:

- Infrastructure as a Service (IAAS). In this model, the provider is bound to provide the entire infrastructure. The entire infrastructure usually consists of servers (often in the form of virtual machines), network and storage (virtual storage machines). The main advantage is that the provider is responsible for uninterrupted operation and maintenance. The SLA between the provider and the customer defines the extent of the service, availability rates and financial penalties the provider must pay in the event of unexpected disruption or data loss.

- Platform as a Service (PAAS). In this model, the provider takes care of the development lifecycle and provisioning of web-based applications and their modules. Software engineering is part of this service.

- Software as a Service (SAAS). In this model, the applications (software products) are licensed as a service that is leased to the customer. Customers are paying to access the application; they are not paying for the application license itself. These applications are hosted on the cloud and are available from anywhere there is an Internet connection.

Cloud solutions provide major benefits to small and midsized companies, which can save a substantial amount of money that would otherwise be invested in the deployment of IT infrastructure. The provider offers the whole infrastructure, its maintenance and configuration, including development of application and provisioning of software. The disadvantage is that all the critical data is located outside the company, posing potential security risks.

Virtualization: the cons

Having read this chapter you may have gotten the impression that virtualization solves all problems and needs the world of IT is facing. However, there are certain limitations and downsides that also need to be taken into consideration before deciding to implement virtualization of servers and storage systems into your organization. A major problem can be the cost of software licenses. The more complex and powerful the solution is, the more it costs. For example, server virtualization with blades is suitable for midsized organizations that need five or more servers. A blade chassis alone can be very expensive, not to mention individual blades.

Every virtual machine needs licenses for the operating system and all additional software. If you purchase one physical server and virtualize it, you need to purchase licenses for each virtual machine. You need to think through your needs and calculate profitability of implementing virtualization.

In storage system infrastructure virtualization, you can encounter several problems. If you use an enterprise level storage system to virtualize external storage or if you use in-band virtualization appliance, this type of solution can potentially become a performance bottleneck. In both implementations of external storage virtualization, all the data blocks from all externally connected storage systems go through one cache and one controller. An out-of-band virtualization appliance can prevent this bottleneck, but it requires a more complicated configuration. Virtualization of external storage can increase vulnerability of infrastructure. If the virtualizing storage system or appliance fails, you cannot use the data stored on external storage because only the virtualizer knows where the data is actually stored. Licenses that enable the virtualization capabilities of the storage system are extremely expensive, and you need to calculate whether the virtualized implementation is going to pay back.

Future of virtualization

Virtualization of IT infrastructure is becoming a mainstream trend. We can encounter a certain degree of virtualization implementation in almost every organization that uses an IT infrastructure. It's likely that blade servers with native virtualization capabilities are going to spread massively. The technology of Hyper-V Server is also undergoing major development and can be expected to increase its share in the virtualization solutions market.

As for storage systems, we primarily use networked storage systems. By networked storage systems we mean either a NAS system or a traditional block-level SAN storage system. Virtualization in storage systems is frequently represented by thin provisioning and automated tiering. In the future, it's likely there will be an increased demand for storage system logical partitioning as IT moves toward the cloud model of IT services distribution. The capability to virtualize external storage is also expected to undergo a boom as the need for consolidation increases. So far, expensive licenses and storage systems capable of external storage virtualization prevent large-scale implementation of this type of solution.

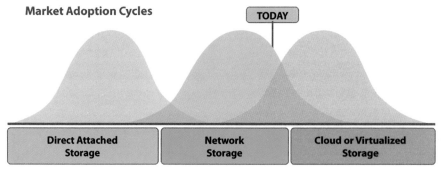

Figure 5.15 — Storage systems are heading towards fully virtualized solutions.

This chapter provided you with all the essential information on virtualization, its layers and areas of application. You were introduced to server virtualization with VMware and Hyper-V software. You should know that blade servers can be especially suitable for virtualization implementation. Some blade servers offer advanced built-in virtualization capabilities we call logical partitioning.

In storage systems, the prevailing virtualization capabilities are represented by thin provisioning and automated tiering. Both of these functionalities allow for greater flexibility, increased performance and improved utilization of a storage system. They also provide simplified management of your IT infrastructure.

High-end enterprise level storage systems can be used to virtualize external storage, which is very helpful when you need to consolidate your heterogeneous IT infrastructure. Logical partitioning is extremely useful when you want to ensure high performance and QoS of a critical application. Logical partitioning of a storage system is extremely useful in large data centers that lease virtual storage machines for money. Cloud solutions can also use and benefit from this functionality.

Archiving and file and content management

What are you going to learn in this chapter?

- Fixed content and its characteristics
- The difference between archiving and backup
- What data objects are and how they differ from other data
- How to describe essential components of a digital archive
- Requirements of archiving solutions on storage systems
- Features of content management

Introduction to archiving

In previous chapters, you learned that there are different types of data. Traditional storage systems, both modular and enterprise, are very efficient when processing structured data, or data in transaction based applications that work with large databases. This efficiency is possible thanks to large, powerful cache and high data throughput on front end and internal busses. Storage systems can handle a large amount of I/O per second (IOPS).

Unstructured data includes text documents, worksheets, presentations, pictures or digitized material, such as scanned copies. This data is represented by individual files. To store this kind of data, we can implement tiering that allows low cost storage of data that isn't accessed frequently. It is also possible to implement a NAS device and share logical volumes of a storage system as network drives, making them easily accessible to users. To effectively organize and manage your unstructured data, you can use content management platforms, such as Microsoft SharePoint or Hitachi Content Platform. A content management application usually runs on a server and offers extensive possibilities of storing, organizing and distributing unstructured data. We will talk about content management platform capabilities in detail later in this chapter.

Apart from structured and unstructured data, we have backup data and data that needs to be archived. Backup data is traditionally stored using low performance hard drives or tape libraries. The purpose of backup data is clear — in the event that we lose primary data, we can restore it from a backup copy.

Archiving data is very different from backing up data. In archiving, we always work with fixed content. Fixed content represents data that will not be changed anymore. We archive data to meet legal requirements (as with medical records and accounting). We also archive data because we want to protect older information that is not needed for everyday operations but may occasionally need to be accessed. Data archiving represents special requirements on storage devices. Archived data needs to be retained for years or even decades. This data can be further divided into online accessible data and offline accessible data.

Archive data can be either structured or unstructured. Structured archive data is represented mainly by locked databases, which are consistent databases that will not be altered by adding or removing individual items. Unstructured data is represented by various files that are not expected to be modified. It is only possible to modify archive data by creating a modified copy. The original must be kept unchanged.

Fixed content

Fixed content consists of data such as digital images, email messages, video content, medical images and check images that do not change over time. Fixed content differs from transaction based data that changes frequently and is marked by relatively short usefulness. Fixed content data must be kept for long periods of time, often to comply with retention periods and provisions specified by government regulations and law. Transaction data needs to be accessed very quickly. However, access times for fixed content data are not so important. Traditionally, fixed content data used to be stored on low cost tapes or optical media — usually with write once read many requirements, while high performance storage systems were used mainly for transaction data. With the price of hardware going down and the application of techniques such as automated tiering, nowadays it's customary to store fixed content data on low performance, inexpensive, online SATA drives installed on storage systems.

Fixed content can be managed through a server running specialized archiving software or by a dedicated appliance. In an organization with many branches, an archiving appliance can be installed in the branch office and feed the archiving solution located in the main data center. This process is called *data ingestion*. Up to 50% of data that companies use possess characteristics of fixed content. Implementation of fixed content management and archiving solutions is therefore becoming a standard, even for small and midsized organizations.

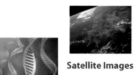

Legal Records   **Email**

Satellite Images   **Digital Video**

Biotechnology   **Medical Records**

Figure 6.1 — Examples of fixed content.

Archiving can be defined as a task of maintaining data over its life-cycle. It is typically used when we need to retain or preserve data for an extended period time. Compliant archiving is the ability to retain data securely for a period of time dictated by a regulation. Archived data must be immutable (cannot be changed) and retrievable (in a timely manner). Archives are designed to hold static data. Static data is also called fixed content. Archived data does not require regular backup.

Other differences between archiving and backup

Generally speaking, backup generates a redundant copy of data. The backup data can be deduplicated or compressed, or it can undergo additional processing that ensures its compactness, but the original data is retrievable through the procedure of recovery process. Archiving does not create redundant copies of data — it only moves it to a separate location designated for data archiving. Archiving makes data backup easier. Only the portion of data that changes is backed up. We are talking mostly about transaction data or files that are frequently accessed and modified. Archived data does not need to be backed up regularly. It can be secured by RAID protection, replicated or duplicated, but it is not subject to conventional backup techniques. Archiving using a digital archive offers extensive features that ensure integrity and authenticity of the data. In other words, it ensures that the original file has not been altered. Remember that a backup is always a copy, while archived data always contains original documents that cannot be further modified.

Motivation for data archiving

There are several reasons for implementing data archiving policies and technical solutions. Some of the most prominent reasons are:

- Effective utilization of high performance tiers
- Cheaper storage for fixed content
- Data retention regulation
- Simplified content management
- Indexing and searching capabilities of a digital archive

Fixed content data should not be stored on high performance tiers that use expensive SSD and SAS hard drives. By moving data from expensive storage media, an organization can save a significant amount of money. A digital archive automatically recognizes fixed content data and moves it to an archive location according to policies set by the administrator. Do not confuse this functionality with automated tiering. Automated tiering can be used with live databases. Automated tiering works on the block level and moves data among the tiers according to frequency of access. All live data, meaning data that is often modified, can be divided into parts that are accessed and modified frequently and can be stored on low performance tiers. This is very different from archiving fixed content. Fixed content is never modified and works on the file level.

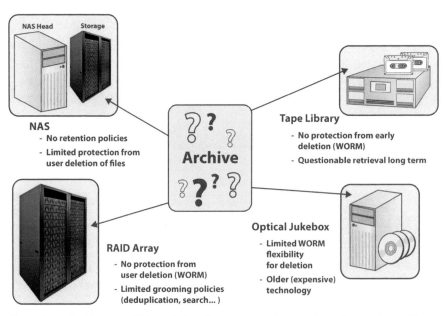

Figure 6.2 — Seeking an archiving solution. The storage systems we have discussed up until now are not very suitable for fixed content storage and archiving.

Unlike traditional storage systems, digital archives are optimized for long-time, low-cost data retention. IT technologies and digitization are reaching almost all fields of human activity. Large quantities of data are coming into existence every day. Digital data is now used in almost all organizations and institutions, replacing documents in paper form, file cabinets and traditional archives and depositaries. With the advancement of information technology, regulations and laws have emerged to govern data management. Retention periods for particular kinds of documents are getting longer. Digital archives need to meet these requirements. In Figure 6.3, you can see what kinds of documents are legally bound to be retained and how long the retention periods are.

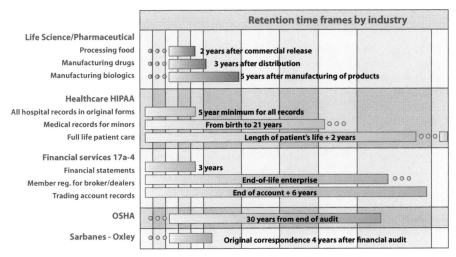

Figure 6.3 — Legal requirements of data retention periods. We can see that many organizations have increasing regulations, especially in the pharmaceutical industry, the food processing industry, healthcare, financial services and auditing. The Sarbanes-Oxley Act very strictly regulates the length of retention of financial records and accounting in companies.

In most companies, the IT equipment for archiving is decentralized and fragmented. Some portion of data is transferred to tapes; the rest is stored in a NAS device or similar location. This fragmentation of an archiving solution can make content management difficult because it does not generally provide advanced search functionality across all archiving devices. In other words, it may be difficult to find the particular document you want to access. A digital archive contains proprietary software that allows an advanced search across all archived data.

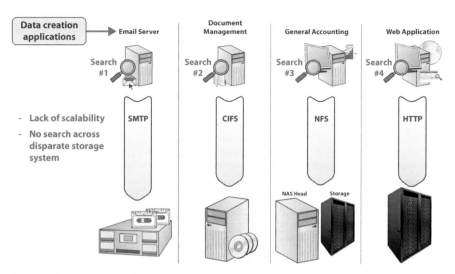

Figure 6.4 — An example of a decentralized and fragmented archiving solution. Disparate storage systems do not provide a common search engine, and they are not very scalable. A digital archive can solve this problem.

Across various industries today, organizations are seeing the creation of new fixed content (data) exceeding that of traditional data. Fixed content requires unique capabilities for effective storage, management and preservation. Business organizations are being challenged to manage fixed content more effectively based on rules and policies because of the growing pressure to comply with regulatory mandates and/or information governance for transparency. Difficulties in searching and retrieving content, as well as producing an auditable chain of evidence for authentic records, is resulting in costly legal discoveries and audit processes. These costs directly affect a customer's bottom line in terms of economic and operational costs (human effort). As a storage environment grows in complexity to handle the growth of fixed content, the cost of management also becomes a significant challenge. Customers need a better method to manage fixed content based on business policies and rules associated with certain content types.

The right format of archived data

One of the first decisions we have to make is to choose the right format for archived data. We can decide to store data in its native format. If we have common files with extensions such as .docx, .jpg, .tiff and .pdf, we can store them as they are. However, we would also have to ensure conservation of the applications able to read these files. As application development progresses and new functions of text editors and similar programs are added, the reverse compatibility with once used standards can turn out to be a problem.

Another possibility is to use digital archive software advanced functionalities that transform our original file into a standardized file format. We can make such a setting that all Microsoft Word documents and images marked as fixed content are automatically converted to standard .pdf files. Another possibility is to convert the data into an archiving data format developed either by a digital archive vendor or third party software provider. The major problem with converting native file formats into standardized file formats is connected with authenticity of the original. This matter has not been fully resolved yet and it is still unclear whether converted documents are still considered as originals by law or whether the legal system sees them as altered and modified copies.

Most companies prefer to archive data in its native format. A few exceptions can be named, though. Organizations that specialize in long-term data preservation can develop their own standard format. NASA Data Active Archive Centers (DAACs) and the U.K.'s National Digital Archive of Datasets are examples of organizations that always convert native formats into their own standardized file formats. The motivation for implementation of a standardized data format can lie in the need to attach extensive additional information about file origin. This information is called *metadata*. If the digital archive capabilities do not fit an organization's needs, it can be the reason for implementing a standardized file format.

Digital archive: object oriented storage system

A digital archive is also called an *object oriented storage system or content aware storage system*. Traditional RAID arrays are working on the block level. The storage system itself does not know what information is stored in the data. It does not even work on the file level (except in NAS devices). Data blocks (ones and zeros) are stored, striped across hard drives or replicated without storage system awareness of what kind of data the blocks represent. A digital archive, on the other hand, is content aware. It is able to store data in the form of objects. As we say that traditional storage systems work on a block level and NAS devices on a file level, digital archives work on an object level.

The object level is hierarchically above blocks and files. An object consists of a file we need to archive. For example, it could be an email, x-ray, MRI, photograph, satellite image or Word document. Aside from the file itself, an object contains metadata. We know that file systems such as NTFS also work with metadata.

The difference between file system based metadata and object metadata is that a storage system administrator can define object metadata. Metadata is encapsulated into the object and cannot be separated from every individual file. In addition, an object also contains definition of policies. These policies may include configuration of the data protection level, indexing, retention periods, shredding and versioning. All these policies will be described in detail later in this chapter.

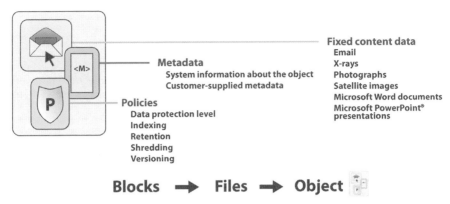

Figure 6.5 — A digital archive works on the object level. Each object contains fixed content data, metadata and description of policies.

Hardware components of a digital archive are not very different from traditional storage systems. In fact, a digital archive consists of dedicated servers that run proprietary software supplied by a digital archive's vendor. These servers process the data and provide management console. Then the data is stored again on a traditional disk array (modular or enterprise). The scheme is similar to a NAS operation. A NAS solution also consists of a NAS head, which is a dedicated server running proprietary software, and a block level storage system. Digital archive servers are linked to storage system tiers equipped with low cost and low performance hard drives. Aside from servers and storage systems, a digital archive may include other components, such as data ingestion appliances that collect data from production servers and send them to a digital archive over distance (through a LAN or WAN connection).

Block Level Storage

LUN Based

Object Level Storage

Object Based

▪ Primary Online Storage	▪ Fixed Content Storage (long-term storage)
▪ SAN Connected to Application	▪ IP Network Connected to Application
▪ High Speed	▪ Object Aware
▪ Huge Capacity	▪ Policy Enforcement
▪ LUN Level Access	▪ Object Level Access

Figure 6.6 — A traditional block level storage system compared to an object level storage system. The object-level storage system consists of powerful proprietary servers and management software. These servers are connected to a RAID array.

A digital archive works with objects. An object contains actual data (a file or files), metadata (data about files and their relationship) and configuration of policies that govern data archiving.

An object aware storage system consists of dedicated proprietary servers and a disk array suitable for long-term data retention. Proprietary software enables fast and efficient management of archive data. A digital archive is fed data from production servers or through data ingesting devices.

Data objects and their components

To illustrate what a data object looks like, we can take a look at a Hitachi Content Platform digital archive. In Figure 6.7, we can see a decomposed data object. Individual elements that have a particular function are represented by individual files, in this case .xml and .txt configuration files. *Xml* represents a data format that was designed to be readable by both humans and computers. The *txt* format represents a universal text file. Both these file types ensures a high level of compatibility and standardization. The data to be archived is represented by the *My Document.doc* file. Additional files contain policy configuration and metadata. The file *created.txt* contains information about the date and origin of the archived file. The file *dpl.txt* contains configuration details for the data protection level. Other metadata files contain retention requirements, indexing information, the shredding policy and hash data. Hashing serves for data authenticity validation. All files can be set to comply with the WORM protection standard; they can be read but cannot be modified or deleted. End users do not access objects in the form depicted in Figure 6.7. End users typically use a web-based interface that allows comfortable searching and previewing of archived content.

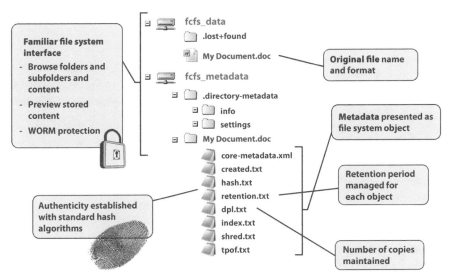

Figure 6.7 — A data object and its components in detail. This example illustrates how objects are handled by a Hitachi Content Platform digital archive.

Digital archive features

A digital archive must ensure long time preservation and authenticity of stored data. High requirements of stored data authenticity are met through active periodical verification of archived documents. Authenticity and credibility of data are key prerequisites, especially for auditing purposes. Additional functionalities of a digital archive increase utilization and economical operation. Active functions of a digital archive are:

- Content verification
- Protection service
- Compression service
- Deduplication service
- Replication service
- Search capabilities

Content verification ensures authenticity and integrity of each data object. A digital archive periodically checks whether the stored data still matches its cryptographic hash value. When we store a document in a digital archive, a special algorithm calculates its hash value. This hash value is generated from the archived file and is unique for each file. In simple terms, a hash value is similar to a finger print. The content verification has two main tasks: to detect corrupted data and to repair corrupted data.

Data can be corrupted if the file is altered or modified accidentally or purposefully, or if a digital archive component malfunctions. To detect data corruption, the digital archive periodically recalculates hash values for all documents and matches them to the originally created hash value. If the old and new hash values for a document are identical, the document is not corrupted and its integrity is not endangered. A violation occurs when the hash values do not match. In this event, the digital archive must repair the data and return it to its original, uncorrupted state.

Corrupted data can be repaired from an existing good copy (such as a RAID or digital archive replica). The digital archive creates a new copy of the data from the good copy and marks the corrupted copy for deletion.

Protection service is implemented in order to ensure stability of the digital archive by maintaining a specified level of archived data redundancy. This level is called the data protection level (DPL) and is set by the digital archive administrator. Different settings can be configured for different types of archived content. DPL configuration tells the digital archive how many copies of the archived document it should keep.

Compression service can be implemented in order to achieve better utilization of storage space assigned to the digital archive. As we described in Chapter 4, compression detects repeating sequences of ones and zeros, searching for repeating patterns. These patterns are then replaced by pointers to the first occurrence of the pattern. Compression effectiveness is determined by the level of data entropy. Please refer to Chapter 4 for more detail.

Deduplication service, which is very well known from backup solutions, can be implemented in a digital archive as well. Unlike compression, which searches for strings of repeating bits, deduplication searches for duplicities in files. Compression works on the level of ones and zeros, while deduplication works on the file level. It's possible for a single document to be marked for archiving from several locations. The digital archive detects duplicities. For two or more files to be deemed identical, their hash values must match. Deduplication can save significant amounts of storage space.

Replication service represents a recommended solution for ensuring redundancy of archived data. It is usually not possible to back up a digital archive by conventional means because it can occupy terabytes or even petabytes of storage. Traditional backup is also not well designed to create copies of fixed content. Replication service replicates the data to another digital archive. This replica can be used for load balancing. In other words, users can access a file on either system, according to its load. Replication service is linked to content verification service. If the corrupted data is found, the replica can serve for data repair.

Search engines allow users to search documents according to information stored in their metadata (such as who created the data, when the data was created and the type of data) or using full text search capabilities (searching for words and strings of words inside text documents).

 Search is a faster way to find desired information within multiple storage resources. Indexing is a process that helps you search content much more quickly. The indexing process creates an interpretation of the content and metadata of a file or object and stores that interpretation in an optimized way for faster, more complete and accurate search results. Search tools query the index for keywords, metadata and more. Results are presented back through the search tool. A digital archive often provides indexing services that help search engines.

Digital archive accessibility

Digital archives should be easily accessible by common access protocols. These protocols include web-based protocols (http, https), network based file systems (NFS, CIFS), mail (SMTP) and file transfer protocols (FTP). Digital archives should also support application programming interfaces (APIs) for command line interface (CLI) based access. In simple words, a digital archive should be accessible and manageable from a command line. A command line interface enables scripting, which leads to automation of management and operations. It also provides a fast and flexible tool for simple installation and integration of a digital archive. According to this information, digital archives should be accessible through:

- Search console — usually a web-based solution with graphical user interface

- Network as a file system — usually by using an NFS or CIFS protocol; data is then displayed as depicted in Figure 6.7

- FTP protocol — an FTP client can connect to a data repository and download documents directly

- SMTP protocol — useful for mail archiving

- CLI — command line interface

End users typically access a digital archive through a web-based GUI, since it provides the simplest and most intuitive interface. End users can also access the repository through an FTP protocol that is more efficient for accessing archived files.

Storage system administrators are likely to access the repository using NFS protocols or CLI.

NFS and CIFS protocols allow connection of a digital archive as a network drive on UNIX and Windows systems. SMTP protocol allows direct connection between an email server and digital archive. Thanks to http and https protocols, authorized users can access the archived data through any compatible web browser.

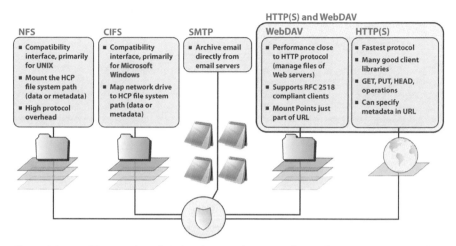

Figure 6.8 — In this example, a digital archive can be accessed using four independent standard protocols. WebDAV (Web-based Distributed Authoring and Versioning) is an extension to HTTP protocol that allows remote management of files stored on web server.

 Open standards based protocols provide applications and users a common and familiar means for interfacing to the repository. Each maintains the familiar and ingrained file system metaphor people have embraced for years and does not require changing the paradigm for how files and content are organized in storage. It also gives independent software vendors (ISVs) options for integrating based on the best approach for their particular application and its specific performance and/ or functional needs. That means multiple applications, and potentially users, share a common repository environment simultaneously.

Digital archive compliance features

Compliance can be defined as a state of being in accordance with established guidance, specifications, rules or legislation. A digital archive needs to comply with such regulations. Digital technology is reaching almost all institutions and organizations, and compliance requirements are becoming stricter and more detailed. Compliance has increasingly become a corporate management concern. Devices such as digital archives must offer functionalities that ensure a standardized level of compliance and simplify compliance management.

So far in this book, we have already mentioned some techniques that help to comply with regulations; we will discuss these now in greater detail. There are also functionalities we have not yet discussed. The most important compliance features of a digital archive are:

- **Write once read many (WORM)**

- **Retention period definition**

- **Data shredding**

- **Data encryption**

WORM functionality was originally introduced in tape libraries. The tapes were designed in such a way that the stored data could not be altered, modified, overwritten or deleted. This functionality is now also available in digital archives. Each object stored in an object oriented storage system can be amended with metadata information that enables WORM functionality. Once enabled, this functionality cannot be disabled. WORM functionality is very popular in archiving solutions and helps to comply with legal standards and regulations.

We have discussed retention periods several times in this book. You have learned that various types of content can be subject to legal regulation with strictly defined retention periods, depending on the information stored in the object and the organization that created the data (such as medical records and MRI images in a hospital). In a digital archive, each object can contain retention period settings. It is also possible to set policies that govern the way each file type is treated. For example, it is possible to set a policy for all .tiff images to be retained for ten years. Once the defined retention period passes, the document is usually destroyed. Effective management of retention periods for different types of records is an important feature digital archives offer.

Data shredding is a data destruction utility designed to securely erase a hard disk or digital storage device. When you delete a file on your hard drive or USB pen drive, the data is not physically removed. The data is just marked as deleted and is available for overwriting. This means that specialized software or hardware can recover the data by searching for and restoring blocks of data marked as deleted. To permanently and securely destroy data, it is therefore not sufficient to just delete it. The shredding utility overwrites data marked for deletion several times with randomly generated meaningless data, preventing possible attempts for deleted data retrieval. Data shredding is a key security utility that ensures deleted data cannot be restored.

Data encryption can be enabled in most storage systems and digital archives. Plain data is coded by a special algorithm. This algorithm makes data unreadable to unauthorized users. Encrypted data need to be decrypted before it can be accessed. Decryption of encrypted data is possible using a password that triggers the encryption algorithm. Storage systems implement this functionality to enhance security capabilities. Encryption is very demanding for the computing performance of an installed CPU. Every block of data needs to be processed by the CPU when we implement encryption, as well as when we need to access (decrypt) the encrypted data. This means that implementation of encryption capabilities can have a negative influence on a storage system's performance. When you employ full-scale encryption, you can expect a 10-20% performance loss, depending on the storage system.

Metadata in digital archives

Generally speaking, metadata is data about data. File systems use metadata to store attributes for each file (such as *read only* or *hidden file*) and access permissions. Object oriented storage systems use their own metadata that stores even more information, such as WORM configuration, retention periods, owners, origin of the data, detailed description. In an object oriented storage system, metadata is often stored in the form of files. The format used for metadata storage is very important. It should be an open standardized format with a clearly defined structure. XML data format represents the ideal standard for metadata storage. XML stands for *Extensible Markup Language*. This markup language is defined by a set of rules for encoding documents in a format that is both human readable and machine readable. Information stored in XML format is standardized, meaning it can be read and accessed by third party software. Digital archives should provide a standardized interface (API). XML contributes to extended compatibility with third party products and supports integration with such products.

Scalability, hardware designing and migrations

The amount of archived data is growing exponentially. A digital archive must allow simple extension of its capacity. This ability is commonly referred to as scalability. A digital archive must be easily scalable in petabytes (PB) to ensure accommodation of large quantities of data. Performance of digital archive must be ready to process such amounts of data. Scalability should also allow you to reach full operability with minimal capacity installed. Additional capacity is installed online without disruption of operation as more storage space is required.

A digital archive must be designed to retain data for decades. Certain types of data are legally required to be stored for indefinite period of time. It is obvious that a single piece of hardware cannot be expected to function for decades or indefinitely. When we consider rapid development of new technologies, we can expect that one device can provide uninterrupted operations only for a limited time — a few years or perhaps a decade — before it becomes obsolete and its maintenance too complicated and expensive. Due to these limitations, each digital archive must support simple data migration by its design. Digital archives are working with objects. The reason for this is to accommodate metadata and related information for each file or set of files that constitutes an object. These objects are also ideal for future data migration. Archived data is stored in the form of objects; the objects are then locked for compliance reasons. Individual objects are created in such a way that they are hardware platform independent. By design, the objects must allow easy manipulation and migration to a new hardware platform.

Integration of a digital archive

It is important to realize that a digital archive is just one component of the complete archiving solution. Similar to a NAS solution, a digital archive consists of servers that run proprietary built-in software. These servers are connected to a traditional block level storage system, either modular or enterprise. The attached storage system is usually equipped with low performance, inexpensive SATA drives. The digital archive must be fed the data. This is called the application food chain. A standalone digital archive provides cheaper, compliant and reliable data storage. It also offers advanced search capabilities and policies management. However, data we need to archive is managed by its parent applications (such as Microsoft Exchange or file servers). That is why we need a component that interconnects the digital archive with the parent application. This component goes through data stored by the particular application and according to set criteria and it chooses the candidate files for archiving.

This missing component, which is responsible for feeding the data to digital archive, is called an *archiving application*. The complete archiving solution is then a chain with three components: application, archiving application and digital archive. An archiving application is linked both to production servers and the digital archive. On the production servers, there are dedicated agents designed to work with a particular application. You learned earlier that archiving does not create copies of data; it moves the original data to the archiving location. The data taken from the parent application is moved to the digital archive and replaced by a link reference to its location in the digital archive. Complete archiving solutions can be differentiated as file archiving, email archiving, enterprise content management (ECM)/electronic resource management (ERM) archiving, enterprise resource planning (ERP) archiving or health care archiving. Before choosing a particular model for a digital archive, we need to think through the process of integration into our existing infrastructure. The right digital archive must be capable of processing data from all important systems running on production servers.

Digital archive cloud features

Digital archive vendors often boast cloud support in their products. In fact, this feature is represented by native support of virtualization. Virtualization allows you to divide one physical digital archive into several logical digital archives. Many organizations, especially small and midsized organizations not legally bound to retain large quantities of data, do not have to purchase the physical digital archive. Instead they can lease a virtual digital archive from a data center. The virtualization capabilities in a digital archive allow the data center administrator to create virtual machines with just enough performance to satisfy the customer's needs.

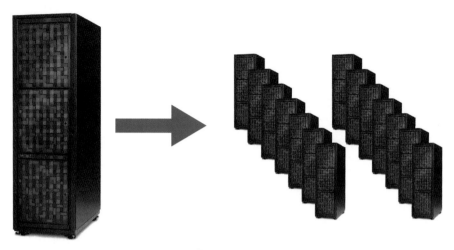

Figure 6.9 — Virtualization of a digital archive. Digital archives are suitable for integration in large data centers. Individual virtual digital archives can then be rented to small and midsized organizations that wish to outsource digital archiving.

Policy based content management

Policy based content management refers to the automatically invoked behavior of a digital archive — movement, retention and disposal according to defined rules. This functionality represents a solution for IT automation. By bringing automation to digital archiving, the policy based content management helps ensure compliance with legal and regulatory requirements. It also safely offers greater control and responsibility to storage consumers.

Let's look at a few examples of how policy based content management simplifies routine administrator's tasks.

Typical IT department:
Policies are defined in such a way that all files that have not been accessed in 90 days are moved off Tier 1 storage. Any .mp3 files that are not stored in specified directories are to be automatically deleted.

Healthcare:

All medical images are automatically replicated to meet regulatory requirements. All treatment records are to be kept for 50 years after a patient passes away. All billing records are to be kept for 10 years after they are paid in full. All MRI images are automatically moved from Tier 1 storage to the archive after 30 days.

Financial Services:

Automation based on defined policies stores mortgage documents on WORM media upon completion and store for the life of the mortgage plus 10 years. Content that has fulfilled all retention requirements is deleted and purged.

Policies are defined using the management console of a digital archive. Each object contains information about related policies and their configuration in the form of metadata.

Archiving and content management

So far we have discussed content management from the perspective of storage systems. The term *content management* can, however, be understood from different perspectives as well. In the context of storage systems, we are talking about specialized servers with proprietary software connected to a traditional block level storage system, either modular or enterprise. This type of solution is called an object oriented intelligent storage system or a digital archive. It provides several types of interfaces through which the content can be accessed. The users typically access content stored on this type of solution through http and https protocols using standard web browsers. The web interface includes an advanced search engine that, in cooperation with content indexing and information stored in metadata, delivers high performance. This is content management, but it is necessary to remember that it is always fixed content management. There are other solutions designed to manage content that is not fixed content that is frequently accessed and modified. This is called live data.

From the perspective of most companies, content management is understood as a process of organizing files, sharing files and information within an organization, and managing workflow. It can be also understood as a traditional information system (IS). Specialized software provided by third party storage vendors runs on production servers. This software can use the internal hard drives of such a server or, in a larger organization, a mapped LUN on traditional storage system connected in a SAN. NAS devices in a LAN environment can also be used as a storage platform that supports this type of solution.

Remember that you need to distinguish between management of fixed content and content management that focuses primarily on live data, or data that is frequently accessed and modified.

In this book, we are focusing on fixed content management because it is closely connected with storage systems.

The traditional view of content management can mean something completely different and unrelated to the topic of storage systems.

Enterprise content management solutions

Before we close this chapter, you should have some insight into enterprise content management solutions of live data. We are not talking about storage systems or digital archives now, but rather about software solutions. We will take Microsoft SharePoint as an example of an enterprise content management system. Data in our organization can be divided among several subgroups. We have live data represented by databases, used by transaction based applications. We have fixed content data, such as MRI images in healthcare or finished accounting reports.

We also have live data that does not fit these categories. Every organization that conducts business needs to work on project documentation. Every organization also needs to share information resources among employees to ensure knowledge is available throughout the company. This documentation is handled very well by content management solutions such as Microsoft SharePoint.

SharePoint is a software based solution independent of the storage system field. It is an application that runs on a production server. Files that are fed into SharePoint are stored in the form of database. This database can be stored on the internal hard drives of a server, on a NAS device or on a mapped LUN in a traditional storage system. The management console allows sharing of documents — mostly text documents, graphs, spreadsheets and similar files — among groups of users that are given permission to access them. SharePoint allows both effective content management and workflow management. Project documentation can be modified, reviewed and versioned by all people involved in the particular project. SharePoint is a file based sharing platform that allows comprehensive and sophisticated organization of documents in relation to users and individual projects or tasks.

Digital archives can support integration with Microsoft SharePoint. Specialized agents are installed on a server that runs SharePoint. Once the particular project is finalized and closed, the live content (project documentation) effectively becomes fixed content, which is no longer accessed frequently. An agent identifies such files and automatically transfers them to the digital archive.

In this chapter, you were introduced to yet another type of storage system. The portfolio of all the most common storage systems is now complete. You are now familiar with traditional block level storage systems, as well as modular and enterprise systems. You know how NAS devices operate. Digital archives, or object oriented intelligent storage systems, are the last product discussed in this book.

Remember that a digital archive consists of servers with proprietary software or a traditional storage system. Data is stored in the form of objects that contains extensive metadata information. Objects are hardware platform independent and can be easily migrated.

Basic functionalities of a digital archive include protection services, compression services, replication services and an advanced search engine. Compliance features of a digital archive consist mostly of WORM capabilities, retention period definition, shredding services and encryption services.

In the following chapter we will look at common tasks storage administrators have to face every day. This should provide you with a more practical perspective on storage system administration and data management.

7

Storage system administration

What are you going to learn in this chapter?

- How to describe everyday storage administrator tasks
- How to configure and monitor a storage system
- What tools are available for a storage system administrator
- Effective allocation of resources and reporting
- Who is responsible for storage system implementation

Who is a storage system administrator?

Unlike other chapters that have presented theoretical knowledge on how things work in data management and storage systems, this chapter should provide you with more practical insight on how things work in real situations. To be more specific, this chapter focuses on people who install and configure storage systems, as well as people who conduct maintenance tasks. This focus gives you yet another perspective on storage systems management.

Before we start with the description of a storage system administrator's duties, it is important to realize who is considered a storage system administrator. A storage system administrator is an employee in charge of maintaining a storage system infrastructure. Vendor policies determine the extent of this employee's duties — a storage system administrator has a specific set of tasks based on the service level agreement (SLA). To make sense of this, you need to understand that there are two kinds of people who perform administrative tasks on a storage system. First, there is always a customer engineer from the vendor — this is the company that supplies the devices. This company also provides a **storage system implementer**, who assembles, installs and integrates the purchased devices. The implementer is specially trained to do these tasks. The service contract strictly lists the number of operations **a storage system administrator** is allowed to perform without breaking service contract maintenance conditions. Under a warranty agreement, the storage system administrators can perform only a limited number of operations on the particular system. The more complicated tasks are performed by a storage system implementer, who works for the company that supplied the equipment and has a partnership contract with the vendor. A storage system administrator is an internal employee of the company that purchased the devices from the vendor through the vendor's partner.

As we mentioned earlier, vendor SLAs determine the extent of a storage admin's duties. Each vendor has different policies. Some vendors prefer that the storage implementer does almost all the tasks, leaving a storage system administrator with very few duties. (In this situation, whenever you need to change the configuration of your storage system, you have to call the support line.) In contrast, some vendors prefer for a storage system administrator to do all the tasks while the implementer performs only the equipment installation. As a result, we will discuss only the most common storage administrator tasks. At the end of the chapter, we will also discuss the most common storage system implementer tasks.

Storage administrator tasks

To illustrate the duties of a storage administrator in this section, we will use the example of a growing organization. Let's say the organization has an existing IT environment but has not yet required an advanced storage system. Now the amount of data that needs to be handled increases to a state not sustainable without an advanced storage system delivering high performance, availability and reliability.

As the project moves forward, the organization buys new servers and storage systems. The internal administrator for this organization is a specialist mainly in servers. (A LAN environment with servers is very common, unlike a SAN environment, which requires additional specialization.) Because the administrator is aware of the importance of data and its secure storage, he recommends purchasing a midrange storage system for a good price and value ratio. The administrator makes a list of storage system requirements and helps find a suitable vendor. He must carefully consider the performance, availability, configuration and required advanced functionalities. Once the administrator finds a suitable device and concludes the purchase, he must specify the configuration requirements and overtake the administration of the storage system from the supplier.

The configuration requirements must include details on how much capacity is required, what hard drives are to be implemented and their performance level. The administrator must assess the importance of various kinds of data, determine what kinds of data need to be stored on high performance hard drives and what data needs to be replicated. The level of protection must be decided upon — especially what RAID level is to be implemented. The supplier provides consulting services that should simplify the procedure for the storage system administrator, who does not yet have extensive knowledge on storage system operations and SAN environments. The consultant from the supplying company gathers details needed to integrate a storage system from the administrator. These details include specifications of the host bus adaptor (HBA) used in servers, the HBA firmware version, the operating systems running on the servers and more. The supplier also provides consulting on operation disruption prevention — the required redundancy level of individual components and the location for replicated data.

The storage administrator also participates in the preparation of additional documentation. The essential documentation and planning includes details on:

- **Capacity management**
- **Availability management**
- **Continuity management**
- **Financial management**

In storage system management, capacity can be considered a basic resource. **Capacity management** deals with the amount of data that needs to be stored, the size and performance of LUN per application (server), the performance of individual hard drives, the performance of I/O and R/W operations, and content characteristics.

In **availability management**, the administrator would configure and sustain protection against component failure. Failure may occur in a hard drive, controller, on HBA, Fibre Channel switches and other components. Availability management also includes replication and backup strategies, as well as data archiving. Data archiving should prevent data loss due to inconsistency caused by application failure.

Continuity management is often part of business continuity planning and disaster recovery procedures. The administrator would need to decide what threats he wants to protect his organization's data against (such as fire, theft or floods). Existing business continuity and disaster recovery documentation needs to be updated every time the IT environment changes.

The administrator also needs to calculate the financial pros and cons of new technology implementation. **Financial management** would include budget preparation, cost calculation and invoicing. ***Total Cost of Ownership (TCO)*** should reflect all costs connected not only with purchase of the equipment, but also with its operations and maintenance. TCO is a very important value that helps determine the real value of an integrated solution.

Once all the documentation is ready and the supplier and purchasing organization agree upon all terms and conditions, installation of the storage systems follows. In our example, and in most cases, this process is completed solely by the supplier. The supplier also provides system management training for the administrator, covering basic system operations, system monitoring and performance tuning.

When the device is integrated and operational, the supplier provides services such as maintenance or monitoring according to the SLA. The supplier then monitors the device's operations remotely. If the supplier detects a problem, the supplier contacts the administrator and discusses the solution. The storage administrator has undergone the usual training to perform basic LUN operations (discussed in the following section), monitoring and performance tuning.

Storage system administration in a SAN environment is different from the common tasks IT administrators face. That is why a storage system administrator needs to be trained to specialize in the field of storage systems. Storage system administrators are required to formulate demands on the new equipment. They must choose the provider and specify the requirements on performance, capacity and additional functionalities. Once the storage system is installed and operational, supplier policies determine the extent of operations a storage system administrator is responsible for. Storage system administrators are usually allowed to perform basic operations with LUNs. Storage system administrators are also responsible for monitoring, basic performance tuning and infrastructure growth planning **In addition, storage system administrators are responsible for maintenance and monitoring of SAN networks, network performance and network security.** They take care of the configuration of Fibre Channel switches, ports and zoning.

Common operations with LUNs and cache

In addition to SAN maintenance and data management, the storage administrator is responsible for storage system monitoring and communication with the supplier, as well as basic operations with LUNs and other configuration tasks according to the SLA and the administrator's training level. Basic LUN operations and configuration tasks include:

- Configuration of RAID groups and volumes (Figure 7.1)
- Implementation of changes in volume configuration
- Data replication optimization
- Configuration of cache
- Cache partitioning
- Backup of storage system configuration

In this section's example, let's say you are the storage administrator performing common operations with LUNs and cache. To configure **a**

RAID group, you need to choose physical hard drives that will be linked together in a RAID array, and you need to select the desired RAID level. Depending on your requirements, you will probably choose a RAID-5 level with a distributed parity that protects against one hard drive failure. If higher data protection is desired, you may choose a RAID-6 level, which protects against two hard drive failures. If the highest possible performance is required, you may even choose RAID-1+0, which implements data striping and disk mirroring. There is no parity in this RAID level. Therefore, there is no need for data reconstruction if one disk fails, since you always have a fully operational mirror disk. To balance performance and cost, you would probably go with RAID-5 or RAID-6.

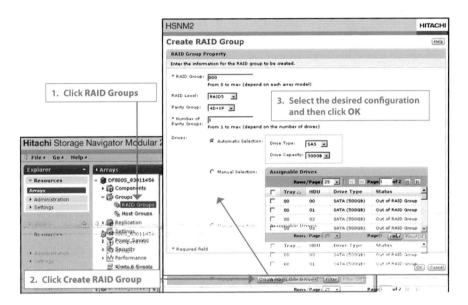

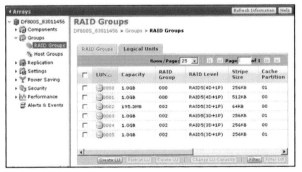

Figure 7.1 — Configuration of RAID groups and LUNs. The picture depicts the interface of a storage system by HDS. The application (Hitachi Storage Navigator 2) with GUI is installed on a server connected to the storage system.

Once you have created RAID groups, you need to decide your LUN allocation policy. You have to decide especially whether you prefer **fat provisioning or thin provisioning.** In the first case, you create a LUN and map it to the server. For thin provisioning, you need to set up a storage pool, create virtual volumes and map the volumes to servers.

As a storage administrator, you need to consider which **front end ports** are used for mapping LUNs. To balance the load, the number of LUNs linked to servers should be even for each port. If you have eight LUNs and four ports, you should configure LUN mapping so that there are two LUNs per port. This important step allows you to achieve high performance, and it prevents bottlenecks that might have occurred if you had linked all eight LUNs through only one or two ports.

In the case of fat provisioning, you should know how to **enlarge the existing LUN.** There are various tools to do so. First the changes in configuration must be made in the storage system's management console. The existing volume is enhanced. To complete this task, you also need to enhance the file system to spread over the volume.

Imagine you have created a 10GB volume and mapped it to a server, which formatted the volume with a file system. When you enlarge the LUN on the storage system's level, the LUN will have, let's say, 20GB, but the file system is still capable of accessing only the originally allocated 10GB. To overcome this issue, you need to perform file system extension operation. At the end of the procedure, you have a 20GB LUN formatted with a file system that is able to use all 20GB. In thin provisioning, when you get an alert that signifies the virtual volume and storage pool are running out of capacity, you need to contact your supplier for installation of additional physical hard drives.

Storage administrator tasks connected with data replication are often limited. Usually, the supplier creates and configures replication pairs, and you can make adjustments, such as changing the **frequency in which snapshots are created**. The default supplier setting (according to organization requirements) is that snapshots are created every 4hrs.

If this becomes insufficient, you can change this to 2hrs. You can also perform pairsplit operations with in-system replication to be able to access data replica located on an S-VOL for the purposes of data mining or data warehousing. However, you cannot usually create new pairs or set up and configure remote replication pairs.

Cache optimization is one of the most difficult tasks you will face as a storage administrator. Cache greatly influences the performance of the whole storage system. We know that hard drives, even with implemented data striping, are still the slowest component of the storage system. Cache is designed to compensate for the performance differential between hard drives and solid state components. Proper configuration is, therefore, essential. You can adjust certain parameters of cache to enhance I/O performance, which is the key for transaction based applications that use large databases. According to the database type, you need to choose the right block size the cache is handling. If a database uses large chunks of data (512K), the cache setting must correspond. When a database works with small chunks of data (16K), you need to adjust the cache settings as well to achieve the best performance and utilization. It is also possible to prioritize certain hosts. I/O requests coming from such hosts are processed with higher priority. Additionally, you can divide cache into logical units when you virtualize the whole storage system (one storage system is divided into several logical storage systems), or when you need to support volumes under high load and the character of the load requires large cache. It is, therefore, possible to assign a certain portion of cache to a particular volume.

You can export the configuration of the whole storage system into a single file. You should export regularly and back up the configuration files. If the configuration is accidentally altered, it is your task as a storage administrator to return the configuration to its working state, which is easy to do using the backed up configuration files.

Monitoring of storage systems

Once the storage system is fully installed and configured, its operations do not require the high attention of a storage system administrator. Everything is fully automatic. Furthermore, all the components in a storage system, as well as all the components in a SAN, are fully redundant, meaning the failure of one component does not affect the operation of the whole device, nor does it cause downtime. A working storage system is not reconfigured every day; once it is fully integrated, it can work for months without requiring the attention of the administrator. However, the administrator should monitor storage system operation regularly. In a storage system, the administrator monitors two major things:

- **Performance of a storage system**
- **Health status of all components installed in a storage system**

Performance is monitored by measuring the IOPS. The data flow can be measured on HBA ports in a server, on ports in the Fibre Channel switch or on the front end ports of a storage system. Other parameters that are monitored include utilization of cache, the CPU load and the load on ports. Monitoring is very important because it helps detect possible bottlenecks. Log files with measurement values also represent a necessary source of information required for performance tuning. (Performance tuning is discussed in detail in Chapter 8.)

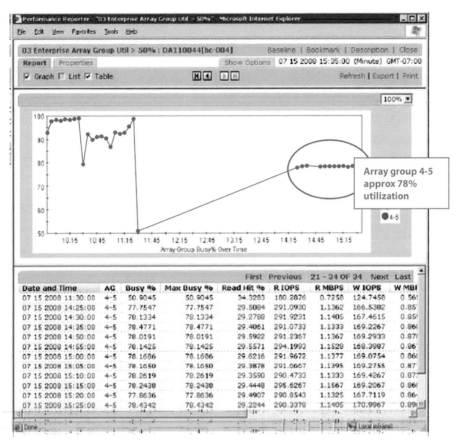

Figure 7.2 — Among IOPS on ports and CPU load, the storage administrator also monitors effective utilization of installed capacity. Here you see an example of a RAID group load and performance monitoring.

The performance of a storage system is measured through various tools. These tools are usually supplied by the storage system vendor. Some software requires the administrator to interpret values, and some software provides automated monitoring. Once a bottleneck is detected, the software sends an alert message to the administrator, who evaluates the situation and ensures the problem is solved. Monitoring can also be provided by the supplier, depending on the SLA.

The health status of all components installed in a storage system is also monitored. A storage system is programmed to detect any possible hardware failure before such a failure happens. Even individual hard drives include these monitoring functions, which are built into firmware (Self-Monitoring, Analysis and Reporting Technology or SMART). A storage system can read and evaluate values provided by hard drives and detect a decrease in performance of a particular hard drive. Once a possible failure is detected, the system sends the storage administrator an alert message. Other components are monitored as well. An alert is also sent when a LUN is near capacity and needs to be enlarged. The storage system administrator's responsibility is to log the alerts and warnings and deal with them appropriately. The storage system administrator never takes care of the replacement of individual failed components. The administrator also cannot replace a broken hard drive with a new one or add new hard drives or expansion units. This is always the supplier's responsibility.

The last thing that requires the regular attention of a storage system administrator is keeping all firmware and software up to date. Whenever there is a new version of firmware installed in a storage system, the administrator should receive this firmware from the supplier. Either the supplier (implementer) or a storage system administrator then performs the firmware update, which can be disruptive (requiring downtime) or nondisruptive (with no downtime). Modern high-end storage systems usually allow nondisruptive firmware updates.

Note that firmware stored in individual hard drives may need regular updates. Management software with a GUI and CLI also needs to be kept up to date.

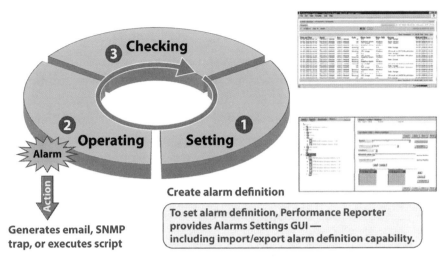

Figure 7.3 — Automated monitoring functionality. You can define situations that trigger an action once they occur. Whenever performance and hardware health values reach the defined status, an alarm (alert, warning) is sent to the storage system administrator. The storage system administrator assesses the situation and ensures the problem is eliminated.

Storage system management software

The management software of a storage system is stored in microcode. However, the microcode itself does not provide any advanced GUI or CLI. To manage disk arrays, you need to install a management software client on the server connected to the storage system. The management software then communicates directly with the storage system microcode. The storage system implementer and administrator make all the necessary configurations through this client. Usually, the configuration is done through the GUI, while the CLI is used mainly for scripting that allows task automation. Scripts that use a CLI are especially useful in replication. By executing the script, you can bring the database stored in the cache and LUN to a consistent state and then perform a pair-split operation. Scripting allows you to do much more than these tasks, but it can be difficult to master.

The storage system administrator helps to design and maintain the SAN infrastructure. For example, the administrator helps to specify the requirements on storage systems and choose the right product and vendor. The day to day tasks mostly include monitoring and slight configuration changes. However, the amount of data that needs to be processed is growing rapidly. To accommodate such growth, the storage system administrator needs to plan expansion of the existing infrastructure, including the purchase of new storage systems, Fibre Channel switches and servers. This time, the administrator can decide to purchase a disk array from a different vendor because it fits the organization's requirements better than the vendor who supplied the first storage system. The administrator's major concerns are issues connected with the management of two different storage systems. With advanced software and technology, these issues can be overcome. The management of a heterogeneous storage system administration can be implemented. This can be done either by virtualizing an external storage system or by network and server based management (an appliance sits on the network between the servers and storage systems). Independent management software, either server based or network based, can:

- Centralize administration and operation for a heterogeneous storage environment under a common management application

- Automate discovery and visualization of a storage infrastructure and network topology

- Analyze all path interdependencies between host servers and storage systems

- Track heterogeneous storage capacity usage so available capacity can be moved where it is needed most

- Integrate with leading enterprise applications to accurately measure storage usage by application when used with host based agents

- Offer modular design for easy integration with advanced storage functions, such as chargeback and storage resource management of file systems

Benefits of such management software include:

- Save both costs and IT resources required to manage multivendor storage networks

- Simplify heterogeneous storage administration by utilizing a common standard based management platform

- Ensure storage availability for mission critical business applications

- Identify underutilized capacity to defer additional storage investments

- Accelerate the deployment of advanced storage functionality without adding administration complexity

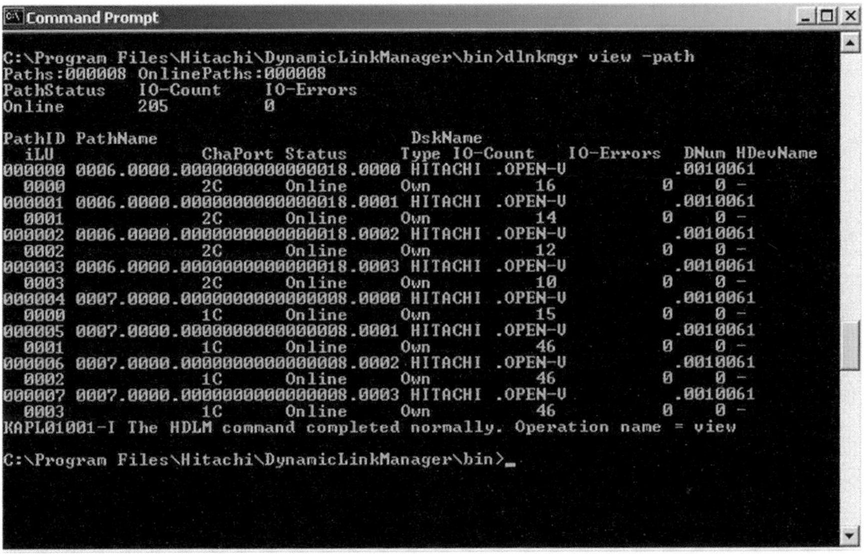

Figure 7.4 — Command line interface. An example of a Hitachi Dynamic Link Manager configuration. This software takes care of path management.

Integration of a new storage system

When purchasing new devices to be integrated into a SAN or LAN environment, the storage administrator must think through the whole implementation process, including the following items:

- The administrator must decide what kind of storage system and connection the solution requires. A traditional midrange or enterprise storage system would be integrated into the SAN.

- The administrator must make sure the existing Fibre Channel switches have enough ports to service the new device. If not, the Fibre Channel switches need to be upgraded.

- Since the whole technology uses optical wires, the cabling needs to be considered as well.

- Switches must be equipped with small form factor pluggable (SFP) transceivers.

- The vendor may supply a rack and rail kit for equipment installation, but this option might be more expensive than using an existing rack.

- The electricity infrastructure must meet the new device's power requirements.

- The server room's air conditioning may also require an upgrade.

- If a NAS device or a digital archive matches requirements on the new equipment better than a traditional storage system, the administrator must consider implementation of such a device within a LAN infrastructure.

Integration of a new device does not always have to be tricky and complicated, but it requires careful planning and design. The cost of training and maintenance need to be considered as well. TCO is a major factor in deciding which vendor to choose.

Effective allocation of resources and reporting

Effective allocation of resources and reporting is a major concern when you wish to provide a storage system as a service. Nowadays, many companies run large data centers focused primarily on data storage. These data centers are equipped with dozens or even hundreds of storage systems and digital archives. When you provide storage as a service, the effective allocation of resources is very important. Virtualization enables the administrator to create made-to-measure virtual storage systems that match customer requirements exactly. SLA contracts with the customer are usually very strict in terms of availability and prevention of data loss. Therefore, effective allocation of resources and their utilization can significantly affect profitability of the business.

Storage system management software allows exporting of various reports that can be very helpful when preparing SLA contracts. These reports are also an inevitable part of documentation required for auditing and compliance with ISO standards. The storage system administrator should be aware of this requirement and collect and manage reports regularly.

Security management

Part of the storage administrator's job is to make sure the data is stored securely. A SAN environment provides inherited security features, mainly because of its isolation from LANs requiring more complex security management. LUN mapping itself can be seen as a security feature because it links a LUN to a designated HBA (according to its WWN) through a selected front end port. Other servers cannot see this LUN. Zoning implemented on Fibre Channel switches is another common method of security enhancement. Zoning is described in detail in Chapter 3. It is also possible to use data encryption on the disk array, but this can affect its performance. In the case of NAS devices connected directly to a LAN, it is desirable to implement a virtual LAN (VLAN) policy. A LAN network can be partitioned into many VLANs. Devices from different VLANs cannot communicate with each other. Authentication services may be provided on a LAN network. An Active Directory Lightweight Directory Access Protocol (AD/LDAP) server is a typical example of this solution. This server verifies the identity of a user who attempts to access data stored on a secured device. In a LAN, other components can be implemented to prevent cyber-attacks from outside — well known hardware firewalls have this feature as a standard. To keep both LAN and SAN environments safe and secure, it is important to update all software and firmware regularly.

Tasks of a storage system implementer

The duties of a storage system implementer can be very different from those of a storage administrator. A storage administrator works in the organization that buys equipment, while the implementer works in an organization that sells equipment. Storage system administrators have limited access to information, while implementers have all the technical documentation at their disposal. This documentation includes maintenance manuals and best practice guidelines. The implementer is also allowed to attend partner trainings (because the company is a partner of a vendor). When a demand from a customer arises, the implementer in cooperation with the IT architect, IT consultant and pre-sales team helps to design the best solution for the customer. The implementer is certified and can perform the installation and initial configuration of a storage system. The storage system administrator cannot. The implementer has a deep knowledge of SAN environments and storage systems and, as a result, is more knowledge than a storage system administrator.

The implementer performs the installation of the equipment and the initial setup. The implementer also provides basic training to familiarize the customer with the new device. The storage implementer is author-ized to conduct all hardware replacement and upgrade procedures. If a disk or other component fails, it is the implementer who can replace the malfunctioning part. The implementer also monitors the storage system remotely and, in cooperation with a storage system administra-tor, helps with performance tuning and advanced operations. Microco-de updates are also the responsibility of a storage implementer.

This chapter provided you with a more practical insight into the du-ties and responsibilities of a storage system administrator. Remember that the storage system administrator is responsible for the whole SAN environment and should be able to configure Fibre Channel switches and server HBAs, as well as perform basic storage system operations. By basic operations we particularly mean the creation and configuration of volumes and their management. A storage system administrator also monitors the operation of a storage system to detect possible malfunc-tions or performance bottlenecks. The storage system administrator is the person responsible for data management, design and infrastructure upgrades that ensure data storage.

Performance tuning, optimization and storage consolidation

8

What are you going to learn in this chapter?

- How to determine whether a storage system is properly tuned for performance

- How to increase and optimize the performance of a storage system

- What tuning possibilities we have for individual components of a storage system

- What values are measured and how to interpret them

- Motivation and goals for consolidation

Motivation for performance tuning

When we purchase and implement a new storage system, the supplier should suggest a configuration that matches the requirements specified in the project documentation. From this perspective, everything works and there should be few items that require immediate attention. However, the amount of data our organization handles can grow quickly. The requirements on our IT infrastructure may change too. The characteristics of load can change in ways we might not anticipate. For example, a server previously under an average load of 30% must now handle more requests. When such situations occur, it is necessary to adjust our IT equipment to these new conditions. Regular monitoring and measurements should provide us with a large amount of input data that needs to be interpreted correctly and transformed into new specifications on the configuration of our storage system, SAN or servers.

We can try to adjust the configuration to match the new requirements. However, if we make the adjustments improperly, we may encounter many significant problems. Once we change the configuration, some LUNs may show degraded performance. The whole storage system may sporadically freeze for a second or two. Under high load, an application requires extreme storage system performance. Storage systems may not be able to handle such peak situations effectively. The application may then show problems that impact the end user.

All these issues can arise when we try to tune the storage system and fail or when our IT environment changes and we do nothing at all. Proper monitoring, performance management and storage system tuning are, therefore, vitally important. The storage system administrator, in cooperation with the supplier, needs to be able to deal with problems that stem from changes in the IT environment.

Introduction to performance tuning

The storage system administrator is responsible for proactive management, which includes performing regular monitoring of the systems and their components. There are several questions that can be answered with careful monitoring of resources:

- Which systems are underutilized?

- How much excess capacity is there?

- Which systems are overutilized or overallocated?

- What bottlenecks exist, and are they easily resolvable?

- Can I be automatically notified when warning thresholds are reached?

The major indicator of storage system performance is I/O response time. If we get a good response time for all I/O coming from all servers, then everything is working smoothly. When the I/O response time is longer than expected, we need to search for the source of the problem. Before we get to that, let's take a look at a typical online transaction. The I/O response time equals the time that is necessary for processing one online transaction.

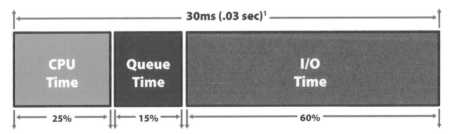

[1]This does not include network time (LAN or WAN)

Figure 8.1 — Typical online transaction processing. A single transaction requires a certain portion of CPU time. Then it queues and is processed further. At the end of the whole process, the transaction is concluded. In other words, the requested data or acknowledgment of a successful write operation is sent back to the host. Notice that the average time for processing a single transaction is 30ms. This does not include the time necessary for delivering data to its destination over the network.

When the I/O response time takes longer than it should, the storage administrator must determine where there is a problem. The simplest performance tuning is based on an even distribution of load over storage systems and their components. If one controller is overloaded, then the first option is to reassign the problematic volume to a different controller or to enable load balancing. The same counts for front end port traffic. When one port becomes overutilized, redirect the data traffic over a different port.

Storage system vendors offer software tools for performance tuning. These tools are designed to cooperate with the most often implemented applications and databases that run on the production servers. These tuning managers can analyze load characteristics and suggest changes in configuration. Modern storage systems allow nondisruptive performance tuning. When we change the storage system configuration, it usually does not happen quickly. For example, when we change the RAID level type, enable load balancing or change LUN characteristics, it takes time to implement these changes (especially because all stored data needs to be moved to a new location). Nondisruptive performance tuning is, therefore, a very important feature.

However helpful the tuning managers are, their area of application is usually limited to storage systems. The bottlenecks may occur on a SAN as well. The tuning managers provide only monitoring and are able to recommend changes in configuration. But in the end, it is always the storage system administrator who must decide which changes to implement and how. To complete this task, the storage system administrator must have the tools to measure the most important characteristics and the knowledge to use them. The administrator (or the storage system implementer, depending on vendor policies) must have tools for implementing a new, improved storage system configuration. The administrator must also be able to write scripts that can provide automation of the most common performance tuning tasks.

Monitoring, analysis of operations and performance tuning are all part of performance management. In performance management, we try to ensure efficient and optimized operation of our IT infrastructure. Monitoring provides us with important values and data. Monitoring is a continuous activity. For performance tuning, current performance values are of little use, as we need to collect performance data over a longer period of time — weeks and months. Performance analysis evaluates this data and provides us with clear information on whether all the components involved in data processing meet expected performance levels.

Performance tuning then implements data collected during the monitoring phase and data evaluated by performance analysis. The most common technique in performance tuning is represented by an even distribution of load over all components. Because the IT environment is changing, characteristics of load are changing as well. The storage system configuration must be adjusted to reflect these changes. The most common tasks in performance tuning include selection of the appropriate RAID level, LUN parameters, front end and back end port configuration, and configuration of individual data paths. Advanced performance tuning is connected with cache reconfiguration and the deployment of services such as automated tiering or wide striping.

What can be measured and what is the output?

Now it's time to get more technical. There are three major areas in our data infrastructure where we can perform measurements and get the performance data we need for analysis and evaluation. These three areas (as depicted in Figure 8.2) are:

- Hosts and HBA components (Section A)

- SAN infrastructure, especially switches and their ports (Section B)

- Storage systems and their components (Section C)

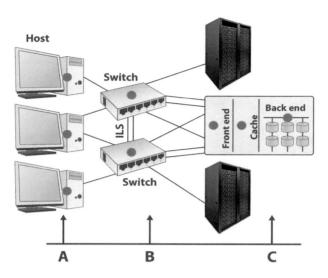

Figure 8.2 — This picture depicts all the locations where we can measure performance. Continu-ous monitoring of these locations provides us with data necessary for performance analysis.

In hosts (servers) we measure read/write response time of mapped storage volumes. The values we receive are in milliseconds. The response time measured in the hosts provides us with a value that includes both network time (time to transfer the I/O request over the network) and I/O transaction processing time in storage systems. In hosts, we also measure the throughput in HBA adaptors (MB/sec), the IOPS, and the disk queue and queue length. The throughput on HBA adaptors shows us the amount of data transferred from one particular host to the SAN. The IOPS shows us how many I/O operations the network and connected storage system can handle per second. The disk queue and queue length values show you how many pending requests are waiting for access to the storage system. These values should be as low as possible. If the disk queue length values are consistently high, it means the storage system is not able to process all the I/O requests without delay. The storage system resources must be reconfigured so that the disk queue length values drop to a low level.

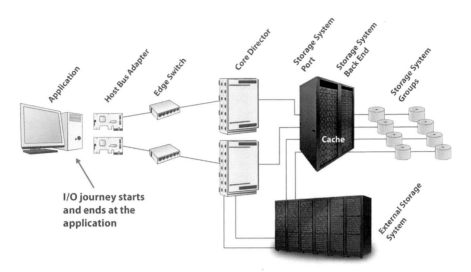

I/O journey starts
and ends at the
application

Figure 8.3 — The I/O journey starts and ends at the application. In the host we can measure the response time, including the sum of time required to process an I/O transaction in each device located in the data path. The response time measured in the host includes network time and storage system I/O transaction response time. This measurement can show you there is a problem with response time, but it does not tell you whether the problem is in the network or the storage system.

In a SAN we focus mainly on Fibre Channel switches. We can measure throughput on individual ports (MB/sec), buffer credits, cyclic redundancy check (CRC) errors and the operations of interswitch links.

The throughput measured on a particular Fibre Channel switch port provides us with the amount of data transferred from all hosts connected to this port. Remember that we connect all our hosts to Fibre Channel switches. These switches are also connected to our storage systems. Depending on your zoning and infrastructure architecture, the port linked to a storage system has to service several ports connected to the host. One Fibre Channel switch port can therefore aggregate traffic coming from several hosts.

As an example, imagine a situation where three hosts are linked to one front end port on a storage system. The throughput measured on the switch should correspond with the throughput measured in the HBA and the storage system's front end port. The Fibre Channel switches need to be configured so that they are able to handle the throughput. There need to be reserves in the available bandwidth to accommodate a peak load without delays or disruptions.

Buffer credit flow control is Fibre Channel switch functionality. Buffer credits represent the number of data frames a port can store. This is particularly useful for long distance Fibre Channel connections (for example, a Fibre Channel offsite connection for synchronous remote replication), where the response time is longer because there are limitations determined by the laws of physics (for example, the response time cannot be faster than the speed of light). If the network is under a high load and its bandwidth becomes insufficient, ports can store several data frames that then wait for processing. If a port cannot store more data frames, the host stops sending I/O requests until space is freed for more data frames. Buffer credit values can show us whether our network has any bottlenecks.

CRC and other error reporting mechanisms operate on the switch level. Their function is to ensure consistency of transmitted data. The switch communicates with the HBA and front end ports in a storage system and detects any possible loss of data frames. Data frame loss can occur mainly if there is a problem with cabling and connectors. If a data frame is lost during the transport, the host must repeat the I/O request, which causes delays. This type of error points to problems with the physical networking infrastructure. All cables and connectors should be checked.

Note that CRC errors are well known in CD and DVD media, as well as hard drives. In CD and DVD media, it usually means the surface of the disk is scratched and the data cannot be reconstructed, which results in missing blocks of data and inconsistency. In a hard drive, the CRC error occurs when the data is stored on a bad sector. This bad sector is then marked as damaged and no longer used for data storage.

An interswitch link is the connection between individual Fibre Channel switches. The status report shows us whether there are any problems with the connection between individual Fibre Channel switches.

In storage systems we have a number of possibilities regarding what and where to measure:

- Cache Write Pending Rate

  - This feature shows us cache is not able to handle all I/O requests efficiently.

  - You must reconfigure cache or upgrade cache capacity.

  - Problems are likely to occur when we have insufficient cache capacity for installed or virtualized capacity (external storage).

- Response time on front end ports

- Throughput on front end ports

- Usage of parity groups

- Back end — FC-AL or SAS operations

- CPU load and load of SAS controller counting parity data

All these values will be described later in this chapter together, with examples of best practices. In Figure 8.4 you can see an overview of performance data we can collect. We have mentioned the most important ones, but there are many more. This should give you an idea how complex performance tuning can be.

Storage Systems:
- Performance IOPS (read, write, total), MB/sec, history, forecast and real time monitor
- By all storage systems
- By port
- By processor
- By processor
- By LDEV
- Cache utilization
- By disk parity group
- By database instance, tablespace, index and more

SAN Switches:
- Bytes transmitted/received, frames transmitted/received by SAN, by switch, and by port
- CRC errors, link errors, buffer full/input buffer full and more

Servers:
- Server capacity/utilization/performance
- I/O performance — total MB/sec, queue lengths, read/write IOPS, I/O wait time
- File system — Space allocated, used, available
- Reads/writes, queue lengths
- Device file — performance and capacity
- CPU busy/wait, paging/swapping, process metrics, IPC Shared memory, semaphores, locks, threads and more
- NFS client detail and NFS Server detail
- HBA bytes transmitted/received

Applications:
- Oracle table space performance and capacity buffer pools, cache, data blocks read/write, tablespaces used, free and logs
- Microsoft SQL Server cache usage: current cache hit %/trends, page writes/sec, lazy writes per second, redo log I/O/second, network: packets sent/received
- DB2 table space performance and capacity buffer pools,
- cache, data blocks read/write, tablespaces used and free, and logs
- Exchange database, shared memory queue, information store, mailbox store, public store and Exchange Server processes

Figure 8.4 — An overview of performance data we can collect. Remember that, for performance analysis and evaluation, you need to collect data over time. Current values are of little use. The measurements should be performed regularly and data for performance analysis should include weeks or months of measurement in order to a get precise and helpful image of the utilization of individual resources.

When you collect all this data, you need to perform analysis. The analysis helps you investigate the tuning possibilities and suggest configuration changes. It should also help you formulate your long term performance strategy. Using reporting tools that operate on all the levels of your infrastructure — including hosts, Fibre Channel switches and storage systems — provides you with output data. To be able to interpret this data meaningfully, you must interpret the meaning of a value from one source in relation to values from the other sources. If you have a response I/O time value from a host, you need to interpret it in relation to the I/O response time measured in Fibre Channel switches and storage systems. To do this you need to analyze the mutual relationship of the values and their meaning, either manually or using specialized software. See Figure 8.5 for reference.

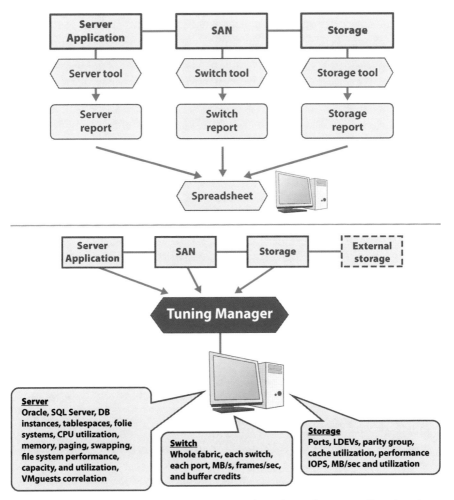

Figure 8.5 — You can analyze collected values and their relationships manually or by using a specialized software tool.

Performance tuning in midrange storage systems

In terms of traditional block level storage systems, we distinguish between midrange and enterprise class monolithic systems. Even though midrange storage systems boast enterprise level functionalities, their performance and configuration possibilities are still limited in comparison to enterprise class storage systems. Before we discuss the best practices for midrange tuning management, remember what a midrange storage system looks like: we have two controllers for redundancy, a limited number of front end Fibre Channel ports, limited number of hard drives that can be installed and relatively small cache. Detailed information on midrange storage system architecture can be found in Chapter 2.

The following examples of best practices in performance tuning are valid for the Hitachi Adaptable Modular Storage 2000 family. This midrange storage system will serve as an example. Note that performance tuning best practices for other midrange storage system from various vendors can differ slightly. In midrange storage systems, we have the following tuning possibilities:

Controller CPU — CPU utilization should be 75% on average. If utilization is higher than 75%, you need to consider whether it is possible to spread some load to the other controller or other storage system. Implementation of load balancing functionality can also help to solve this situation.

Cache Write Pending (CWP) — This value can show us whether our cache is working properly. The cache serves as a buffer that compensates for insufficient performance of physical hard drives. When the cache gets full, the data must be destaged from cache to individual disks. This happens asynchronously. When a host sends a write request, the storage system stores the data to be written on hard drives in cache and sends acknowledgment to the host, confirming successful write operations. This block is then destaged from cache to the hard drive. The cache does not send each write transaction immediately to the physical disks. Instead it waits until there are several write requests for the same destination on the physical disks and then sends all these write requests to the physical disks together. If the cache gets full and the physical hard drives have too many pending requests waiting to be destaged to disk to store all the data in cache, we have a few options for resolutions. We can upgrade the cache if possible, or we can employ cache partitioning, which assigns a portion of cache to the application causing the high load. These resolutions allow uninterrupted operations of other applications.

When a front end Fibre Channel port is overutilized, we can try to employ load balancing, or we can manually change paths to other LUNs so that all front end ports are utilized evenly.

When we take a look at a storage system's back end, the major focus that affects the performance of the whole system is on individual disks and parity groups. The utilization of a hard disk unit (HDU) should be less than 75%. If this limit is exceeded, there is more than a 75% chance of waiting on a physical I/O request to the back end array group. When we monitor HDU activity and discover a performance imbalance, we can try to:

- Spread the load to another RAID group

- Change the RAID level to one more appropriate for the workload

- Use faster disks

- Add more disks to the RAID group

- Move some of the load to the other storage system

The LUN response time is also monitored. In a Microsoft SQL Server environment, the LUN read response time for the database disk should be below 20ms on average, and spikes should not be higher than 50ms. The response time of a particular LUN can be evaluated as follows:

- Less than 10ms — very good

- Between 10ms and 20ms — okay

- Between 20ms and 50ms — slow, needs attention

- Greater than 50ms — serious I/O bottleneck

Enterprise storage performance basics

Compared to midrange storage systems, enterprise level systems are much more robust and powerful. They offer a significantly higher number of front end ports, extremely large cache and their back end architecture allows connection of many expansion units with hard drives. This robust architecture provides many more possibilities for performance tuning. Performance tuning in enterprise storage systems can be very complicated because of configuration complexity. Let's take a closer look at individual areas of an enterprise level storage system that are particularly interesting from the perspective of performance tuning:

- Response time factors

- Port utilization and throughput

- Cache utilization

Response time is affected by utilization of the particular front end Fibre Channel port, cache and individual parity groups. These are the hardware limitations. However, response time is also affected by load characteristics. It really depends on whether we are using applications that store data sequentially or applications that request random I/O. As we discussed previously, traditional enterprise storage systems work on the block level (as opposed to the file or object level). The size of blocks is also important. Let's look at the operations associated with enterprise level front end Fibre Channel ports in more detail.

Port load balancing is important and should be employed in an enterprise level storage system. A single physical front end Fibre Channel port is able to process thousands of I/O requests. It is also possible to create virtual front end ports to prioritize the traffic to certain hosts. Front end ports need time to process protocol instructions and virtual port operations; this process is known as *performance overhead*. In contemporary storage systems, the overhead associated with protocol time on a physical port is very low. It is currently calculated in microseconds, where it previously was calculated in milliseconds. The performance overhead still needs to be considered, especially when implementing a high number of virtual ports per physical port. Block size is critical for planning and analysis. A single Fibre Channel port can process thousands of I/O requests before reaching the saturation point. This point is reached faster in cases where the average block size is large (64K and higher). Performance problems would be seen when load balancing is not performed properly during configuration and/or capacity planning. Performance problems could occur if too many virtual ports are created on a single physical port or if there are too many active LUNs on the same physical ports. Front end port virtualization and port priority assignment are configured on the storage system level.

With port utilization and throughput optimization, you may still face a few problems. If you have a high number of IOPS with small blocks, the port capacity is saturated later than if you have a smaller number of IOPS with large blocks. However, a high number of IOPS with small blocks stresses the CPU and creates a performance bottleneck. You need to carefully plan how many hosts you will connect through a single Fibre Channel port, how many virtual ports you will use and what type of load the port will deal with. It is important to find a balance to avoid the problems connected with lack of performance.

Cache utilization is a key element for great I/O performance. Remember that you want to avoid CPU and hard drive utilization higher than 75%. In cache, you want to do the exact opposite. The more cache you utilize, the better. The cache utilization target is 90% or more. As for the cache sizing, remember that a larger cache is important, especially for random I/O. A large cache permits a frame to remain in cache longer, which increases the chance of a read hit. If you send the frequently used data into a storage system with a large cache, it can happen that this data remains in the cache until the server sends a request to read this particular data. In other words, if you have a large cache, frequently used data can stay there for repeated reading of data. A high read hit rate is desirable because the storage system can handle the read request much faster when the desired data is stored in cache than if this data has already been destaged to hard drives. You can imagine this as the highest tier — when frequently used data stays in cache, it can be accessed much faster than if it was stored on a hard disk or even a solid state disk. Note that by frequently accessed data we mean data that is accessed several times a minute. It is therefore a very small portion of data compared to the total capacity of a storage system.

When it comes to cache configuration, another thing to remember is that sequential workloads use smaller amounts of cache memory as compared to random workloads. The key to success, therefore, is in understanding how an application utilizes cache. Applications have different cache utilization characteristics.

Impact of cache size on performance

A positive impact will be seen using larger cache, especially on workloads that are predominantly random read/write activity. The larger the cache is, the longer a frame will stay in cache, thus increasing the chance of a read hit on the same frame. Sequential workloads use small amounts of cache memory and free cache segments as soon as the job is completed. As a result, cache sizing generally has little to no impact on sequential workloads.

The size of cache you should use, therefore, largely depends on how your application works. However, there are some basic rules for cache sizing. When you upgrade your infrastructure with a new storage system, you should use at least as much cache as the storage system being replaced. Increase cache proportionally to any increase in storage capacity. If you do not have any current performance data to start with, configure at least 1.5GB to 2GB of cache per TB of installed capacity. Start with the current hit rate if you know it. Remember the guideline that doubling cache size reduces the miss rate by half. For example, if your read hit rate is 80% with 16GB of cache, then doubling cache size to 32GB should improve hit rate to 90%.

The last thing you need to consider when configuring cache is what portion of cache will be used either for read or read/write operations. The correct settings of cache proportions help to achieve higher performance. If these settings are not correct, the write and read operations may perform more slowly than desired.

In addition to ports and cache, we can optimize LUN response time and parity group performance. The LUN response time characteristics and optimization are practically the same as in midrange storage systems and have been discussed earlier in this chapter. Parity group performance optimization is, again, similar to the midrange storage systems, so let's just look at a few of the most important tips:

- Treat every sequential I/O request as four random I/O requests for sizing purposes.

- Do not allocate more than four *hot* LUNs per parity group. The LUN is characterized as hot when its utilization reaches 70% or more.

- Do not allocate more than eight *medium hot* LUNs per parity group. The LUN is characterized as medium hot when its utilization ranges between 50% and 70%.

Remember that to tune your storage system to the highest possible performance, you need to consider not only the hardware capabilities and the evenness of the workload distribution, but also applications that access the storage system. You should know whether your applications access data sequentially or randomly. The data block size is also important.

Please refer to Figure 8.6 for a clear and straightforward enumeration of the most important performance tuning metrics.

Metric Name	Value Description	Normal Value	Bad Value
I/O rate	I/Os per second	N/A	N/A
Read rate	I/Os per second	N/A	N/A
Write rate	I/Os per second	N/A	N/A
Read block size	Bytes transferred per I/O operation	4096	N/A
Write block size	Bytes transferred per I/O operation	4096	N/A
Read response time	Time required to complete a read I/O (millisecond)	10 to 20 (DB) 2 to 5 (log)	>20 >5
Write response time	Time required to complete a write I/O (millisecond)	10 to 20 (DB) 5 to 10 (log)	>20 >10
Avarage queue length	Average number of disk requests queued for execution on one specific LUN	1 to 8 8 is the maximum queue depth value	>8
Read hit ratio	% of read I/Os satisfied from cache	25% to 50%	<25%
Write hit ratio	% of write I/Os satisfied from cache	100% (0% on Hitachi Virtual Storage Platform)	<100%
Average write pending	% of the cache used for write pending	1% to 35%	>35%

Figure 8.6 — Overview of metrics relevant to performance tuning and recommended normal and bad values.

Software for performance tuning and automated optimization

Tuning management software is a storage performance management application that maps, monitors and analyzes storage network resources from the application to the storage device. It provides end-to-end visibility you need to identify, isolate and diagnose performance bottlenecks with a focus on business applications, such as:

- Oracle
- Microsoft SQL Server

- Microsoft Exchange

- IBM® DB2®

This software correlates and analyzes storage resources with servers and applications to improve overall system performance. It continuously monitors comprehensive storage performance metrics to reduce delay or downtime caused by performance issues. It facilitates root cause analysis to enable administrators to efficiently identify and isolate performance bottlenecks. It allows users to configure alerts for early notification when performance or capacity thresholds have been exceeded. In addition, it forecasts future storage capacity and performance requirements to minimize unnecessary infrastructure purchases.

Among other features of advanced tuning management software, we can find tools that provide in-depth performance statistics of storage systems and all network resources on the application's data path. It works together with storage functionalities such as thin provisioning or automated tiering pools for usage analysis and optimization.

This software provides customizable storage performance reports and alerts for different audiences and reporting needs.

When we implement such software, we can benefit from:

- Simplification of performance reporting and management of the storage environment

- Improvement of service quality through accurate performance reporting

- Increased application availability through rapid problem identification and isolation

- Reduction of storage costs through proper forecasting and planning of required storage resources

Automation of performance tuning is usually available only on enterprise level storage systems. Prerequisites for such automation are implementation of thin provisioning and automated tiering. Some storage systems have utilities for performance monitoring and tuning inbuilt in the microcode.

Good tuning management software focuses not only on storage systems but also on the SAN and hosts. It can happen that we look for problems in the storage systems when the problems are actually caused by incorrect application settings.

Consolidation — when and why?

The issues companies face nowadays are mostly connected with a heterogeneous IT infrastructure and the complexity of its management. The consolidation should address these issues and bring us to a lower TCO. The consolidation provides a long term effect; while we do not save money immediately after the consolidation of an IT infrastructure, we will see savings in the following years. The target of consolidation is to:

- Centralize and simplify management
- Save electricity and space
- Reduce complexity and heterogeneity of IT environment
- Reduce number of personnel that perform administration and maintenance
- Save money on licensing, as well as personnel training and certification
- Unify and standardize hardware platforms and hardware operations

The means that allow consolidation include blade servers, server virtualization, modern storage systems with lower electricity consumption, storage system virtualization, outsourcing to large data centers and cloud computing. Effective equipment utilization, which is connected with performance tuning, also helps to lower the costs.

We should consolidate our IT infrastructure when we detect increasing costs related to storage system operations and maintenance. We consolidate servers, network devices, storage systems and applications.

Consolidation project

When we realize that our company is spending too much money on IT infrastructure operations, we should take action. The consolidation starts with a consolidation project, which can be divided into four stages. To illustrate how a consolidation project looks and what it should include, we will use consolidation of servers and storage systems as an example situation. The stages of a consolidation project are:

- Analysis of the current IT infrastructure state

- Development of consolidation plan

- Migration to new consolidated platform

- Optimization of the new solution

The first step is to analyze the current IT infrastructure state. To do so, you need to write down all your hardware and software resources. Among hardware resources there are servers, networking components, storage systems and workstations. Software resources include operating systems and applications. When you complete this list, you need to focus on how all these resources work together and what performance they deliver. You need extensive, detailed information on how your hardware resources are implemented, interconnected and secured. As for the software resources, you need to know the versions of the operating systems and applications are being used, a history of updates and patches, and a detailed licensing analysis. You could use performance reports together with the performance monitoring history. Bills for electricity and personnel training may come in handy as well.

Essentially, we can say that the first stage of consolidation, the analysis stage, focuses on three levels: technical, financial and performance statistics. You can see that there are plenty of factors that need to be considered. Because of the consolidation project's complexity, it is not something that can be completed overnight. It can take up to several months and the efforts of both IT management and IT administrators.

In the second stage of IT infrastructure consolidation, we take the output of the analysis we made in the first stage and suggest a solution. There are many strategies on how to do this, but the key is to have comprehensive knowledge of the products available on the market that could help in consolidation. We also need to calculate operating expense savings to prove the profitability of the new solution. Nowadays, most consolidation projects include migration to blade servers and virtualization. Virtualization in servers is usually much simpler and cheaper to implement than virtualization of storage systems.

The third stage is the migration to a new consolidated platform. To perform a seamless migration, we should stick to the well known Information Technology Infrastructure Library® (ITIL®) methodology. Migration can be physical to virtual (P2V). Virtual to virtual (V2V) migration is an option when we are talking about consolidation in an environment that has already been virtualized.

Once we have migrated to the new solution, the last stage takes place. We perform regular monitoring to determine whether the expected results of consolidation have been reached.

In this chapter, you learned performance tuning basics. You are now familiar with basic performance metrics. You know where in your IT equipment you can make performance measurements, and you are able to interpret the output of these measurements. We have also discussed what software tools you can use for performance tuning and what these tools usually offer. Remember that the values presented in this chapter represent general information. Recommended performance values for your storage system can differ from what is mentioned here. Please refer to the documentation that was supplied with your storage system for more detail.

Business challenges

9

What are you going to learn in this chapter?

- How to see a storage systems infrastructure from the perspective of IT managers
- What business challenges companies face
- How to accommodate accelerating data growth
- How to describe advanced data classification and tiered storage
- Environmental concerns connected with data center operations
- The importance of TCO, CAPEX and OPEX calculations

Business challenges

Previous chapters of this book dealt mostly with the technical aspects of storage systems and SANs. You also gained insight into storage system administration and maintenance. In this final chapter, we will provide you with yet another perspective on storage systems. We will show you what challenges companies face today and what solutions help IT managers meet these challenges. This chapter will therefore be particularly useful to IT managers. The data provided in this chapter originated from complex research conducted by Hitachi Data Systems on its customers. You will learn what the most painful issues are and the options we have to overcome them. You will also be introduced to some functionalities of storage systems that are designed to be environmentally friendly.

At the beginning, it's necessary to realize that different companies have different needs and they encounter different challenges. Your organization may face extremely fast data growth and need more and more capacity to accommodate such growth. Another possibility is that your organization does not suffer from a lack of storage capacity, but instead has serious problems with high availability — this happens when your data becomes so important that you cannot afford any disruptions. You may also have problems with a lack of physical space to place new racks, insufficient cooling systems unable to service newly integrated devices and other issues. As a result, we will need some clear classification of business challenges to avoid getting lost in the myriad of possibilities. We can classify the challenges as follows:

- **Accelerating storage growth** — need more and more capacity

- **Increasing requirements on high availability** — cannot afford any disruptions because our data has become too important for our business

- **Fast and effective response to business growth** — need to be able react quickly to new conditions

- **Heterogeneous infrastructure** — result of fast infrastructure growth, which was not properly planned, causing TCO to increase rapidly

- **Compliance and security challenges** — need to process, protect and retain data according to legal requirements and regulations

- **Power and cooling challenges** — pay too much for electricity and cooling and may be running out of space in the server room

- **Data center challenges** — specific needs for those whose business is focused primarily on cloud type provision of storage and computing capacity

In the following subsections of this book, we will address each issue.

Data growth forecast

To be able to keep up with the storage capacity requirements, you need to perform data growth analysis and implement capacity management. You need to gather information about capacity requirements of all the applications and users, and forecast how these requirements will grow in the horizon of the next months and years. To be able to forecast storage capacity for the future, you need to analyze and evaluate data from the past. To make a prediction, you need to know whether the data growth has been linear or geometrical. You need to have clear statistics on capacity requirements for storage tiers as well. The demand for high performance data storage can grow more quickly than the demand for low performance storage, or vice versa. You also need to consider requirements on RAID protection and data replication because data must be stored in several copies for redundancy and other purposes.

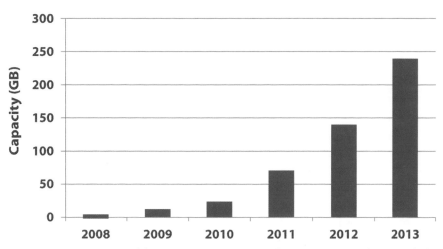

Figure 9.1 — An overview of the storage requirements in the past years provide you with the necessary information to forecast data growth.

The demand for storage capacity can be linear. If your storage infrastructure has not been consolidated yet, it can happen that the amount of stored data drops once you centralize and consolidate your storage. During consolidation, you also classify data and implement tiering. A portion of your data can be archived to tapes, freeing space for live data. Linear data growth is represented by a straight line in a graph. If the growth is linear, you can forecast growth easily.

However, more often, the demand for storage capacity is geometrical, meaning the amount of data coming into existence is growing exponentially. Exponential growth is often caused by an increase of unstructured data, large quantities of metadata or an increased demand for in-system replication, where S-VOLs are used by data mining or warehousing applications.

> **Let's take a look at some example data growth forecasts:**
>
> **Linear growth** — our analysis showed that each year the amount of stored data increased by 30TB. In the horizon of five years, we will need 150TB of capacity.
>
> **Geometrical (exponential) growth** — our analysis showed that each year the amount of stored data increased by 120% compared to the previous year. The growth is depicted as a curve on the graph.

To achieve economical utilization of all resources, we also need to anticipate what kind of data will grow in what amount. Structured data and unstructured data have different hardware requirements. Structured data, represented mainly by databases, should be stored on a suitable storage system. Traditional block level storage systems offer high performance in processing transaction based data. Conversely, unstructured data (such as pictures and PDF files), are best processed and organized by NAS devices and digital archives. We need to anticipate how we will grow both structured and unstructured data to plan development of our storage systems accordingly. For example, if we know the amount of unstructured data will grow much more quickly than the amount of structured data, we can plan a capacity and performance upgrade in the NAS device or digital archive.

We also need to perform an analysis of tier utilization to learn what data requires what performance. Depending on our analysis, we may learn that data saved on high performance tiers will grow much more quickly than data stored on low performance tiers, or vice versa. See Figure 9.2 and Figure 9.3 for reference.

Data growth forecast — tier view

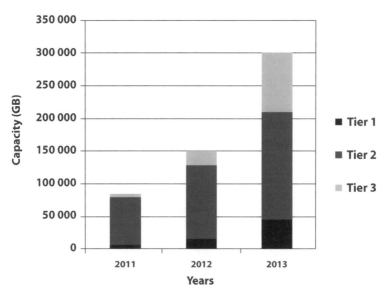

Figure 9.2 — Data growth forecast in relation to performance tiers.

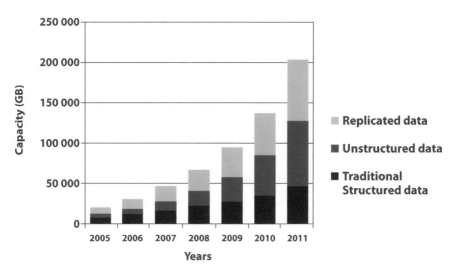

Figure 9.3 — Structured, unstructured and replicated data growth.

Advanced data classification and tiering

In Chapter 5, we discussed the automated tiering functionality, which is offered in modern enterprise level storage systems. Automated tiering uses a virtualized storage pool, which is spread across several tiers. One example would be parity groups using hard drives with different performance and price characteristics. The storage system then stores data automatically on individual tiers according to the frequency of access. This functionality offers great performance and allows you to achieve high utilization of expensive resources. However, to economically use all your storage resources, you need to design and implement tiered storage systems that distribute data to individual tiers according to many criteria — not only frequency of access. Tiered storage (not to be confused with automated tiering functionality) represents the whole infrastructure of storage systems, where all resources are effectively utilized and where data is stored on hard drives according to its requirement on availability, security and performance. See Figure 9.4 for reference.

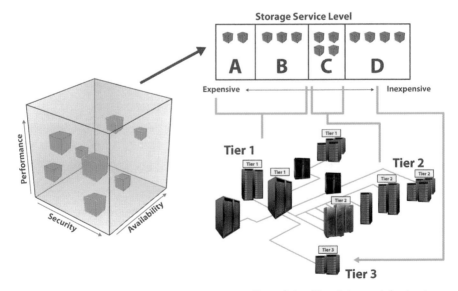

Figure 9.4 — Tiered storage infrastructure.

Implementation of a tiered storage infrastructure is a very powerful solution, which can offer many benefits, especially in terms of TCO. Implementation of a tiered storage infrastructure would, however, be useless without careful classification of data. This is the task of IT managers who are responsible for IT infrastructure design, development and maintenance, including a SAN. Data classification is primarily a manual process that cannot be fully automated. It is the IT manager who has to discover and evaluate information assets and determine whether or not this information has worth for your business. Data classification is, therefore, not only based on frequency of access, but also on data value. For reference, visit the Storage Networking Industry Association (SNIA) Data Management Forum at www.snia.org. SNIA defines information classes in the following categories:

- Mission-critical

- Business vital

- Business important

- Important productive

- Not important

- Discard

At this point, it's good to realize that we also need to determine what kind of data can be deleted. Companies and their employees are reluctant to erase data, but there should be certain policies governing data shredding as well. These should be included in the information lifecycle planning. To assign data to one of the above mentioned categories, we can use various metrics:

- Usage pattern of the information — frequent, regular, periodic, occasional, rare, on demand or request, or never

- Information availability requirement — immediate, reasonable, defined time frame, extended time frames, limited, not defined or unnecessary

- Financial impact of information unavailability — significant long-term and/or short-term, potential long-term, possible, unlikely or none

- Operational impact of information unavailability — significant and immediate, significant over time, probable over time, possible over time, doubtful or none

- Compliance impact of information unavailability — definite and significant, eventual, probable, potential or possible, or none expected

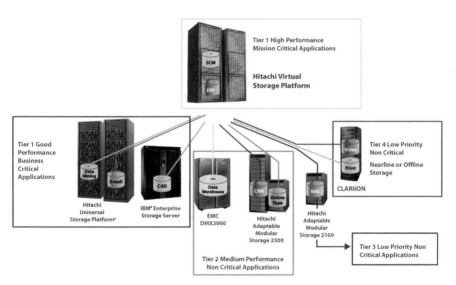

Figure 9.5 — Overview of virtualized multitiered storage infrastructure with implemented data classification.

As you can see, plenty of criteria should be considered. Assessing data importance and classification, together with maintaining policies in this respect, is time consuming and resource intensive. For this reason, IT managers often neglect data classification and avoid implementing a multitiered storage approach, but this decision results in unnecessarily high TCO.

Data classification is the responsibility of IT managers, and it results in the division of data among data groups that require specific handling. Each company can use different data classification procedures. The goal is to assess the value of information for a particular business. According to the data groups, we define Storage Service Levels (SSL). SSLs contain detailed information about hardware resources. New equipment is purchased in accordance with SSLs.

Data classification is a prerequisite to implementation of multitiered storage infrastructure. As you can see in Figure 9.4 and Figure 9.5, a multitiered storage infrastructure represents a whole solution that includes implementation of different kinds of storage systems. In a multitiered storage infrastructure, we can have enterprise level storage systems, midrange storage systems, NAS devices, digital archives and tape libraries.

A multitiered storage infrastructure is a powerful and complex solution. Implementation of this solution can be the result of storage infrastructure consolidation.

A multitiered storage infrastructure is different from automated storage tiering because it considers various criteria, not only frequency of access. Virtualization and thin provisioning are often part of capacity and tier management.

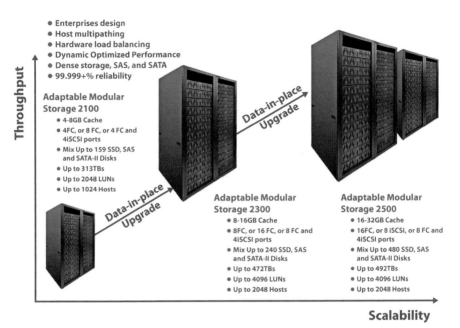

Figure 9.6 — *Not all organization are big enough to implement a multitiered storage infra-structure. For small and midsized organizations and companies, there are modular storage systems designed to meet their needs. In this picture, you can see the Hitachi Adaptable Modular Storage 2000 family and its scalability. This scalability and the possibility of easy upgrades are important features that should be considered when designing a storage system infrastructure.*

High availability challenges

When your data becomes so important that your business cannot have any service disruption, your major concerns are protection against data loss and business operation continuity.

The solution can be found in the advanced replication and backup functionalities offered in enterprise level storage systems. Modern enterprise level storage systems offer unified out-of-region data protection that ensures the availability of up-to-date data replicas. To deliver the best protection available, you can implement three data center multitarget replication. Please refer to Chapter 4 for more details. The benefits of such a solution lie in fast data synchronization with long distance recoverability and in reduced storage cost by dynamically provisioning pools at backup sites.

The universal replication feature, which is available in modern enterprise storage systems, supports synchronous and asynchronous replication for both internal and external virtualized storage. A single replication framework for all externally attached arrays by different vendors represents a powerful solution that can effectively address all issues connected with high availability clustering. There is no requirement to implement multiple, disparate business continuity solutions across each array. This significantly minimizes costs, reduces infrastructure and simplifies disaster recovery management and implementation. This single framework approach to managing business continuity also eases IT manager concerns related to having a consistent, repeatable, enterprise wide disaster recovery process.

Virtualization of external storage also simplifies backup solutions since the backup infrastructure only needs to be zoned to one storage system, no matter how many different physical storage systems are virtualized behind it. This simplifies the overall management of the entire centralized backup infrastructure.

Fast and cost-effective response to business growth

The response time to meet business needs for additional storage and the cost of provisioning for unplanned data storage are business challenges as well. When our capacity planning fails and we unexpectedly need to purchase more capacity, we realize this problem can be very painful.

We can solve this issue by implementing thin provisioning, which speeds the availability of additional storage and reduces the risk of having insufficient storage. Benefits of thin provisioning include improvement of access to information, increased productivity and risk mitigation and elimination of costs associated with not meeting fast changing business needs.

Thin provisioning functionality is available both on internal and external virtualized storage. It uses storage pools and virtual volumes. Through thin provisioning, the storage system administrator can assign virtual capacity to hosts even though the physical capacity is not yet installed. Virtual volumes are mapped to servers and capacity is provided by storage pools. The storage system monitors storage pool usage continuously and sends alerts to the administrator when it is necessary to install more physical capacity. The important feature is that capacity expansion can be done nondisruptively.

Load balancing and active-active architecture maximize performance without allowing the actions of one set of users to affect the quality of service of others, thus, readily accommodating new classes of users and applications.

Nondisruptive data migration capabilities are also critical. In-system replication able to create volume clones across externally connected storage systems ensures data migration is as simple as it can be. When you create a volume clone, you do not encounter decreased performance or service disruption.

Compliance and security challenges

With new regulations and legal requirements on data processing, protection and retention, companies are struggling to comply and cut risks. A solution that addresses these challenges should be capable of blocking unauthorized access and protecting data with no performance impact.

As high profile data indiscretions continue, the response is tighter data security regulations to control sensitive information. Increasingly, these regulations are being enforced to protect sensitive data, and the risks associated with noncompliance to these tough regulations are significant. Organizations and companies are employing all prudent measures at their disposal. The storage level data encryption feature is one such measure.

Modern high-end storage systems are available with a controller based data-at-rest encryption option compatible with both open and mainframe systems. This encryption can be used to encrypt the internal drives, using strong encryption (AES-256). In modern powerful storage systems, this encryption introduces absolutely no throughput or latency impact for data I/O. The feature also includes an integrated key management functionality, which is both simple and safe.

Beyond the cryptographic characteristics, the data-at-rest encryption feature can be used to introduce encryption within a storage ecosystem with little to no disruption to the existing applications, infrastructure or network.

This feature has the added benefits of being data center friendly because it uses very little additional power (approximately the equivalent of a 25W lightbulb for 1PB of data), produces negligible amounts of additional heat and requires no additional rack space. Other benefits include reduced complexity and decreased encryption cost.

Power requirements and cooling

As requirements for more and more storage space rise, IT managers are increasingly worried about the cost of electricity and cooling. Nowadays, costs related to electricity consumption and cooling requirements are among the top three issues.

What is the greatest facility problem with your primary data center?

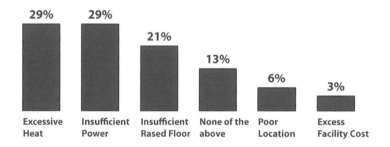

29%	29%	21%	13%	6%	3%
Excessive Heat	Insufficient Power	Insufficient Rased Floor	None of the above	Poor Location	Excess Facility Cost

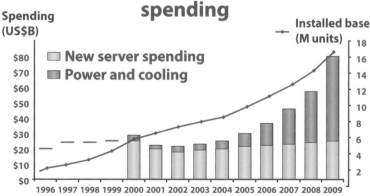

Figure 9.7 — Greatest issues organizations and companies face.

Electricity and cooling costs are not the only motivation for reducing power consumption and implementing electricity saving features. The onset of global warming is expected to increase the demand on existing cooling systems, leading to costly investments in new plants. More efficient use of an existing storage infrastructure can reduce the demand for new storage, ease the demand for power and cooling and enable a business to reduce costs and address its green obligations. Some of the challenges facing data centers in respect to electricity, cooling and environmental requirements include:

- Running out of power, cooling and space

- Growing energy costs

- Increasing regulatory compliance issues

- Data center expansion without consideration for future power and cooling requirements

- Data storage configured without adequate consideration to heat distribution (equipment racks should be installed with cold rows and hot rows — this will be discussed later in this chapter)

- Difficulty relieving data center hot spots without disrupting applications

The solution capable of addressing these issues should provide features that lead to cost-effective and energy efficient management and operation of storage systems. It should also provide the ability to extend the life of existing storage assets.

When you design a storage infrastructure, you need to analyze the power and cooling requirements as well as the requirements on the space in your server room. In addition to power consumption metrics in kW, there are other metrics that should be considered:

- Total five-year power and space costs

- Heat loading (kW/sq ft)

- Space requirements (sq ft)

- Floor loading (lbs/sq ft)

Aside from these metrics, you should look for a vendor that designs, manufactures and supports environmentally friendly storage infrastructures throughout their entire lifecycle — including end-of-life disposal. You should also keep in mind that innovations such as controller-based virtualization and thin provisioning yield substantial environmental advantages because they reduce the need for storage capacity.

Virtualization and consolidation of hardware platforms are the key to reduced power and cooling costs. Without virtualization, data centers may be stuck with existing physical configurations leading to an increased need for cooling. Virtualization strategies must embrace as much of the storage infrastructure as possible to optimize utilization and save on power and cooling. Virtualization must be easy to manage through one common user interface, technology and application.

Consolidation is important because disparate storage is inefficient. Assets are typically underutilized, unnecessarily consuming power, cooling and space resources. Planning future storage capacity and performance avoids hitting any limitations that would impact the environmental savings model.

HDD and fan power savings

Thin provisioning and virtualization are advanced features that affect the management and operations of a whole storage infrastructure. Their implementation is reflected in lower TCO. However, there are features that work on the HDD and fan level and lead to significant power savings.

Modern storage systems, both modular and enterprise are in most cases able to spin down drives in selected RAID groups. When properly configured, SATA drives will park heads when idle for more than 2hrs. Modern storage systems must also constantly assess cooling requirements and dynamically adjust fan speeds to maintain correct temperatures.

It would be useless to implement a spin down feature on RAID groups that are highly utilized (production volumes used by transaction based applications). However, there are disk functions eligible for spin down solutions. These include:

- Mirrored drive groups involved in backup to tape

- Virtual tape library drive groups involved in backups

- Local (internal) backup copies of data

- Drive groups within archive storage

- Unused drive groups

The capability to turn off hard drives after they are not accessed for 2hrs can increase power savings by 23%. This functionality is often implemented together with smart algorithms that minimize HDD usage. These algorithms ensure that sequential writes and reads are done in massive batches. Data to be written to a particular hard drive is kept in cache as long as possible. Imagine that within a few hours there are only four write requests for that particular hard drive. The algorithm ensures these four write requests are sent to the hard drive in a batch instead of accessing the hard drive four times.

The storage system controller also varies the fan speed to the internal temperatures to reduce power requirements for fan operation.

Green data center

An environmentally aware data center that meets requirements on performance, capacity and high availability, all while remaining eco friendly and power efficient, is now possible. In 2009, this ideal data center was built and began its operations. See Figure 9.8 for reference.

Applies principles from Eco friendy Data Center Project and IT Power Saving Plan

- Location: Yokohama
- Operation: 2009
- Dimension: 10,000m²
- Power Usage
  effectiveness rating: 1.6

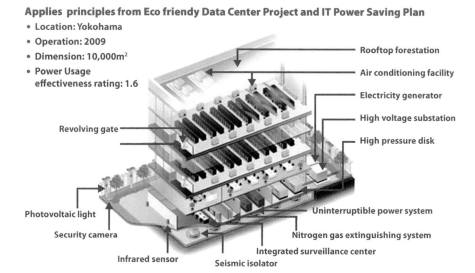

Figure 9.8 — Environmentally friendly and energy efficient data center.

In large data centers, racks with storage systems and servers are placed in rows. Modern storage systems are designed for such positioning. The goal is clever distribution of heat by managing air flow. As a result, you get hot rows and cold rows. In simple words, you arrange racks in alternating rows with cold air intakes facing one way and hot air exhausts facing the other. Typically, the front side of a storage system is designed to face the cold row, where cold air is distributed from the air conditioner. The rear side of a storage system is then pouring heated exhausts into hot rows. Typically, hot rows face air conditioner return ducts, which take the hot air away.

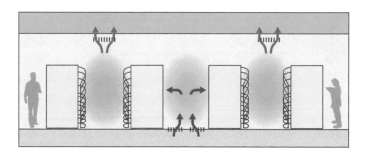

Figure 9.9 — The concept of hot and cold rows.

Total cost of ownership

Throughout the book, we have encountered the term Total Cost of Ownership (TCO) many times, and we have explained it briefly. You learned that the initial cost of a new storage system or server is only the beginning of a long succession of other related costs. TCO is, therefore, a focus for all IT managers and provides the basis for the storage economics field. Each IT manager needs to carefully calculate TCO for each device to decide whether it is an economical purchase. Vendors often use TCO values in their marketing to persuade companies to buy their products. At this point, it is good to take a closer look at TCO and list all the items that constitute it. TCO includes all costs related to a particular device throughout its lifecycle — from the purchase to end-of-life disposal. TCO is important for budgeting IT resources and for decision making related to old technology replacement.

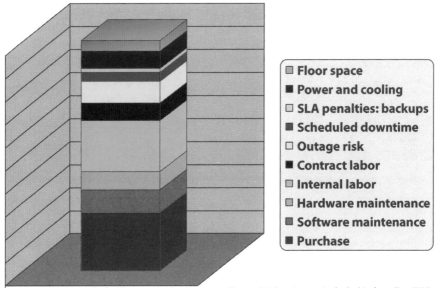

- ☐ Floor space
- ■ Power and cooling
- ☐ SLA penalties: backups
- ■ Scheduled downtime
- ☐ Outage risk
- ■ Contract labor
- ☐ Internal labor
- ☐ Hardware maintenance
- ■ Software maintenance
- ■ Purchase

Figure 9.10 — Items included in baseline TCO.

Throughout this chapter, we have discussed many business challenges. Most of the challenges presented are related to TCO, and most of the solutions presented help to lower TCO.

> Common TCO items include hardware acquisition costs, hardware maintenance, software licensing costs, software maintenance, storage management labor, backup, migration and remastering, power and cooling costs, floor space, and SAN resources.

In addition to considering TCO, an IT manager must consider distribution of costs over time, such as the costs at purchase, the costs after one year and the costs after five years. These expenses are calculated through two other values — capital expenditure (CAPEX) and operational expenditure (OPEX). CAPEX represents mostly the initial purchase and the investments into technology. In other words, CAPEX is how much you have to spend to get new equipment, licenses and personnel. OPEX represents the costs for maintenance, electricity and cooling.

CAPEX can be lowered by implementing functionalities such as thin provisioning and zero page reclamation. OPEX can be lowered by virtualization and consolidation of infrastructure through higher utilization of hardware resources.

The motto for lowering TCO, CAPEX and OPEX can be best described as: "Reduce costs by implementing technology!" By now you have learned that virtualizing and consolidating storage infrastructure can result in major cost savings. Implementing data tiers is also very important. All these factors represent major investments, but when properly calculated, they will pay you back through long term cost savings. Companies are often reluctant to invest large quantities of money into storage infrastructure, but the financial figures are clear — it is not efficient to maintain old technology that is no longer supported. From a long-term perspective, it is always best to keep your hardware up to date.

Self-assessment test

1. In the context of storage systems, a volume is a:

    a) Logical interface used by an operating system to access data stored on a particular medium

    b) Physical hard drive

    c) Record containing information on partitioning of the disk

    d) Unique identification number of a partition

2. In a disk array, data striping is a functionality that is:

    a) Controller based and ensures the data is mirrored to two disks

    b) Controller based; the controller distributes data over several physical hard drives to enhance storage system performance

    c) Server based; the file system distributes data into stripes according to frequency of access

    d) Controller based and ensures the organization of data in the storage system's cache

3. The RAID functionality is important because it:

    a) Provides economical storage of data on hard drives

    b) Allows to create several logical disks over a single physical hard drive

    c) Redundancy feature that prevents data loss in case one physical hard drive fails

    d) Access data stored on hard drives through TCP/IP protocol

4. **The most important components of a midrange storage system are:**

   a) Controller, switch and expansion units with hard drives

   b) CPU, hard drives and RAID controller

   c) Four controllers for redundancy, cache and SAS back end

   d) Front end ports, cache, back end and hard drives

5. **To connect a server to a SAN, we need:**

   a) HBA installed in the server, Fibre Channel cable and Fibre Channel switch with available ports

   b) Twisted pair cable with RJ45 connector

   c) To configure storage system and register server WWN

   d) Fibre Channel switch

6. **The implementation of zoning in SAN environment helps to:**

   a) Ensure QoS for I/O operations

   b) Secure SAN network

   c) Distribute load evenly over two or more data paths in SAN

   d) Interconnect two Fibre Channel switches

7. The main difference between a SAN and NAS is that:

    a) NAS works on the block level with a TCP/IP connection, while a SAN works on the file level with a Fibre Channel connection

    b) NAS works on the file level with a TCP/IP connection, while a SAN works on the block level with a Fibre Channel connection

    c) NAS works on the file level with a Fibre Channel connection, while a SAN works on the block level with a TCP/IP connection

    d) NAS works on the block level with a Fibre Channel connection, while SAN works on the file level with a TCP/IP connection

8. The purpose of business continuity planning is to:

    a) Minimize the negative impact of anticipated threats on a business process

    b) Create a disaster recovery plan with step by step instructions for recovery

    c) Optimize the total cost of ownership

    d) Describe remote replication requirements

9. A backup strategy to support 99.999% availability includes implementation of:

    a) Advanced backup on tape libraries

    b) Snapshots, in-system replication and offsite tapes

    c) Remote replication and geoclusters

    d) RAID 6, which prevents data loss in the event of failure of two physical hard drives

10. **Implementation of thin provisioning allows us to:**

   a) Share LUNs among several servers

   b) Access the hard drive over iSCSI

   c) Access data stored on S-VOLs (secondary volumes of a replication pair)

   d) Allocate more disk space than is actually installed in a storage system

11. **Storage virtualization:**

   a) Enables you to view an entire SAN as one storage pool independent of physical location

   b) Allows you to allocate more disk space on a single storage system

   c) Creates LUNs that can be mapped to virtualized servers

   d) Automatically stores frequently accessed data on the fastest hard drives

12. **The difference between data archiving and backup is:**

   a) Archiving requires more storage space than backup

   b) Archives are designed to ensure integrity and retention of fixed content, while backup creates copies of data for recovery

   c) Backup provides faster recovery, while recovery from an archive can take days or weeks

   d) There is no difference; data archiving is part of the backup strategy

13. **Fixed content is defined as:**

    a) Files that can be effectively compressed and deduplicated

    b) Infrequently accessed data stored on inexpensive and low performance storage

    c) Data that could not (or at least should not) be modified or altered

    d) Data that complies with legal regulations and requirements

14. **To ensure that the stored data has not been modified, the digital archive:**

    a) Periodically checks whether the stored data still matches its cryptographic hash value

    b) Performs a pair split operation, which disconnects the volume from production severs

    c) Uses password protected file access and encryption

    d) Needs to be regularly audited by an external auditing company

15. **The desirable value of a LUN read response time is:**

    a) Less than 65%

    b) Less than 20ms

    c) More than 100ms

    d) At least 4Gb/sec

16. In the context of storage systems, we have several classification categories. We can classify data according to:

   a) Data source, data author and requirements on data security

   b) Its importance, performance and availability requirements

   c) Amount of stored data

   d) Media used for data storage

17. Automated tiering is implemented because it:

   a) Allows storage system scalability and upgrade

   b) Ensures the best utilization of installed hard drives by automatically storing frequently used data on the most efficient and powerful hard drives

   c) Allows consolidation and centralized management of a heterogeneous IT environment

   d) Monitors storage system performance

18. Enterprise level storage system implementation helps us when we need to:

   a) Ensure high performance for more than five servers

   b) Use enormous disk space for video processing

   c) Consolidate management of several midrange storage systems from different vendors

   d) Employ remote replication and ensure high availability

19. We can ensure economical operations and high utilization by:

a) Replacing old storage systems with new storage systems equipped with large hard drives

b) Implementing virtualization both in servers and storage systems

c) Replacing all hard drives with modern solid state disks

d) Implementing modern racks and air conditioning

20. Which of the following items is NOT included in TCO calculation?

a) Insurance of the hardware

b) Hardware acquisition costs

c) Floor space

d) Software licensing costs

Glossary

A

AaaS — Archive as a Service. A cloud computing business model.

Actuator (arm) — Read/write heads are attached to a single head actuator, or actuator arm, that moves the heads around the platters.

AD — Active Directory

Address — A location of data, usually in main memory or on a disk. A name or token that identifies a network component. In local area networks (LANs), for example, every node has a unique address.

AL — Arbitrated Loop. A network in which nodes contend to send data, and only one node at a time is able to send data.

AL-PA — Arbitrated Loop Physical Address

AMS — Adaptable Modular Storage

API — Application Programming Interface

Application Management — The processes that manage the capacity and performance of applications

Array Group — Also called a parity group, is a group of hard disk drives (HDDs) that form the basic unit of storage in a subsystem. All HDDs in a parity group must have the same physical capacity.

Array Unit — A group of hard disk drives in one RAID structure. Same as parity group.

ASSY — Assembly

Asymmetric virtualization — See Out-of-band virtualization.

Asynchronous — An I/O operation whose initiator does not await its completion before proceeding with other work. Asynchronous I/O operations enable an initiator to have multiple concurrent I/O operations in progress. Also called Out-of-band virtualization.

ATA — Advanced Technology Attachment. A disk drive implementation that integrates the controller on the disk drive itself. Also known as IDE (Integrated Drive Electronics) Advanced Technology Attachment.

Authentication — The process of identifying an individual, usually based on a username and password.

Availability — Consistent direct access to information over time

B

Back end — In client/server applications, the client part of the program is often called the front end and the server part is called the back end.

Backup image — Data saved during an archive operation. It includes all the associated files, directories, and catalog information of the backup operation.

Big Data — Refers to data that becomes so large in size or quantity that a dataset becomes awkward to work with using traditional database management systems. Big data entails data capacity or measurement that requires terms such as Terabyte (TB), Petabyte (PB), Exabyte (EB), Zettabyte (ZB) or Yottabyte (YB). Note that variations of this term are subject to proprietary trademark disputes in multiple countries at the present time.

BIOS — Basic Input/Output System. A chip located on all computer motherboards that governs how a system boots and operates.

BPaaS — Business Process as a Service. A cloud computing business model.

BPO — Business Process Outsourcing. Dynamic BPO services refer to the management of partly standardized business processes, including human resources delivered in a pay-per-use billing relationship or a self-service consumption model.

Business Continuity Plan — Describes how an organization will resume partially or completely interrupted critical functions within a predetermined time after a disruption or a disaster. Sometimes also called a Disaster Recovery Plan.

C

Cache — Cache Memory. Intermediate buffer between the channels and drives. It is generally available and controlled as two areas of cache (cache A and cache B). It may be battery-backed.

Cache hit rate — When data is found in the cache, it is called a cache hit, and the effectiveness of a cache is judged by its hit rate.

Cache partitioning — Storage management software that allows the virtual partitioning of cache and allocation of it to different applications.

Capacity — Capacity is the amount of data that a storage system or drive can store after configuration and/or formatting.

Most data storage companies, including HDS, calculate capacity based on the premise that 1KB = 1,024 bytes, 1MB = 1,024 kilobytes, 1GB = 1,024 megabytes, and 1TB = 1,024 gigabytes. See also Terabyte (TB), Petabyte (PB), Exabyte (EB), Zettabyte (ZB) and Yottabyte (YB).

CAPEX — Capital expenditure — the cost of developing or providing non-consumable parts for the product or system. For example, the purchase of a photocopier is the CAPEX, and the annual paper and toner cost is the OPEX. (See OPEX).

CBI — Cloud-based Integration. Provisioning of a standardized middleware platform in the cloud that can be used for various cloud integration scenarios.

An example would be the integration of legacy applications into the cloud or integration of different cloud-based applications into one application.

CCI — Command Control Interface

CCIF — Cloud Computing Interoperability Forum. A standards organization active in cloud computing.

CDP — Continuous Data Protection

Centralized management - Storage data management, capacity management, access security management, and path management functions accomplished by software.

CF — Coupling Facility

Chargeback — A cloud computing term that refers to the ability to report on capacity and utilization by application or dataset, charging business users or departments based on how much they use.

CIFS protocol — Common internet file system is a platform-independent file sharing system. A network file system accesses protocol primarily used by Windows clients to communicate file access requests to Windows servers.

CLI — Command Line Interface

CLPR — Cache Logical Partition. Cache can be divided into multiple virtual cache memories to lessen I/O contention.

Cloud Computing — "Cloud computing refers to applications and services that run on a distributed network using virtualized resources and accessed by common Internet protocols and networking standards. It is distinguished by the notion that resources are virtual and limitless, and that details of the physical systems on which software runs are abstracted from the user." — Source: *Cloud Computing Bible*, Barrie Sosinsky (2011)

Cloud computing often entails an "as a service" business model that may entail one or more of the following:
- Archive as a Service (AaaS)
- Business Process as a Service (BPaas)
- Failure as a Service (FaaS)
- Infrastructure as a Service (IaaS)
- IT as a Service (ITaaS)
- Platform as a Service (PaaS)
- Private File Tiering as a Service (PFTaas)
- Software as a Service (Saas)
- SharePoint as a Service (SPaas)
- *SPI* refers to the Software, Platform and Infrastructure as a Service business model.

Cloud network types include the following:
- Community cloud (or community network cloud)
- Hybrid cloud (or hybrid network cloud)
- Private cloud (or private network cloud)
- Public cloud (or public network cloud)

- Virtual private cloud (or virtual private network cloud)

Cloud Enabler — a concept, product or solution that enables the deployment of cloud computing. Key cloud enablers include:
- Data discoverability
- Data mobility
- Data protection
- Dynamic provisioning
- Location independence
- Multitenancy to ensure secure privacy
- Virtualization

Cloud Fundamental — A core requirement to the deployment of cloud computing. Cloud fundamentals include:
- Self service
- Pay per use
- Dynamic scale up and scale down

Cloud Security Alliance — A standards organization active in cloud computing.

Cluster — A collection of computers that are interconnected (typically at high-speeds) for the purpose of improving reliability, availability, serviceability or performance (via load balancing). Often, clustered computers have access to a common pool of storage and run special software to coordinate the component computers' activities.

CM — Cache Memory, Cache Memory Module. Intermediate buffer between the channels and drives. It has a maximum of 64GB (32GB x two areas) of capacity. It is available and controlled as two areas of cache (cache A and cache B). It is fully battery-backed (48 hours).

Community Network Cloud — Infrastructure shared between several organizations or groups with common concerns.

Concatenation — A logical joining of two series of data, usually represented by the symbol "|". In data communications, two or more data are often concatenated to provide a unique name or reference (e.g., S_ID | X_ID). Volume managers concatenate disk address spaces to present a single larger address spaces.

Connectivity technology — A program or device's ability to link with other programs and devices. Connectivity technology allows programs on a given computer to run routines or access objects on another remote computer.

Controller — A device that controls the transfer of data from a computer to a peripheral device (including a storage system) and vice versa.

Controller-based virtualization — Driven by the physical controller at the hardware microcode level versus at the application software layer and integrates into the infrastructure to allow virtualization across heterogeneous storage and third party products.

Corporate governance — Organizational compliance with government-mandated regulations

CSV — Comma Separated Value or Cluster Shared Volume

D

DAS — Direct Attached Storage

Data block — A fixed-size unit of data that is transferred together. For example, the X modem protocol transfers blocks of 128 bytes. In general, the larger the block size, the faster the data transfer rate.

Data Duplication — Software duplicates data, as in remote copy or PiT snapshots. Maintains two copies of data.

Data Integrity — Assurance that information will be protected from modification and corruption.

Data Lifecycle Management — An approach to information and storage management. The policies, processes, practices, services and tools used to align the business value of data with the most appropriate and cost-effective storage infrastructure from the time data is created through its final disposition. Data is aligned with business requirements through management policies and service levels associated with performance, availability, recoverability, cost, and what ever parameters the organization defines as critical to its operations.

Data Migration — The process of moving data from one storage device to another. In this context, data migration is the same as Hierarchical Storage Management (HSM).

Data Pool — A volume containing differential data only.

Data Protection Directive — A major compliance and privacy protection initiative within the European Union (EU) that applies to cloud computing. Includes the Safe Harbor Agreement.

Data Striping — Disk array data mapping technique in which fixed-length sequences of virtual disk data addresses are mapped to sequences of member disk addresses in a regular rotating pattern.

Data Transfer Rate (DTR) — The speed at which data can be transferred. Measured in kilobytes per second for a CD-ROM drive, in bits per second for a modem, and in megabytes per second for a hard drive. Also, often called data rate.

Device Management — Processes that configure and manage storage systems

Direct Attached Storage (DAS) — Storage that is directly attached to the application or file server. No other device on the network can access the stored data.

Director class switches — Larger switches often used as the core of large switched fabrics

Disaster Recovery Plan (DRP) — A plan that describes how an organization will deal with potential disasters. It may include the precautions taken to either maintain or quickly resume mission-critical functions. Sometimes also referred to as a Business Continuity Plan.

Disk Array — A linked group of one or more physical independent hard disk drives generally used to replace larger, single disk drive systems. The most common disk arrays are in daisy chain configuration or implement RAID (Redundant Array of Independent Disks) technology.
A disk array may contain several disk drive trays, and is structured to improve speed and increase protection against loss of data. Disk arrays organize their data storage into Logical Units (LUs), which appear as linear block paces to their clients. A small disk array, with a few disks, might support up to eight LUs; a large one, with hundreds of disk drives, can support thousands.

DLM — Data Lifecycle Management

DNS — Domain Name System

DRP — Disaster Recovery Plan

DWDM — Dense Wavelength Division Multiplexing

E

ENC — Enclosure or Enclosure Controller. The units that connect the controllers with the Fibre Channel disks. They also allow for online extending a system by adding RKAs.

Ethernet — A local area network (LAN) architecture that supports clients and servers and uses twisted pair cables for connectivity.

Exabyte (EB) — A measurement of data or data storage. 1EB = 1,024PB.

F

FaaS — Failure as a Service. A proposed business model for cloud computing in which large-scale, online failure drills are provided as a service in order to test real cloud deployments. Concept developed and proposed by the College of Engineering at the University of California, Berkeley in 2011.

Fabric — The hardware that connects workstations and servers to storage devices in a SAN is referred to as a "fabric." The SAN fabric enables any-server-to-any-storage device connectivity through the use of Fibre Channel switching technology.

Failback — The restoration of a failed system share of a load to a replacement component. For example, when a failed controller in a redundant configuration is replaced, the devices that were originally controlled by the failed controller are usually failed back to the replacement controller to restore the I/O balance, and to restore failure tolerance. Similarly, when a defective fan or power supply is replaced, its load, previously borne by a redundant component, can be failed back to the replacement part.

Failed over — A mode of operation for failure tolerant systems in which a component has failed and its function has been assumed by a redundant component. A system that protects against single failures operating in failed over mode is not failure tolerant, since failure of the redundant component may render the system unable to function. Some systems (e.g., clusters) are able to tolerate more than one failure; these remain failure tolerant until no redundant component is available to protect against further failures.

Failover — A backup operation that automatically switches to a standby database server or network if the primary system fails, or is temporarily shut down for servicing. Failover is an important fault tolerance function of mission-critical systems that rely on constant accessibility. Also called *path failover*.

Failure tolerance — The ability of a system to continue to perform its function or at a reduced performance level, when one or more of its components has failed. Failure tolerance in disk subsystems is often achieved by including redundant instances of components whose failure would make the system inoperable, coupled with facilities that allow the redundant components to assume the function of failed ones.

Fault Tolerant — Describes a computer system or component designed so that, in the event of a component failure, a backup component or procedure can immediately take its place with no loss of service. Fault tolerance can be provided with software, embedded in hardware, or provided by some hybrid combination.

FC — Fibre Channel or Field-Change (microcode update) or Fibre Channel. A technology for transmitting data between computer devices; a set of standards for a serial I/O bus capable of transferring data between 2 ports

FC-0 — Lowest layer on fibre channel transport. This layer represents the physical media.

FC-1 — This layer contains the 8b/10b encoding scheme.

FC-2 — This layer handles framing and protocol, frame format, sequence/exchange management and ordered set usage.

FC-3 — This layer contains common services used by multiple N_Ports in a node.

FC-4 — This layer handles standards and profiles for mapping upper level protocols like SCSI an IP onto the Fibre Channel Protocol.

FC-AL — Fibre Channel Arbitrated Loop. A serial data transfer architecture developed by a consortium of computer and mass storage device manufacturers, and is now being standardized by ANSI. FC-AL was designed for new mass storage devices and other peripheral devices that require very high bandwidth. Using optical fiber to connect devices, FC-AL supports full-duplex data transfer rates of 100MB/sec. FC-AL is compatible with SCSI for high-performance storage systems.

FCIP — Fibre Channel over IP, a network storage technology that combines the features of Fibre Channel and the Internet Protocol (IP) to connect distributed SANs over large distances. FCIP is considered a tunneling protocol, as it makes a transparent point-to-point connection between geographically separated SANs over IP networks. FCIP relies on TCP/IP services to establish connectivity between remote SANs over LANs, MANs, or WANs. An advantage of FCIP is that it can use TCP/IP as the transport while keeping Fibre Channel fabric services intact.

Fibre Channel — A serial data transfer architecture developed by a consortium of computer and mass storage device manufacturers and now being standardized by ANSI. The most prominent Fibre Channel standard is Fibre Channel Arbitrated Loop (FC-AL).

FICON — Fiber Connectivity. A high-speed input/output (I/O) interface for mainframe computer connections to storage devices. As part of IBM's S/390 server, FICON channels increase I/O capacity through the combination of a new architecture and faster physical link rates to make them up to 8 times as efficient as ESCON (Enterprise System Connection), IBM's previous fiber optic channel standard.

Frames — An ordered vector of words that is the basic unit of data transmission in a Fibre Channel network.

Front end — In client/server applications, the client part of the program is often called the front end and the server part is called the back end.

FS — File System

FTP — File Transfer Protocol. A client-server protocol that allows a user on one computer to transfer files to and from another computer over a TCP/IP network.

G

Gb — Gigabit

GB — Gigabyte

Gb/sec — Gigabit per second

GB/sec — Gigabyte per second

GbE — Gigabit Ethernet

Gbps — Gigabit per second

GBps — Gigabyte per second

GBIC — Gigabit Interface Converter

Global Cache — Cache memory is used on demand by multiple applications. Use changes dynamically, as required for READ performance between hosts/applications/LUs.

GUI — Graphical User Interface

H

HA — High Availability

HBA — Host Bus Adapter - An I/O adapter that sits between the host computer's bus and the Fibre Channel loop and manages the transfer of information between the two channels. In order to minimize the impact on host processor performance, the host bus adapter performs many low-level interface functions automatically or with minimal processor involvement.

HDD — Hard Disk Drive. A spindle of hard disk platters that make up a hard drive, which is a unit of physical storage within a subsystem.

Head — See read/write head

Heterogeneous — The characteristic of containing dissimilar elements. A common use of this word in information technology is to describe a product as able to contain or be part of a "heterogeneous network," consisting of different manufacturers' products that can interoperate.
Heterogeneous networks are made possible by standards-conforming hardware and software interfaces used in common by different products, thus allowing them to communicate with each other. The Internet itself is an example of a heterogeneous network.

Homogeneous — Of the same or similar kind

Host — Also called a server. Basically a central computer that processes end-user applications or requests.

Host LU — Host Logical Unit. See also HLU.

Host Storage Domains — Allows host pooling at the LUN level and the priority access feature lets administrator set service levels for applications.

Hub — A common connection point for devices in a network. Hubs are commonly used to connect segments of a LAN. A hub contains multiple ports. When a packet arrives at one port, it is copied to the other ports so that all segments of the LAN can see all packets. A switching hub actually reads the

destination address of each packet and then forwards the packet to the correct port. Device to which nodes on a multi-point bus or loop are physically connected.

Hybrid Cloud — "Hybrid cloud computing refers to the combination of external public cloud computing services and internal resources (either a private cloud or traditional infrastructure, operations and applications) in a coordinated fashion to assemble a particular solution." — Source: Gartner Research.

Hybrid Network Cloud — A composition of two or more clouds (private, community or public). Each cloud remains a unique entity but they are bound together. A hybrid network cloud includes an interconnection.

Hypervisor — Also called a virtual machine manager, a hypervisor is a hardware virtualization technique that enables multiple operating systems to run concurrently on the same computer. Hypervisors are often installed on server hardware then run the guest operating systems that act as servers.

Hypervisor can also refer to the interface that is provided by *Infrastructure as a Service (IaaS)* in *cloud computing*.
Leading hypervisors include VMware vSphere Hypervisor™ (ESXi), Microsoft® Hyper-V and the Xen® hypervisor.

I

I/O — Input/Output. Term used to describe any program, operation, or device that transfers data to or from a computer and to or from a peripheral device.

IaaS — Infrastructure as a Service. A cloud computing business model — delivering computer infrastructure, typically a platform virtualization environment, as a service, along with raw (block) storage and networking. Rather than purchasing servers, software, data center space or network equipment, clients buy those resources as a fully outsourced service. Providers typically bill such services on a utility computing basis; the amount of resources consumed (and therefore the cost) will typically reflect the level of activity.

IDE — Integrated Drive Electronics Advanced Technology. A standard designed to connect hard and removable disk drives.

Index Cache — Provides quick access to indexed data on the media during a browse/restore operation.

iFCP — Internet Fibre Channel Protocol. Allows an organization to extend Fibre Channel storage networks over the Internet by using TCP/IP. TCP is responsible for managing congestion control as well as error detection and recovery services. iFCP allows an organization to create an IP SAN fabric that minimizes the Fibre Channel fabric component and maximizes use of the company's TCP/IP infrastructure.

In-band virtualization — Refers to the location of the storage network path, between the application host servers in the storage systems. Provides both control and data along the same connection path. Also called symmetric virtualization.

Interface — The physical and logical arrangement supporting the attachment of any device to a connector or to another device.

Internal bus — Another name for an internal data bus. Also, an expansion bus is often referred to as an internal bus.

Internal data bus — A bus that operates only within the internal circuitry of the CPU, communicating among the internal caches of memory that are part of the CPU chip's design. This bus is typically rather quick and is independent of the rest of the computer's operations.

IP — Internet Protocol

iSCSI — Internet SCSI. Pronounced eye skuzzy. An IP-based standard for linking data storage devices over a network and transferring data by carrying SCSI commands over IP networks.

ITaaS — IT as a Service. A cloud computing business model. This general model is an umbrella model that entails the SPI business model (SaaS, PaaS and IaaS — Software, Platform and Infrastructure as a Service).

J

Java — A widely accepted, open systems programming language. Hitachi's enterprise software products are all accessed using Java applications. This enables storage administrators to access the Hitachi enterprise software products from any PC or workstation that runs a supported thin-client internet browser application and that has TCP/IP network access to the computer on which the software product runs.

Java VM — Java Virtual Machine

JBOD — Just a Bunch of Disks

L

LAN — Local Area Network. A communications network that serves clients within a geographical area, such as a building.

LBA — Logical block address. A 28b value that maps to a specific cylinder-head-sector address on the disk.

LC — Lucent connector. Fibre Channel connector that is smaller than a simplex connector (SC).

LDEV — Logical Device or Logical Device (number). A set of physical disk partitions (all or portions of one or more disks) that are combined so that the subsystem sees and treats them as a single area of data storage. Also called a volume. An LDEV has a specific and unique address within a subsystem. LDEVs become LUNs to an open-systems host.

Load balancing — The process of distributing processing and communications activity evenly across a computer network so that no single device is overwhelmed. Load balancing is especially important for networks where it is difficult to predict the number of requests that will be issued to a server. If one server starts to be swamped, requests are forwarded to another server with more capacity. Load balancing can also refer to the communications channels themselves.

LPAR — Logical Partition (mode)

LU — Logical Unit. Mapping number of an LDEV.

LUN — Logical Unit Number. 1 or more LDEVs. Used only for open systems.

M

MAC — Media Access Control. A MAC address is a unique identifier attached to most forms of networking equipment.

MAN — Metropolitan Area Network. A communications network that generally covers a city or suburb. MAN is very similar to a LAN except it spans across a geographical region such as a state. Instead of the workstations in a LAN, the workstations in a MAN could depict different cities in a state. For example, the state of Texas could have: Dallas, Austin, San Antonio. The city could be a separate LAN and all the cities connected together via a switch. This topology would indicate a MAN.

Mapping — Conversion between two data addressing spaces. For example, mapping refers to the conversion between physical disk block addresses and the block addresses of the virtual disks presented to operating environments by control software.

Mb — Megabit

MB — Megabyte

Metadata — In database management systems, data files are the files that store the database information; whereas other files, such as index files and data dictionaries, store administrative information, known as metadata.

MIB — Management Information Base. A database of objects that can be monitored by a network management system. Both SNMP and RMON use standardized MIB formats that allow any SNMP and RMON tools to monitor any device defined by a MIB.

Microcode — The lowest-level instructions that directly control a microprocessor. A single machine-language instruction typically translates into several microcode instructions.

Mode — The state or setting of a program or device. The term mode implies a choice, which is that you can change the setting and put the system in a different mode.

MP — Microprocessor

MTS — Multitiered Storage

Multitenancy — In cloud computing, multitenancy is a secure way to partition the infrastructure (application, storage pool and network) so multiple customers share a single resource pool. Multitenancy is one of the key ways cloud can achieve massive economy of scale.

(LAN) or wide area network (WAN). The terms "computing" and "cloud computing" refer to services offered on the public Internet or to a private network that uses the same protocols as a standard network. See also *cloud computing*.

NFS protocol — Network File System is a protocol that allows a computer to access files over a network as easily as if they were on its local disks.

Node — An addressable entity connected to an I/O bus or network, used primarily to refer to computers, storage devices, and storage subsystems. The component of a node that connects to the bus or network is a port.

Node name — A Name_Identifier associated with a node

N

NAS — Network Attached Storage. A disk array connected to a controller that gives access to a LAN Transport. It handles data at the file level.

NAT — Network Address Translation

NDMP — Network Data Management Protocol is a protocol meant to transport data between NAS devices.

NetBIOS — Network Basic Input/Output System

Network — A computer system that allows sharing of resources, such as files and peripheral hardware devices.

Network Cloud — A communications network. The word "cloud" by itself may refer to any local area network

O

OPEX — Operational Expenditure. This is an operating expense, operating expenditure, operational expense, or operational expenditure, which is an ongoing cost for running a product, business, or system. Its counterpart is a capital expenditure (CAPEX).

Out-of-band virtualization — Refers to systems where the controller is located outside of the SAN data path. Separates control and data on different connection paths. Also called asymmetric virtualization.

P

PaaS — Platform as a Service. A *cloud computing* business model — delivering a computing platform and solution stack as a service. PaaS offerings facilitate deployment of applications without the cost and complexity of buying and managing the underlying hardware, software and provisioning hosting capabilities. PaaS provides all of the facilities required to support the complete life cycle of building and delivering web applications and services entirely from the Internet.

PACS — Picture archiving and communication systems

PAN — Personal Area Network. A communications network that transmit data wirelessly over a short distance. Bluetooth and Wi-Fi Direct are examples of personal area networks

Parity — A technique of checking whether data has been lost or written over when it is moved from one place in storage to another or when it is transmitted between computers.

Parity Group — Also called an array group. This is a group of hard disk drives (HDDs) that form the basic unit of storage in a subsystem. All HDDs in a parity group must have the same physical capacity.

Partitioned cache memory — Separate workloads in a "storage consolidated" system by dividing cache into individually managed multiple partitions. Then customize the partition to match the I/O characteristics of assigned LUs

PAT — Port Address Translation

PATA — Parallel ATA

Path — Also referred to as a transmission channel, the path between two nodes of a network that a data communication follows. The term can refer to the physical cabling that connects the nodes on a network, the signal that is communicated over the pathway or a sub-channel in a carrier frequency.

Path failover — See Failover.

PB — Petabyte

PCI — Power Control Interface

PCIe — Peripheral Component Interconnect Express

Performance - Speed of access or the delivery of information

Petabyte (PB) — A measurement of capacity - the amount of data that a drive or storage system can store after formatting. 1PB = 1,024TB.

PiT — Point-in-Time

PL — Platter. The circular disk on which the magnetic data is stored. Also called motherboard or backplane.

Port — In TCP/IP and UDP networks, an endpoint to a logical connection. The port number identifies what type of port it is. For example, port 80 is used for HTTP traffic.

Private Cloud — A type of cloud computing defined by shared capabilities within a single company; modest economies of scale and less automation. Infrastructure and data reside inside the company's data center behind a firewall. Comprised of licensed software tools rather than ongoing services. Example: An organization implements its own virtual, scalable cloud and business units are charged on a per use basis.

Private Network Cloud — A type of cloud network with three characteristics: (1) Operated solely for a single organization, (2) Managed internally or by a third-party, (3) Hosted internally or externally.

Protocol — A convention or standard that enables the communication between two computing endpoints. In its simplest form, a protocol can be defined as the rules governing the syntax, semantics, and synchronization of communication. Protocols may be implemented by hardware, software, or a combination of the two. At the lowest level, a protocol defines the behavior of a hardware connection.

Provisioning — The process of allocating storage resources and assigning storage capacity for an application, usually in the form of server disk drive space, in order to optimize the performance of a storage area network (SAN). Traditionally, this has been done by the SAN administrator, and it can be a tedious process. In recent years, automated storage provisioning (also called auto-provisioning) programs have become available. These programs can reduce the time required for the storage provisioning process, and can free the administrator from the often distasteful task of performing this chore manually.

Public Cloud — Resources, such as applications and storage, available to the general public over the Internet.

P-VOL — Primary Volume

Q

QoS — Quality of Service. In the field of computer networking, the traffic engineering term quality of service (QoS)

refers to resource reservation control mechanisms rather than the achieved service quality. Quality of service is the ability to provide different priority to different applications, users, or data flows, or to guarantee a certain level of performance to a data flow.

R

RAID — Redundant Array of Independent Disks, or Redundant Array of Inexpensive Disks. A group of disks that look like a single volume to the server. RAID improves performance by pulling a single stripe of data from multiple disks, and improves fault-tolerance either through mirroring or parity checking and it is a component of a customer's SLA.

RAID-0 — Striped array with no parity

RAID-1 — Mirrored array and duplexing

RAID-3 — Striped array with typically non-rotating parity, optimized for long, single-threaded transfers.

RAID-4 — Striped array with typically non-rotating parity, optimized for short, multi-threaded transfers.

RAID-5 — Striped array with typically rotating parity, optimized for short, multithreaded transfers.

RAID-6 — Similar to RAID-5, but with dual rotating parity physical disks, tolerating two physical disk failures.

RAM — Random Access Memory

RAM DISK — A LUN held entirely in the cache area.

RD/WR — Read/Write

Read/Write Head - Read and write data to the platters, typically there is one head per platter side, and each head is attached to a single actuator shaft.

Redundancy — Backing up a component to help ensure high availability.

Reliability — (1) Level of assurance that data will not be lost or degraded over time. (2) An attribute of any commuter component (software, hardware, or a network) that consistently performs according to its specifications.

Round robin mode — A load balancing technique which distributes data packets equally among the available paths. Round robin DNS is usually used for balancing the load of geographically distributed Web servers. It works on a rotating basis in that one server IP address is handed out, then moves to the back of the list; the next server IP address is handed out, and then it moves to the end of the list; and so on, depending on the number of servers being used. This works in a looping fashion.

Router — A computer networking device that forwards data packets toward their destinations, through a process known as routing.

RTO — Recovery Time Objective. The length of time that can be tolerated between a disaster and recovery of data.

S

SaaS — Software as a Service. A cloud computing business model. SaaS is a software delivery model in which software and its associated data are hosted centrally in a cloud and are typically accessed by users using a thin client, such as a web browser via the Internet. SaaS has become a common delivery model for most business applications, including accounting (CRM and ERP), invoicing (HRM), content management (CM) and service desk management, just to name the most common software that runs in the cloud. This is the fastest growing service in the cloud market today. SaaS performs best for relatively simple tasks in IT-constrained organizations.

SAN — Storage Area Network. A network linking computing devices to disk or tape arrays and other devices over Fibre Channel. It handles data at the block level.

SAP — (1) System Assist Processor (for I/O processing), or (2) a German software company.

SAS — (1) SAN Attached Storage. Storage elements that connect directly to a storage area network (SAN) and provide data access services to computer systems. (2) Serial Attached SCSI.

SATA — Serial ATA. Serial Advanced Technology Attachment is a new standard for connecting hard drives into computer systems. SATA is based on serial signaling technology, unlike current IDE (Integrated Drive Electronics) hard drives that use parallel signaling.

SCSI — Small Computer Systems Interface. A parallel bus architecture and a protocol for transmitting large data blocks up to a distance of 15m to 25m.

Server — A central computer that processes end user applications or requests, also called a host.

Server Virtualization — The masking of server resources, including the number and identity of individual physical servers, processors, and operating systems, from server users. The implementation of multiple isolated virtual environments in one physical server.

Service-level Agreement — SLA. A contract between a network service provider and a customer that specifies, usually in measurable terms, what services the network service provider will furnish. Many Internet service providers (ISP) provide their customers with a SLA. More recently, IT departments in major enterprises have adopted the idea of writing a service level agreement so that services for their customers (users in other departments within the enterprise) can be measured, justified, and perhaps compared with those of outsourcing network providers.

Some metrics that SLAs may specify include:
- The percentage of the time services will be available
- The number of users that can be served simultaneously
- Specific performance benchmarks to which actual performance will be periodically compared
- The schedule for notification in advance of network changes that may affect users
- Help desk response time for various classes of problems
- Dial-in access availability
- Usage statistics that will be provided

Service-Level Objective — SLO. Individual performance metrics built into an SLA. Each SLO corresponds to a single performance characteristic relevant to the delivery of an overall service. Some examples of SLOs include: system availability, help desk incident resolution time, and application response time.

SFP — Small Form-Factor Pluggable module Host connector. A specification for a new generation of optical modular transceivers. The devices are designed for use with small form factor (SFF) connectors, offer high speed and physical compactness, and are hot swappable.

SLA — Service Level Agreement

SM — Shared Memory or Shared Memory Module. Stores the shared information about the subsystem and the cache control information (director names). This type of information is used for the exclusive control of the subsystem. Like CACHE, shared memory is controlled as 2 areas of memory and fully non-volatile (sustained for approximately seven days).

Snapshot Image — A logical duplicated volume (V VOL) of the primary volume. It is an internal volume intended for restoration.

SNIA — Storage Networking Industry Association. An association of producers and consumers of storage networking products, whose goal is to further storage networking technology and applications. Active in cloud computing.

SNMP — Simple Network Management Protocol. A TCP/IP protocol that was designed for management of networks over TCP/IP, using agents and stations.

SPaaS — SharePoint as a Service. A cloud computing business model.

Spare — An object reserved for the purpose of substitution for a like object in case of that object's failure.

SSD — Solid-state Drive or Solid-State Disk

Storage pooling — The ability to consolidate and manage storage resources across storage system enclosures where the consolidation of many appears as a single view.

Striping — A RAID technique for writing a file to multiple disks on a block-by-block basis, with or without parity.

Subsystem — Hardware or software that performs a specific function within a larger system.

Switch — A fabric device providing full bandwidth per port and high-speed routing of data via link-level addressing.

Symmetric virtualization — See In-band virtualization.

Synchronous — Operations that have a fixed time relationship to each other. Most commonly used to denote I/O operations that occur in time sequence, i.e., a successor operation does not occur until its predecessor is complete.

T

Target — The system component that receives a SCSI I/O command, an open device that operates at the request of the initiator

TB — Terabyte. 1TB = 1,024GB.

TCO — Total Cost of Ownership

TCP/IP — Transmission Control Protocol over Internet Protocol

Terabyte (TB) — A measurement of capacity, data or data storage. 1TB = 1,024GB.

Thin Provisioning — Thin provisioning allows storage space to be easily allocated to servers on a just-enough and just-in-time basis.

Throughput — The amount of data transferred from 1 place to another or processed in a specified amount of time. Data transfer rates for disk drives and networks are measured in terms of throughput. Typically, throughputs are measured in kb/sec, Mb/sec and Gb/sec.

Tiered storage — A storage strategy that matches data classification to storage metrics. Tiered storage is the assignment of different categories of data to different types of storage media in order to reduce total storage cost. Categories may be based on levels of protection needed, performance requirements, frequency of use, and other considerations. Since assigning data to particular media may be an ongoing and complex activity, some vendors provide software for automatically managing the process based on a company-defined policy.

Tiered Storage Promotion — Moving data between tiers of storage as their availability requirements change

TLS — Tape Library System

Topology — The shape of a network or how it is laid out. Topologies are either physical or logical.

Track — Circular segment of a hard disk or other storage media.

Transfer Rate — See Data Transfer Rate.

U

UPS — Uninterruptible Power Supply - A power supply that includes a battery to maintain power in the event of a power outage.

V

VI — Virtual Interface. A research proto-type that is undergoing active development, and the details of the implementation may change considerably. It is an application interface that gives us-er-level processes direct but protected access to network interface cards.

This allows applications to bypass IP processing overheads (for example, copying data, computing checksums) and system call overheads while still preventing 1 process from accidentally or maliciously tampering with or reading data being used by another.

Virtualization — Referring to storage virtualization, virtualization is the amalgamation of multiple network storage devices into what appears to be a single storage unit. Storage virtualization is often used in a SAN, and makes tasks such as archiving, backup and recovery easier and faster. Storage virtualization is usually implemented via software applications.

There are many additional types of virtualization.

Virtual Private Cloud (VPC) — Private cloud existing within a shared or public cloud (for example, the Intercloud). Also known as a virtual private network cloud.

Volume — A fixed amount of storage on a disk or tape. The term volume is often used as a synonym for the storage medium itself, but it is possible for a single disk to contain more than one volume or for a volume to span more than one disk.

V-VOL — Virtual Volume

W

WAN — Wide Area Network. A computing internetwork that covers a broad area or region. Contrast with PAN, LAN and MAN.

WORM — Write Once, Read Many

WWN — World Wide Name. A unique identifier for an open-system host. It consists of a 64b physical address (the IEEE 48b format with a 12b extension and a 4b prefix).

WWNN — World Wide Node Name. A globally unique 64b identifier assigned to each Fibre Channel node process.

WWPN — World Wide Port Name. A globally unique 64b identifier assigned to each Fibre Channel port. A Fibre Channel port's WWPN is permitted to use any of several naming authorities. Fibre Channel specifies a Network Address Authority (NAA) to distinguish between the various name registration authorities that may be used to identify the WWPN.

Y

YB — Yottabyte

Yottabyte — A highest-end measurement of data at the present time. 1YB = 1,024ZB, or 1 quadrillion GB. A recent estimate (2011) is that all the computer hard drives in the world do not contain 1YB of data.

Z

Zettabyte (ZB) — A high-end measurement of data at the present time. 1ZB = 1,024EB.

Zone — A collection of Fibre Channel Ports that are permitted to communicate with each other via the fabric

Zoning — A method of subdividing a storage area network into disjoint zones, or subsets of nodes on the network. Storage area network nodes outside a zone are invisible to nodes within the zone. Moreover, with switched SANs, traffic within each zone may be physically isolated from traffic outside the zone.